INDIA.

VOL. I.

LONDON: PRINTED BY
SPOTTISWOODE AND CO., NEW-STREET SQUARE
AND PARLIAMENT STREET

Yours very sincerely
Rammohun Roy

Ob. SEPT 27TH 1833.

London: Longmans & Co.

SCOTTS IN INDIA

London: Longmans & Co.

422749

SIX MONTHS IN INDIA.

BY

MARY CARPENTER,

AUTHOR OF
'OUR CONVICTS,' 'LAST DAYS OF RAMMOHUN ROY,' ETC.

IN TWO VOLUMES.

VOL. I.

LONDON:
LONGMANS, GREEN, AND CO.
1868.

TO

𝕮𝖍𝖊 𝕳𝖔𝖓𝖔𝖚𝖗𝖊𝖉 𝕸𝖊𝖒𝖔𝖗𝖞

OF

THE RAJAH RAMMOHUN ROY,

THE GREAT REFORMER OF INDIA,

WHO FIRST EXCITED IN THE AUTHOR'S MIND

A DESIRE TO BENEFIT HIS COUNTRY,

𝕿𝖍𝖊𝖘𝖊 𝖁𝖔𝖑𝖚𝖒𝖊𝖘

ARE

RESPECTFULLY DEDICATED.

PREFACE.

IT WAS NOT MY INTENTION, when I went to India, to write an account of my travels: my visit was purely one of friendly sympathy. Circumstances recorded in the following narrative, led me to modify my original intention, and greatly extended my sphere of observation. The light afforded me by my past experience, as well as the sympathy in my work of the Supreme Government and that of each Presidency, and the friendly confidence of the native inhabitants, enabled me, in my brief visit, to see and learn much which does not usually come under the notice of travellers. Everything, invested with the charm of novelty, produced a very vivid impression on my mind; and though I had no time while in the country to record in writing many of these impressions, yet I had peculiar opportunities of comparing them with those of official gentlemen, and of experienced residents in the country, and thus of correcting or strengthening them.

On my return to England, it appeared to those who are most desirous to benefit India, that an important means of drawing attention to that great country would be lost, if I did not record my observations and impressions for publication. On reflection, I accorded with this opinion, and now respectfully offer to my countrymen and countrywomen these volumes for their kind consideration.

I must crave from my readers some indulgence for the many defects they will discover, in consideration of the fact that, during my preparation of the work, my attention has been forcibly claimed for the various institutions under my care, some of which had suffered from my absence.

RED LODGE HOUSE, BRISTOL:
February 5, 1868.

CONTENTS

OF

THE FIRST VOLUME.

CHAPTER I.

THE OUTWARD VOYAGE.

	PAGE		PAGE
Malta	5	Arrival at Bombay	18
Alexandria	7	Official Letters	24
The Red Sea	9	The First Journey	26
Aden	11	Surat	31
Alarm of Fire at Sea	17	Arrival at Ahmedabad	34

CHAPTER II.

AHMEDABAD AND ITS INSTITUTIONS.

Tropical Vegetation	39	Need of Female Normal Schools	64
Animated Nature	41	Soirée of Hindoo Ladies	69
Court of Justice	42	Hindoo Dinner-party	70
The Jail	48	Picnic at Sirkhej	71
A Girls' School	53	Tomb of Shah Alum	74
High School	55	Jain Temple	75
Visits of Native Ladies	57	Widow Remarriages	76
Normal Training School	58	Reformatory Schools	77
Lunatic Asylum	61	Native Christian Mission Station	78
Native and English Inhabitants	63		

CHAPTER III.

SURAT, BOMBAY, AND POONA.

	PAGE		PAGE
History of Surat	83	Mission Boarding School for Girls	106
Watering-place	85	Journey over the Bhore Ghaut Incline	107
English Cemetery	86		
Girls' School	89	Government and Mission Schools	109
Soirée of Hindoo Ladies	90		
Morning Reception of English and Natives	93	Mission Boarding School for Girls	113
Native Inspectors	94	The Jail	115
Mission Chapel and Station	95	Heathen Temple on Parbati Hill	117
The Jail	98		
Arrival at Bombay	99	Baptisms at Mission Chapel	119
Anglo-Indian Residence	100	Female Normal Training School	120
The Cocoanut	101		
The Jail	103		

CHAPTER IV.

MADRAS.

	PAGE		PAGE
Parsee Dinner-party	127	The Hospital	150
Voyage to Beypoor	128	Museum	151
The Journey	129	School of Industrial Arts	152
Arrival at Madras	130	Visit from Native Gentleman and Lady	155
Mission Schools	133		
Presidency College	139	Veda Somaj	156
Mahometan School	141	Cathedral	159
Military Orphan Asylum	143	The Monsoon	160
Vepery College	145	Departure from Madras	161
Conference with Native Gentlemen	148		

FIRST VOLUME. xi

CHAPTER V.

CALCUTTA.

	PAGE		PAGE
The Ganges	164	Country Missionary Excursion	190
The Landing	166	Visit to Heathen Temple	195
The City	167	Brahmo Worship	197
Religious Movement	169	Medical College	199
Rajah Rammohun Roy	170	Alipore Jail	200
Keshub Chunder Sen	179	Female Prison	202
Brahmo Prayer Meeting	180	Lunatic Asylum	203
Native City	181	Institutions	203
Tea-party of Native Gentlemen and Ladies	183	School for Neglected Children	207
		Christmas Day	209
Mission Schools	185	Female Normal School	213
Church Female Normal School	187	Social Science Association	218
Zenana Teaching	188	Drawing Room	220
Bethune Girls' School	189		

CHAPTER VI.

THE SUBURBS OF CALCUTTA.

	PAGE		PAGE
Bishop's College	223	Ooterparrah	239
Horticultural Gardens	224	Native Public Library	244
Howrah	227	Burranagore	248
Bhowanipore	231	Ranaghat	255
Serampore	234	Kishnaghur	257
Konnegur	236	The Jail	266

CHAPTER VII.

FAREWELL TO CALCUTTA—MADRAS—CALICUT.

	PAGE		PAGE
Bamabodhini Shova	271	Triplicane	284
Departure from Calcutta	273	Monegar Choultry	286
Arrival at Madras, Guindy Park	275	Address at Evangelistic Hall and at Patcheappah Hall	289
Female Normal School Memorial	277	Coimbatore	290
Native Address	280	Calicut	292
Veda Somaj	281	The Jail	296
Mission Chapel	282	Industrial Exhibition	298

SIX MONTHS IN INDIA.

CHAPTER I.

THE OUTWARD VOYAGE—ARRIVAL IN INDIA—
THE FIRST JOURNEY.

Wednesday, Sept. 5, 1866.—We went on board the 'Syria,' and soon steamed off from Marseilles. We now felt we were actually *en route* for India.

The bay looked very glorious, surrounded by the old historic city, the Massilia of the ancient Romans. This entrance from the East to civilised Europe has not been standing still during the two thousand years in which its name has been known as a fine harbour; and though some of the streets we traversed on the preceding day were dingy and unpromising enough, yet we were well rewarded for spending a few hours in exploring the city, by observing splendid new rows of buildings, handsome broad streets arranged so as to terminate with some fine monument, beautiful drives, and lovely public gardens, in which advantage was so skilfully taken of the natural features of the site, as to lead one on, almost insensibly, to a splendid view over the city to the surrounding country, bounded by the graceful outline of blue hills or mountains. The spirit of the imperial capital seemed spreading here, and gave one a striking impression of the power which made itself felt even in the new buildings of this distant part of the empire.

As we steamed swiftly along, we saw disappear, one after another, the buildings we had visited on the preceding day; the hills faded from us so quickly that the pencil could scarcely catch their outline. Then a bold rocky coast succeeded—cliffs bright and glistening in the sunlight, with a clear azure sky above, and washed below by the blue waters of the Mediterranean. Their fantastic turreted forms looked like actual castles crowning some steep massive rock, such as are seen on the banks of the glorious Rhine. One longed to stay and take a nearer view of them, and penetrate the caverns at their base; but we passed swiftly on: the forms of the cliffs and the rocky islets were changing their relative positions perpetually, and we had scarcely time to make simple outline sketches of them, before they receded from our view.

We had now bid adieu to the shores of Europe.

Very different feelings must have animated the various passengers who were now to be our companions until our arrival at Alexandria. Several were gentlemen who had some official position in India and who were returning to their duties, with or without their families; others were going out for the first time on engagements of different kinds.

Our own small party was composed of very various materials. I had been requested by a friend to take charge of a young Hindoo lady, the daughter of Dr. Goodeve Chuckerbutty, of Calcutta. He had become a Christian, and had sent his daughter to England for education. As she had been absent for six years, he was glad of this opportunity for her to come home, and the young lady herself was not a little rejoiced to return to her native land. An estimable young Jewish lady, who was going to Bombay to meet her betrothed, placed herself under my care, and by her agreeable character added much to the pleasure of the voyage. We all had the escort of Mr. Monomohun Ghose, a Hindoo gentleman from Calcutta, who, after spending between four and five years studying in England, had been called to the English Bar. He was leaving with much regret the country where a new and civilised life had been opened to him; where he had seen the natives of our marvellous island of Great Britain in their true light, and where he had received the courteous hospitality which we always desire to show to strangers. It was with many anticipations of difficulties, many fears of what he would have to encounter in his own land, and yet with hopes of being able to contribute something to the elevation of his countrymen, that he now bid adieu to the Western World, to the continent that had been the object of his earliest aspirations, which had been more than realised. As for myself, the desire of many years was about to be gratified. The visit to England, now four-and-thirty years ago, of the Rajah Rammohun Roy, the first great reformer of his countrymen—the first who had publicly called on them to renounce idolatry and superstition, who had presented to them the 'Precepts of Jesus, the Guide to Peace and Happiness,' who had devoted his life to their elevation—had left an indelible impression on my mind; that impression was perpetuated by the circumstance that his mortal remains are deposited in the beautiful cemetery of Arno's Vale, near Bristol. Other duties and engagements had long called away my attention from India; but six years before, my interest in that great country had been revived by a visit from a young Brahmin convert to

Christianity. He had given, in a public lecture, so graphic and fearful a picture of the condition of Hindoo women, as to lead me to form the solemn resolve to do something to ameliorate their condition, whenever an opening should present itself; if possible, to visit India whenever I should be able to do so, and, if I could do nothing more, extend to them the sympathy of an Englishwoman. The work which I had already undertaken for the neglected children of my own country, and especially the criminal children of my own sex, was not then sufficiently matured to be left with safety. But the visits of other Hindoo gentlemen to Bristol, the anxiety they manifested for the elevation of the women of India, together with their assurances that a visit from me to their people would be useful, decided me to undertake the journey as soon as possible. It is unnecessary to state the difficulties which had to be overcome, arising from the fears of friends, and the arrangements that required to be made to secure the safety of my work in my absence: all these did but increase the thankfulness and joy with which I found myself actually embarked on my enterprise, and inspired me with courage to surmount any future obstacles.

Nothing of peculiar interest presented itself before we reached our first goal, Malta, for we passed by Sardinia in the night, and did not catch a glimpse of Caprera, which we had longed to see.

But every day the sea was so marvellously calm—such a lovely blue, so delicate and tender! It was unlike anything I had seen before, though I had always thought previously that the waters washing the southern coast of my native Devon must transcend any others in beauty. The fleecy clouds of the soft autumnal sky were exquisitely reflected in it, and sometimes a sail in the distance carried on the eye to the horizon, which was often scarcely discernible, so nearly blended were the heavens above with the waters below. Each evening revealed other glories, for the moon cast her full splendour on the waters—a flood of liquid silver—and justified her title to be Empress of the Night; while Venus, with a loveliness all her own, threw her radiance over the sea, too bright to be obscured by the more powerful lustre of the moon. And as our beautiful vessel glided along with unerring course, her paddles left in the waters a double track of foam, which, receding even to the horizon, marked a pathway in the sea made by the marvellous mind of man.

It was well worth some few discomforts and difficulties to have uninterrupted leisure to enjoy such beauty, and to be able to rise from it to Him who is the source of all!

However delightful a voyage may be, ship passengers do nevertheless eagerly hail the first sight of land. So did we the island of Malta. At first faintly discerned on the horizon, then a long strip of land, then the features of the country were clearly defined, and then—almost before we were prepared for it—the harbour of the famous town and fort of Valetta burst upon us. But there was no landing for us unfortunate beings! Though our crew and passengers appeared quite free from any contagion, yet we had left some few undisputed cases of cholera at Marseilles, and we must not inflict on the island the danger of infection. Only those landed who had reached their destination, and we did not envy their lot, as they would be subjected to all the annoyance and expense of performing quarantine. We were not, however, doomed to complete disappointment, for the setting sun gave us one of the most brilliant effects that I have ever beheld. We may think the brilliancy of Turner's painting unnatural, poetical, and exaggerated, but none that I have ever seen exceeded this. The sun shed a rich golden light on the buildings at the entrance of the harbour, on the left side a little elevated and defended by a massive fort; on the right, rising in terraces up the steep cliff, was the city, crowned by the church of St. Paul, built by our good Queen Adelaide, the last spire we should see for many a day. All these were built of white stone, and, with the fortifications rising behind them, looked dazzlingly brilliant as they reflected the rays of the setting sun. The soft blue sky had melted by the most delicate gradations into a golden tint, so brilliant that it could be but faintly represented by the richest chromes; these again melted into a roseate hue, and this again into the softest warmest grey possible, which relieved the buildings, and seemed to rest on the flood of glowing red below.

The water reflected the buildings above with such marvellous delicacy and exactitude, that Canaletti and even Turner would have confessed themselves quite unequal to the task of reproducing the effect on canvas. I felt it to be presumptuous to attempt to note it down in colours, yet the slightest memorial of such a scene is most valuable to the possessor.

Sept. 9, *Sunday morning.* — The stewardess announced that it was a 'fresh morning.' It was bright and beautiful, as one loves to see a Sabbath at home, but the flitting clouds indicated a little more animation in the sea than was quite agreeable to some of us. The ship-bell took the place of church-bells, and we obeyed its summons to join in the worship, which was impressively conducted by our fellow-passenger, the Archdeacon of Calcutta. Thus isolated from the rest of the world, and on the mighty waters, one feels peculiarly under the care of Him who rules them, and the prayers for those who are 'travelling by land or by sea' have a deeper meaning to us.

ALEXANDRIA.—Our first introduction to the Eastern World. The bay, surrounded by the city connected with so many old associations, was beautiful and glorious in the morning sun. But alas! we were not permitted to see it any nearer than from our ship, as we were under ban, and two not very respectable-looking Egyptians came on board with soiled yellow ribbons, indicating that they were officers appointed to take care that the quarantine laws were strictly observed. They did not appear to have any repugnance to food forbidden by their religion, but rather glad of an opportunity of indulging in it freely without unpleasant surveillance; they also invited some of the gentlemen to go on shore under their escort to see the city, on condition of 'backshish.' This of course was refused. We were officially informed that, as a great favour, we should be permitted to travel by night through Egypt in carriages specially provided for the purpose, and thus saved the necessity of remaining, at enormous expense and inconvenience, fourteen days in quarantine. There were no very pleasant prospects before us, as the most experienced of our fellow-passengers informed us. At decline of day we were put on shore, all communication with the inhabitants of Alexandria being strictly forbidden. We hoped that this prohibition would protect us from the officiousness of the rough Egyptian porters—but quite in vain. It was with difficulty that we protected our luggage and portable effects from them, as they crowded round us; they, indeed, might have easily carried infection, if any was to be taken from us, into every part of the Pasha's dominions. Our troubles, however, were not yet begun. To our dismay, we were then thrust into some long covered wooden vans, boarded almost to the top, and without windows, so that the only means of seeing anything of the country we passed through was to stand on the narrow seats, and look through a small round hole, or over the top of the boarding. This was our first introduction to Egypt, the land of ancient story, which had taken so important a place in the early civilisation of the world, and which was so remarkably associated with the religious history of the chosen people. The mere fact of being on that soil hallowed by so many sacred memories was most interesting, though we could not catch even a passing glimpse of the objects around us, except occasionally of Venus, our faithful attendant, who was now shedding her silver rays no longer over the sea but on a branch of the Nile. But it was impossible thoroughly to enjoy even this, miserably imprisoned as we were, the gentlemen in one van and the ladies in another, and enjoined not to alight until we should arrive at Suez. One poor lady was very ill, and passed a night of agony on the narrow wooden benches, groaning piteously; the poor children were of course full of discomfort, which they expressed after their own peculiar fashion—some fretfully, some passionately, in one very inharmonious chorus. No comfort of any kind could be procured, few could obtain even short snatches of broken sleep. Thus we passed the night—we who had each paid our four pounds ten shillings for the transit through Egypt.

At length daylight dawned, and having passed unknowingly by the Pyramids and Cairo, we found ourselves at the end of our journey, near Suez, and realised the idea of being actually in the East, when we noticed very shaggy-looking Egyptians go forth from their mud cabins to their daily occupations, or groups of travellers on camels, and saw around us the real 'sandy desert' of the Israelites. We carried away some sand as a trophy.

Every thoughtful person who is for the first time on the Red Sea, and beholds the bare jagged mountain cliffs of the Sinaitic range, must feel inspired with indescribable emotions. However the Scripture narrative may be viewed by different religionists, yet the simple fact that this region has been for thousands of years associated with marvellous events connected with the rise of revealed religion in the world, that the memories linked with that 'great and terrible wilderness' have ever been held sacred both by Jews and Mahometans as well as by Christians—all these recollections inspire the mind with feelings which cannot be expressed, and which draw off the thoughts from surrounding discomforts. The very Mount Horeb of the Ten Commandments cannot be seen from the ship, being too far inland, but the Sinaitic range looked very glorious as the setting sun shed his rays on it. The sky being of the richest hue far above the horizon, it will be easily imagined how very brilliant the rocks must have been to come out brightly as intense orange against it; while the more distant range was of a soft delicate red, and the sea, which we had noticed in the morning as of a deep but vivid blue, was now a soft and warm grey.

The Red Sea is generally the most dreaded part of the voyage, and the intense heat we should have to encounter was much feared for us by our friends. We were thus prepared for something very trying to our health. For myself I may bear witness that, looking back on this voyage now after my return home, I do

not remember having found this part of it peculiarly
unpleasant, nor do I recollect that those of our fellow-
passengers who had usually been on deck found it so
either. The cabins must have been extremely hot and
oppressive, and we thankfully accepted the arrangement
made for us by the captain, to separate off part of the
deck for us ladies, that we, as well as the gentlemen,
might pass the night there. It was very wonderful to
look up from our lowly bed, and find ourselves canopied
by the cerulean vault spangled with the brightest diamond stars imaginable, and to trace out our old familiar
constellations in their changed places. But one passenger
felt the heat more than she could bear. The poor invalid
who had suffered so much in that dreadful night of the
transit through Egypt was not to accompany her husband
to the end of his voyage; she became worse and worse,
and expressed a presentiment which was strong in her
mind that the Red Sea would be fatal to her. Her
young native servant was very assiduous in her attention to her sick mistress, and the ship's doctor did all
he could. But one afternoon her husband was called
away from the dinner-table; her sufferings were nearly
ended—she soon breathed her last. Early next morning
we heard the tolling of the ship's bell, and knew that
the last solemn ceremony was being performed of com-
mitting the mortal remains to the sea. We seldom saw
again any of that party; we all felt much for them.

Sunday, Sept. 16.—Again a Sabbath on the water!
After breakfast all the ship's crew are assembled on
deck in clean Sunday trim, to have the roll called
over. We had now a number of Hindoo sailors on
board, and their gay clothing was varied and picturesque:
some clean white garments gave a brilliancy to their
dark complexions, and we should hardly have recognised
them as the same persons whom we had seen in their

dingy working-dress. Every little incident of this kind pleasantly breaks the monotony of ship life. Our religious service was this time on deck, which was far pleasanter than in the saloon, though perhaps more trying to the voice of the preacher. During the course of it, our attention was a little distracted by an island in sight, perhaps the very one on which the 'Alma' was wrecked many years ago. There were others not far off, all desolate and burnt up by the intense heat. Our careful captain anxiously watched to keep his vessel clear of them. Will civilisation ever attempt to people such spots? We may look to the time when even these may become the abode of man, and when springs may be drawn by his marvellous skill out of these barren rocks.

ADEN.—The long-desired termination of our Red Sea voyage. The close oppressive heat was now succeeded by a fresh breeze, after passing the straits. We felt ourselves indeed in a foreign region. The strangest human figures, in boats equally strange, soon surrounded our ship, some bringing various articles for sale, others wishing to exhibit their skill in diving for a piece of money. Many passengers threw a coin into the water, and the dexterity was wonderful with which these boys caught it before it reached the bottom. The transparency of the sea enabled us to watch their curious motions in diving; they seemed in their natural element, and to feel perfect masters of it. Most of our passengers landed, but I did not, thinking it unwise to encounter any unnecessary fatigue. Notwithstanding the miseries caused by coaling, which involves a perfect babel of discordant voices, with dust and dirt in every direction, the calm evening beauty of the scene around us was most refreshing to the spirit. Withdrawing the attention from Steamer Point itself, and the not very picturesque but useful ridges of coal near it, the eye rests on precipitous bare rocks and mountains opposite, which cannot sustain the smallest vegetation against their arid sides; they are cleft apparently by some tremendous volcanic action into a frightful gorge, terminated by still higher mountains, whose ruggedness is softened by distance. No ordinary mountain scenery can give the smallest conception of this, in its extraordinary burnt dreary aspect. But distance and the transparent warm atmosphere of these southern regions can lend enchantment even to these gloomy peaks. The sky was of the most exquisite delicate grey gradually melting into gold. On one side of this central chasm, opposite to us, the jagged peak, grey and distinct, rose against the evening sky, receding to the horizon; on the other, the fort stood on an isolated cliff, with distant hills in the background. The sea on every side was most calm and serene, reflecting like a lake the picturesque little vessels that were scudding about with the strange-looking natives, or some steamers which might be going off to the African coast. Our fellow passengers returned with various treasures of ostrich-feathers, beautiful coral, baskets, &c., which they had purchased; but many were somewhat annoyed to find how exorbitant a price they had paid, through their inexperience, without obtaining really choice articles.

We bid adieu to the last land we should behold before arriving at our destination. The voyage across the Arabian Sea is the least interesting of any part of the overland route to India. We were indeed isolated from the inhabited portion of the globe, for there was no land to interrupt the rolling waters of the oceans which were between us and the ice-girt southern pole. We did not find the weather perceptibly cooler as we were led to expect, but it was somewhat rougher. Lassitude crept over most of us during the greater part of the day, and those who had attempted in the earlier stages of the voyage to employ their time to some profit, gradually succumbed to the influences around them. A few of the passengers, kindly seconded by the captain and some of the officers, got up some amusing theatricals for evening entertainment, and our Hindoo friend gave an excellent Shakespearian recitation; this being in a language foreign to him was very striking to us all, as he seemed perfectly at home in the full meaning and spirit of the piece, which was Clarence's dream. The heavenly bodies presented a never-failing source of interest, the waters as in the Mediterranean reflecting their splendour; we had also the pleasure of observing the wonderful phosphorescence of the waves wherever moved by the vessel, arising from multitudes of minute animalcules. One evening, before going down to our seven-o'clock tea, there was an unusual gloom over the sky; the moon seemed to be under a heavy cloud, for her brightness was so veiled that the fixed stars were more visible than they had been for some time. While below we were informed that there was an eclipse of the moon in progress. We hastened on deck, and then found that there was indeed a total one. The phenomenon, always interesting, was on this occasion peculiarly so; the obscuration was total, but the moon was visible, of a deep red colour. It was a remarkable sight, and we watched it with extreme interest, until the moon gradually emerged from the shadow, and shone forth with intense splendour, dimming the light of all the heavenly bodies, except our beautiful planets, our faithful attendants, Venus and Jupiter.

During the voyage I availed myself of the opportunity presented to me by my fellow-passengers of obtaining some information respecting the country I was about to visit, and its inhabitants. The very different, and even contrary statements I received from them, severally and independently, confirmed my belief that the accounts of India and the Hindoos which we hear in England are greatly coloured by the character and views of the narrator; I perceived, especially, that what may be true of one part of India is very incorrect of another. I had already heard much from my Hindoo friends, and had read much on the subject; I was not, therefore, going to a country or state of society entirely unknown to me. I soon perceived, however, that though everything I heard from gentlemen or ladies who had lived long in the country was most valuable, in showing me what had to be learnt, and in aiding me to form a judgment, yet that I must not allow my mind to be influenced by the representations of individuals, however intelligent or however long they had resided in India. One gentleman, for instance, would assure me that the natives could never be trusted, and were most dishonest as servants; another spoke of their great fidelity and personal attachment to their employers, remaining with them under every difficulty, and serving them with a consideration and kindness, as well as honesty, seldom found among English servants. I was struck by observing that the Hindoo sailors, when required to act together in drawing up the line or cable, &c., seemed to find it impossible to work in concert, as our English sailors do, giving 'a long pull, and a strong pull, and a pull all together;' each one appeared to exert his strength quite independently, and thus lost much of that power which is gained by union.

In order to help them to keep time in their work, a fiddle was brought out and played to them on these occasions, which proved a poor substitute for the English sailors' united chorus. I expressed my surprise to a gentleman who employed many natives in his business, that the captain did not train these men to do their work better. He looked at me with amazement, and replied, 'He cannot; it is impossible to train these people. I have been working with them a dozen years, and if I appear to improve them a little, when I leave them for a time, everything is lost that I have taught them. They *cannot* be improved.' This remark, and the hopelessness which it indicated, led me to consider closely, in my future intercourse with the natives, whether this despondency respecting the possibility of their improvement was well-founded, or whether this difficulty in ameliorating their condition arose from want of such friendly interest in them, as would lead to a study of their nature, and the best way of improving it, and that it was increased by the want of early training adapted to remedy defects. The conclusions I arrived at after further opportunities of observation will be stated in a later part of this work. Many spoke of the natives with a contempt and dislike which reflected great discredit, in my opinion, on those who indulged in such feelings towards a race totally different from our own, and which ought to be treated with consideration as in some degree dependent on us. The Hindoos ought not be judged by the same standard as Englishmen, who have so long enjoyed the advantages of education and Christianity.

I could not avoid expressing some indignation when I heard a military gentleman call the natives 'niggers,' a term peculiarly improper, as the Asiatic race is perfectly different from the African, and no term of contempt ought to be applied to the negro or any other human being. He excused himself on the plea that the Hindoos did not object to it. Little do those who use such language from simple thoughtlessness, without any unkind feeling, know how deep a dislike to our countrymen, what rankling in the heart, they thus excite in the nation with regard to whom they use this language. One young gentleman, who was going out to take an office in India, appeared to seize opportunities of inflicting divers kicks and blows on any unfortunate coloured persons he might come across; this, however, was speedily checked by his fellow-passengers. Such conduct is no longer tolerated in India, and British justice enables any one who is thus treated at once to obtain his remedy by law. A specimen of the arrogant pretensions of some English was given by a fellow-passenger, who actually informed my Hindoo friend, a gentleman of birth and very superior education, that the 'conquered race' ought always to do homage to the conquerors, and that all natives should salaam every Englishman they meet! As he was treated respectfully and on a perfectly equal footing by the passengers generally, I endeavoured to show him the absurdity of the remark, and to turn it off as a joke—but it was not so to him; he felt it most painfully, and frequently afterwards referred to it, as an indication of the real feelings of Englishmen towards them. Other gentlemen, however, spoke and acted very differently. One especially, who was returning to an influential position in Northern India, spoke with much interest of the efforts he and others were making to bring forward native gentlemen into situations where they were preparing for the difficult art of self-government. He was, however, the only one on board who appeared to have had intercourse with the educated and superior classes of the Hindoos.

Sunday, Sept. 22.—Our Sabbath calm was somewhat interrupted in the afternoon by a slight alarm of fire in one part of the machinery. The captain appeared little disturbed by it, having all arrangements made for such a catastrophe, and it was quickly extinguished. Our speed, however, was considerably slackened, and it appeared that some injury was done. The 'Geelong' had been intended for an Australian voyage, for stormy not hot weather, and the great heat had caused the accident. Not wishing to alarm the passengers, nothing was done on that day to remedy the mischief. It was therefore very startling during the night to find the vessel stop, and hammering continued for a couple of hours. At length we went on as usual, and though our arrival was somewhat retarded, we were still two days before we were due.

Monday, Sept. 23.—Our last day on board. What varied hopes and fears animated us fellow-passengers! Almost all were anticipating delightful meetings with friends or relatives, or looking forward to some definite object in life—except myself. I knew not a single person in Bombay, whether native or English; for a letter received at Aden informed me that the Parsee friend, Mr. Manockjee Cursetjee, who had recently visited England a second time, and who had offered me one of his villas, was now with the Court at Poona; and announced the melancholy news of the death of Mr. Ramchunder Balchrishna, a most enlightened Hindoo, who had visited Bristol, and expressed most earnest interest in the elevation of the women of India.

On his return to Bombay he had been much discouraged by the caste prejudices excited against him in consequence of his journey to England, and the improvement he wished to make in his own family. He became much depressed, and pecuniary losses completely prostrated him. He had died of fever a short time before my arrival, universally lamented. The young Jewish lady was in high spirits at the prospect of her reception by the hospitable and distinguished family, who had promised to have her met, and conducted to their beautiful abode at Poona; and we all sympathised with her joyous feelings. She hoped also that her betrothed would have arrived from his station at Rangoon.

Tuesday, Sept. 24.—Very early in the morning the cannon announced our arrival in the harbour of Bombay. Shortly after, boats arrived with missives. A kind invitation for me to the wedding at Poona from the Sassoons, Miss J.'s hospitable hosts, was declined with many thanks, as this would interfere with the object of my journey. This, however, showed me that I was not to be regarded as a stranger in a strange land. On going early on deck, to my great surprise, I found an official waiting from the Governor, Sir Bartle Frere, who informed me that his Excellency had kindly arranged for the reception of myself and party at his marine bungalow, and that breakfast was awaiting our arrival. We therefore took leave of our friends, and left the vessel which had been our temporary home, truly grateful that our voyage had been accomplished so well, and with so little discomfort. I had indeed felt it a season of rest and quiet, greatly needed to prepare for such exertion as might be before me. So we went with our conductor in the Government boat, and soon reached the landing-place at Bombay.

ARRIVAL IN INDIA.

Everything is so strange and wonderful on first landing on a new continent!

Not having been on shore since we left the European soil at Marseilles, except during our miserable transit through Egypt, every object attracted my attention, and almost bewildered me. My native friend Mr. G. welcomed me to the land of his birth, and before we could reach the carriage provided for us, I had other greetings. The landlord of the Adelphi Hotel brought a letter from my Parsee friend requesting me to remain there on his account until his arrival from Poona, and Mr. G. quickly recognised by the crest of the Tagores —an elephant, with the motto 'Work will win '—on the turban of a native servant, a messenger from our friend Mr. Satyendra Nath Tagore, C.S., apologising for not being there to welcome us. He had just been appointed assistant-judge, and could not leave his duties; he begged us, however, to proceed at once to Ahmedabad, under escort of his butler, so soon as we were sufficiently rested from our voyage—an invitation which we accepted with pleasure; it was, indeed, one of long standing.

The beautiful Oriental palms, especially the graceful cocoanut trees, were most striking, and at once reminded me that I was in India. Everywhere, the appearance of the men, women, and children was sufficiently novel and curious. The deficiency of clothing in the men struck me peculiarly. They seem to consider that a black skin supersedes the necessity of raiment, and in this respect the lower orders appear perfectly devoid of any sense of decency. I never became reconciled to this, and believe now, as I did then, that living thus in a sort of savage state in the midst of a civilised people increases that want of proper self-respect and that separation from the higher classes which is so painfully characteristic of Hindoo society.

We were not aware of the Indian mode of hospitality, which consists in putting a house at the disposal of guests. Forgetting that the Court was at Poona, we expected on arriving at the Government bungalow, Malabar Point, to be received by some members of the household. We were therefore somewhat surprised at passing between rows of native liveried servants, and being ushered into a central apartment, of which, and the whole house, we were expected to take possession, making ourselves perfectly at home! It was fortunate that my Hindoo friend was with me, as few of the native servants understood any English, and the young lady with me had quite forgotten her native language. Mr. G. was located in a small bungalow adjoining, and we all greatly enjoyed the cool commodious rooms, and the shady verandah overlooking the sea. Many friends called, and some had been to the ship to offer me kind hospitality—among others, the Rev. Dr. Wilson, who, with his excellent wife, are always ready to show kindness to those who want help, and are the friends of all, of whatever creed or race. On calling that evening at his beautiful villa overlooking the sea, we were surprised to see a native gentleman walk in with his wife, a spectacle which greatly astonished my Calcutta friend; as in that city no lady is ever allowed to come out in public, and in the house it is considered indecorous for a gentleman to speak to his wife, or even to notice her, in presence of strangers. This incident led me to perceive what I had previously suspected—that what I had been told respecting India by gentlemen long resident in Calcutta, or the Bengal Presidency, did not apply to India generally, and certainly not to Bombay. I afterwards found, as I had also anticipated, that the Calcutta of fifteen, ten, or even five years ago, is very different in many important respects from the Calcutta of to-day. I therefore determined to remain in the position I had chosen, that of a learner.

When we established ourselves in our delightful temporary home, our ignorance of Anglo-Indian life made our position appear very strange to us. It is usual for visitors to take their own personal attendants with them —I was travelling without one. The servants in India, being generally Hindoos or Mahometans, do not live in the house, and the culinary department is always separated from it to avoid the heat of the fires. My young lady-friend and I were therefore quite alone in the bungalow, with none but menservants near, who had their domiciles in the compound or enclosure round the house. I was assured, however, by Mr. Ghose that we need feel no uneasiness; and, indeed, it was so, for nothing could be more kind and thoughtful than the manner in which all our wants were abundantly supplied.

Sept. 25.—The next day Mr. G. went into town to telegraph to Mr. Tagore our arrival and intention to visit him, and to deliver some of my letters in Bombay. He was much surprised at the friendly courteous manner in which he was received by all the English gentlemen he met. Remembering the general tone of society towards native gentlemen in Calcutta five years ago, before he left India, he was agreeably surprised by the very great difference he observed here. In the evening we drove to a public promenade along the beach, where we saw a glorious sunset on the bay: numerous carriages were there also, and the seats along the road were covered with persons enjoying the freshness of the evening air and the beauty of the scene. These were principally Parsees, who form an opulent and influential class in Bombay, and who are also considered more advanced than the Hindoos in social reform. But these gentlemen were enjoying their ride alone. I at once felt I was very far from my native island, where the ladies of a family share all the innocent gratifications of the other sex, and where evening enjoyment after a day of labour is considered incomplete without their presence.

A pleasant surprise awaited us on our return. Dr. A. P., the Hindoo gentleman who had conducted his wife to call on me the preceding day, now brought his three young daughters, and those of his deceased friend, Ramchunder Balchrishna, to the Government bungalow to see me. They had been educated in the Alexandra School for young Parsee ladies, which had been founded chiefly through the exertions of Mr. Manockjee Cursetjee, and in which it is attempted to give a good English education to the pupils. These young ladies did great credit to the institution. They were dressed simply and nearly in the English style, and their manners were unaffected and easy. Though they had received only two years' instruction, they were able to speak English fluently, and to enjoy seeing strangers and hearing of distant England. I regret to state that this was the only visit of the kind I received while in India, and that the pupils of this school and Mrs. Tagore were the only young Hindoo ladies I met with who could speak English. On all other occasions I was obliged to avail myself of an interpreter to communicate with native ladies, except in the case of those who had been connected with the missionaries, or were converts to Christianity. Surprise has often been expressed that I did not acquire 'the language' before coming to India. It would have been impossible for me, under the circumstances, to have devoted time and attention to the acquisition of a new language so radically different from the classical and modern tongues with which I was already acquainted; but the acquisition of any one language would have been but of little use to me. My first visit would have required a knowledge of Guzerathi, the second, Marathi. At Madras I should have required Tamil, Telugu, or Canarese; at Calcutta, Bengali; while on my return I should have needed Malayalim or some other language, to enable me to converse with the native ladies. It may be said that Hindostani is a *lingua franca*, which would have been useful everywhere. It would, doubtless, have been an advantage to me to be acquainted with it on many occasions; but all I heard while in India led me to the conclusion that though it is very necessary for persons resident in the country to master it, as it is the ordinary language of servants, yet it does not appear to be a cultivated language, or one rich in literature; besides, in the different parts of the country, it becomes so much mingled with the vernacular of the district, that what is used in one part can hardly be understood by those inhabiting a distant province. With very rare exceptions, all the educated classes in the parts of the empire I visited understood English, and generally were masters of the language; hence I had not the least difficulty in communicating with the gentlemen of the country, and through them with the ladies.

It has been already stated that my visit to India was not undertaken with any intention of special work there, but as a proof of friendly sympathy, and in the hope of gaining such information as might lead to future help in the matter of female education. I anticipated also obtaining that rest and refreshment which I needed. It was, then, with great astonishment, and at first with some regret, that I received the following official document, which was handed to me on the evening of this day:—

OFFICIAL LETTERS FROM THE GOVERNMENT OF BOMBAY.
No. 531 of 1866.
EDUCATIONAL DEPARTMENT.
From C. Gonne, Esq., Secretary to Government, Bombay, to Sir Alexander Grant, Bart., Director of Public Instruction.

Sir,—His Excellency the Governor is informed that Miss Mary Carpenter is likely to arrive by the mail steamer now expected, and that she hopes to give a portion of her time in India to the same questions, connected with education generally, with youthful and other reformatories, and with convict discipline, to which she has devoted so much time and attention in England.

2.—On questions connected with these and other cognate subjects, I am desired to state, Miss Carpenter's opinion has, for many years past, been sought and listened to by legislators and administrators of all shades of political opinion in England; and his Excellency in Council looks forward to her visit to Bombay as likely to be of great public benefit, by aiding in the solution of many problems with regard to which much has yet to be learnt in India, from the results of late European enquiry and discussion.

3.—I am accordingly instructed to request that you will be good enough to furnish Miss Carpenter with any statistical or other information on subjects connected with her enquiries which your records may supply, and afford her every facility to visit and inspect the institutions under your control.

I have the honour to be, Sir,
Your most obedient servant,
(Signed)   J. KING,
For Secretary to Government.

Bombay Castle, September 26, 1866.

The same to—

The Inspector-General of Prisons—The Inspector-General of Medical Department (for communication to all officers in charge of Lunatic Asylums)—All Departments of the Government Secretariat—The Director of Public Instruction—The Inspector-General of Hospitals and Officers in charge of Lunatic Asylums—The Inspector-General of Prisons.

This printed circular was enclosed in the following letter :—

No. 544 of 1866.

From C. Gonne, Esq., Secretary to Government, Bombay, to Miss Mary Carpenter, Bombay.

EDUCATIONAL DEPARTMENT.

Madam,—I am directed by his Excellency the Governor in Council to enclose, for your information, a copy of the instructions which have been given to the Heads of Departments under this Government, with the view of aiding the objects of your visit to Western India.

I have the honour to be, Madam,
Your most obedient servant,
(Signed)   J. KING,
Acting Under-Secretary to Government.

Bombay Castle, September 26, 1866.

It was evident, then, that my journey must now include a much more extended sphere than I had hitherto contemplated. An opportunity so courteously given of studying the different institutions of the country must not be lost. To some of these—hospitals and lunatic asylums—I had not in my work hitherto directed special attention, and it did not seem desirable to me to enter on a new sphere of labour, though I might visit these as occasion offered. To education generally—the education and reformation of the neglected and destitute classes of children—and to prison discipline, with the treatment of the criminal classes, my work had been hitherto given. To these, wherever I went, I resolved henceforth, as far as lay in my power, to devote my thoughts and attention. I therefore gratefully acknowledged to the Governor in Council the obligation he conferred on me by his missive.

BOMBAY, *Sept.* 26.—At an early hour we were at the railway station, which was indeed a scene of inconceivable din and confusion. To attempt to describe the motley groups around would be useless. We should have been perfectly bewildered but for the help of our native friend. At length we were comfortably seated in one of the first-class carriages, which, on the Indian railways, are very large and commodious. An English gentleman and a native of rank were our travelling companions. The country offered no peculiar objects of interest, but was generally verdant, having been refreshed by the rains. The cocoanut trees, so characteristic of a tropical country, disappeared as we proceeded inland. The other trees did not seem at first sight very different from our own, but a closer observation showed us that not one was exactly the same. Our chief forest trees (the oak, elm, beech, ash, &c.) are not known here. The fir-trees of the more northern regions do not appear, but we occasionally saw some which bore considerable resemblance to these, as well as to our other old familiar friends. Mr. Ghose could not enlighten us respecting their names and nature, as they were generally different from what he had been accustomed to see in Bengal. Some very strange-looking fruits, as they seemed, attracted our attention. On approaching nearer we found that they were the hanging nests of a tribe of birds, which adopt this plan as a protection from their enemies, the monkeys and the snakes. It was very interesting to observe in their natural state these very curious contrivances suggested by instinct, which we had formerly seen only in a museum.

Some woody mountains at no great distance bounded our view on the right, and formed a striking object. We had good opportunities for observing the lower classes of the population, since the stations were frequent, and as the arrival of the train appeared to be the great event of the day in these regions, numbers of natives crowded round, every time we stopped; their unregulated manners, loud discordant jabbering, and insufficient clothing, did not impress the mind with a favourable idea of the peasantry of the country, but we felt that it would be unfair to select such a concourse as a type of the people. As the railways are under the control of English companies, we did feel a right to complain of the neglectful conduct of the railway officials, whose attention we found it very difficult to obtain; and the stations themselves were so roughly built, that it was seldom possible for a lady to alight there, or to obtain any refreshment.

At length, after passing over several smaller rivers, we came to the beautiful Nerbudda, whose wide sandy banks indicate that during the rains it must be of considerable width. The bridge which crosses it is long, and it had been recently repaired after some damage from the rains. This stream is held sacred by the superstitious natives, and considerable indignation was felt at the idea of its being crossed, in defiance of the goddess of the river, by the sacrilegious machinery. On the appointed day, therefore, when all was prepared for the opening of the railway, immense multitudes of the natives assembled on the banks of the sacred stream, expecting to see its titular divinity execute vengeance on the perpetrators of this impious outrage. The train arrived and began to cross the bridge, when, in the very middle of its course, there was a sudden stoppage! The power of the goddess was now manifest to the assembled multitudes; she was about to be avenged. Hideous shrieks and yells arose with the most tremendous excitement. But in a few moments there was another shout such as is never heard from Hindoos— a true British hurrah from the triumphant officials mounted on the train, who set on the steam again, and gloriously crossed the river. Then the astonished natives changed their minds, and said it was a god! Cocoanuts and other votive offerings were showered in profusion; and even now at times such presents are made, to gain the favour of so powerful an agency.

The railway must indeed appear something supernatural to these ignorant inhabitants of districts which before had seldom been disturbed by the inroads of civilisation. The real effects on the population are more wonderful than fiction would dare to represent; in a variety of ways the railroad is probably producing a greater change in the population than any other single agency. The mere fact of connecting by an easy and agreeable day's travelling, places which formerly could be reached only by tiresome and expensive journeys of weeks, is of incalculable importance in breaking down the narrow ignorance which characterises most parts of India, and in promoting friendly intercourse between different parts of the country, as well as in facilitating commerce, &c. The railway carriages are also extremely useful, indirectly, in leading the most exclusive natives to disregard the regulations of caste. A Brahmin has frequently been known to draw back on entering a carriage, when perceiving it filled with persons of other castes, with whom contact would, in his opinion, be pollution. He retreats to seek another, but all are equally infected; he appeals for protection to the railway official, who coolly informs him that his remedy is easy; he may take a first-class ticket, and enjoy solitary state in a carriage to himself. But this greatly-increased outlay is not at all to his mind, and as his business is pressing he swallows the indignity, and steps into the carriage with the other passengers. An amusing story was told us of a proud Brahmin thus being unexpectedly shut in with a number of persons of the most despised class, on whom he had been accustomed to heap every species of insult. Finding him now in their power, they returned to him some of the contemptuous treatment which he had lavished on them, and he was obliged to bear it from his fellow-passengers until the train stopped. Christianity had not taught him that we are all children of the same Heavenly Father, nor them that we are to forgive injuries and to overcome evil with good; the railway was giving this arrogant man a lesson that he had better in future restrain himself in his treatment of his humbler fellow-beings. My friend Mr. G. saw some persons of different castes drinking together in a railway carriage; on his pointing out to them their impropriety, they excused themselves on the ground that the current of air which passed through the carriage when in motion removed contamination from them! Habits of punctuality and attention to duty are also taught, both directly and indirectly, by the railway. At first, passengers were constantly too late, or arrived just as the train was starting, and being thus unable to take their tickets, had the mortification of seeing it go off without them. Persons of consequence were at first very indignant on the occasion, but soon learnt that they, too, must submit to the inexorable law of railroads, which, like time and tide, wait for no man. The railway officials, who are chiefly natives, are here obtaining unconsciously an excellent training, of more value to them than any pecuniary recompense. While, then, we were frequently annoyed by many inconveniences and discomforts on this journey, we could not but feel that under the circumstances the Indian railways are very wonderful, and show the possibility of improving even the inferior portions of the native races, under judicious government and proper training. Our English fellow-passenger, whose duties in the Civil Service gave him much opportunity of forming a judgment on these subjects, fully corroborated my opinion. He spoke much of the importance of cotton cultivation in this district. By his extensive knowledge of the country, and the friendly manner in which he conversed in the vernacular with the native gentleman, and spoke of the natives generally, he gave us a very favourable impression of the tone of feeling existing in this province between the English and the natives. Having heard much of the unhealthy effect of the Indian climate on our countrymen, I was astonished to learn from him that he had been more than twenty years in the country, since his florid appearance indicated the healthy condition of an English country gentleman. This he attributed to regular active exercise, and to having his mind fully occupied by his work. A similar testimony I received from many in various parts of the country. The native gentleman could speak a little English, and showed us with much pride likenesses of the Queen and Royal Family in lockets appended to his handsome gold watch-chain. He politely asked us to occupy his villa on our return.

At length we reached Surat, where we were rejoiced to meet our friend Mr. Tagore, who had come from Ahmedabad that morning to meet us. Though we had sent him a telegram announcing our journey on the morning preceding, he had not received it until the middle of the night, and had kindly started at once to make every possible arrangement for our comfort. We had been informed that we could pass the night at the railway station; all the accommodation provided there, however, for passengers, consisted of cane sofas in very uncomfortable-looking ladies' waiting-rooms, with miserable dirty dressing-rooms. There seemed to be nothing like an hotel in the place, and Mr. Tagore had therefore telegraphed to a native gentleman who had borrowed from a friend a beautiful villa or 'garden house' in the neighbourhood, where a dinner in English style was kindly provided for us. We afterwards learnt that, had the time of our coming been known, many of the English families resident in or near Surat would have shown us hospitality; having, however, no introductions to this city, I had not calculated on any such courtesy.

SURAT, *Sept.* 27.—The next morning we were up betimes to reach the station early, and we drove through this famous old town. Few traces of its ancient splendour remain, after the various vicissitudes it has gone through; indeed, we were chiefly struck with the air of desolation pervading all the streets; this was heightened rather than diminished by occasional remains of ancient carving over some miserable abode where half-dressed natives were standing, fixing on us a dull stupid gaze as we passed. What we saw gave us a far from pleasant impression of a Hindoo city, and when the Hindoo gentleman who had kindly arranged for our comfort pressed me to stay there a few days on my return, I certainly did not feel any anxiety to accept the invitation. Little did I anticipate how much of progress I should find in the midst of what appeared very unpromising at Surat.

Nothing of peculiar interest presented itself on this second day's journey; indeed, if there had been much to observe, we should hardly have noticed it, so intent were the two friends who had long been separated on giving and receiving news from each other—so glad was I to learn from my young friend the assistant-judge everything about his present position, and of what he thought was wanting for India. He informed us that on his return to his own city, Calcutta, about two years before, after having passed his examination for the Civil Service, he was received with the greatest honour by his countrymen; indeed, his success was regarded by them as a national triumph. He was appointed by the Government to the Bombay Presidency, and he determined to take with him his young bride, to whom he had been long betrothed. Having witnessed in England the comfort and happiness of our domestic life, and perceiving the immense benefits resulting to society from the elevation of women, he resolved to depart entirely from the customs of his country—which impose strict seclusion on ladies of position, and oblige them to treat their husbands with a deference bordering on servility—and to regard his wife in every respect as an equal. Staying for some months at Bombay before proceeding to his destination, his bride had been most kindly received, and gradually introduced into the customs of English society. The change was indeed great to her from the seclusion of the zenana to the freedom of our life, but she had shown herself equal to it, under the protection of her husband. When settled at Ahmedabad, she again met with English ladies, who took a generous pleasure in bringing forward their young Eastern sister; and intercourse with them was facilitated by her having become sufficiently acquainted with English for ordinary purposes, through the sedulous instructions of her husband. They were fortunate in being at Ahmedabad in the midst of a native society considerably advanced in ideas on the subject of female elevation, so that they had not the immense difficulties to encounter which would have beset them had they remained at Calcutta. On one occasion, indeed, they gave an entertainment to English and native gentlemen and ladies, a brilliant account of which appeared in the local newspapers. How much moral courage all this must have required I did not fully know until after I had visited Calcutta. We heard also from our friend that he had an important case in hand—a gang of thirty-two men and boys who had been roving the country stealing, and who, after many remands by the magistrates, owing to the difficulty of obtaining reliable evidence, were now on trial. We wished much to see him in his new dignity. The time thus passed rapidly as we travelled through a rich and beautiful country, revived by the recent rains. There was no place of refreshment during the whole journey, so we were thankful that we had been liberally supplied with provisions at the Government bungalow, and that our friend had also brought his contribution, a custom which appears general and necessary in railway travelling in India. We were, however, unpleasantly reminded of being in a tropical region by the rapidity with which sandwiches became uneatable, and sweet cakes were made the abode of a colony of ants. We found some compensation in the fruit of the banana or plantain, a most valuable article of food in India, very plentiful, cheap, nutritious, and refreshing; it is equally acceptable to rich and poor, and is prized by all. Those who know it only as procured in English fruit-shops can little appreciate its real excellence.

At length, as evening advanced, we perceived that we were approaching a city, and drove into the station at Ahmedabad, the termination of this line of rail. As this is the capital of an extensive cotton district, the place was very crowded, and the scene of many greetings and much bustle; but our friend soon perceived his carriage waiting for us, and having put our luggage into his bullock-cart to follow, we drove off, all highly gratified that this long-expected visit was now actually to be accomplished. There were many interesting objects on our way, but they did not attract much attention from us; we were anxious to see his Eastern home, and the lady who was at the head of it. At length we passed through a large wooded compound to a handsome-looking house with a portico, and were introduced to drawing-rooms fitted up in English style, where Mrs. Tagore kindly received us, and led Miss C. and myself to our apartments, which she had taken pains to arrange so as to promote our comfort. When dinner was announced she conducted us in, doing her part as hostess admirably.

The table was spread as in an English gentleman's house, and, except the presence of Hindoo servants, there was little to remind me that I was separated from my native land by nearly a whole hemisphere. There was even less to make me realise the idea, as we were conversing with animation in English round the hospitable table, that I was the only individual there of Saxon race,—that the young lady with me, to whom English had become more familiar than her own language, and who was a Christian, was the daughter of a Coolin Brahmin, one of the highest and most exclusive of sects,—and that my other friends, who had not embraced Christianity, were of the ancient unmixed races of Hindoos who had, without renouncing their nationality, broken through the bonds imposed by ancient custom, and were anxious to bring Western civilisation into their own country. This meeting was a happy one to all of us, and we felt it to be an omen that we should realise long-cherished hopes and aspirations.

CHAPTER II.

AHMEDABAD AND ITS INSTITUTIONS.

THE city of Ahmedabad is said to have been founded A.D. 1412 by the Sultan Ahmed Shah, as the capital of the then rich empire of Guzerat, and he named it after himself. Ancient Hindoo capitals supplied materials for raising many of the structures of the new city. It was built along the river Sabarmati, which forms the base of a city of semicircular form. It remained a powerful place under various rulers, until in the eighteenth century the Marathas obtained possession of it. In 1780 the English stormed and seized it. Afterwards it was restored to the Marathas, and remained in their hands until 1818, when, on the fall of the Peishwa, it finally reverted to the British. The city is surrounded by a substantial wall, averaging fifteen feet in height and five in thickness, which is more than five miles in length. There are bastions at almost every fifty paces and eighteen gates. The walls are in substantial repair, for in 1832 the municipal authorities levied a special tax for their thorough restoration.

Three centuries of Mahometan rule left many traces of grandeur in the architecture of the city; the splendid tombs and mosques, built with much richness of detail and often beauty of design, show that it was once inhabited by a very superior race. But great devastations are evident everywhere, and the general appearance of the city indicates rather departed grandeur than present prosperity. Yet the fine old walls with their bastions and gates have a very striking appearance, and the Mahometan buildings, which are seen in every direction, tempt the traveller to spend many days in exploration. Murray tells us in his guide-book that a week at least will be required to view over the principal sights of the place, and many interesting excursions may be made to remarkable places in the neighbourhood. Yet this extraordinary city is so little known on the other side of India, that when at Calcutta some months afterwards I spoke to an educational inspector about schools in Ahmedabad, he remarked, 'You may as well speak in England of what is done in the school of some remote village in Russia, as to us here of such a place as Ahmedabad.'

The interesting relics of antiquity in this wonderful city I had, however, little power of exploring. The weather was still hot, and all my time and strength were required to become acquainted with the institutions and the inhabitants of the place.

Our kind host adopted the mode of living usual with the Anglo-Indian gentry. At six o'clock an early cup of tea is generally served to every one in private; this is a very much-prized custom of the country. All members of the family are at their own disposal until they assemble for a substantial breakfast at about ten, earlier or later according to circumstances. Sometimes special excursions are planned for these cool early hours; sometimes there is literally a 'morning call' from friends, generally by appointment; no one, however, is expected to be ready to admit visitors between seven and eight A.M. unless previously notified. After breakfast the gentlemen go to their business, and do not appear until it is finished. The ladies usually receive company before two, when 'tiffin' is announced, after which they are supposed to be in retirement until they dress for the evening ride, and return to dinner at half-past seven or eight. Little is done after the long ceremony of that meal, and all retire early, often at ten, to rise betimes, and enjoy the cool of the early morning. On Sunday we are reminded mournfully of being in a heathen country—no 'sound of the church-going bell;' we did not even hear the old familiar tones of a church clock, or even of a house clock; there seemed little note of time, except the announcement of meals. The camp church is about four miles from the city, and the same clergyman officiates at a small church near Mr. Tagore's residence, but on this occasion there was no service. So we had family worship at home, each one taking a part in it, on this the first Sabbath in the country of the great Indian reformer Rammohun Roy: this course we adopted on each succeeding Sabbath.

Guzerat is famed for the luxuriance of its vegetation, and for its abundant and varied animal life. Of the former we had seen numerous indications on our journey, and on our rides we were struck with observing high hedgerows of hothouse plants, which did not, however, indicate careful nurture such as ours receive in England; they were wild and straggling, and not beautiful, though certainly useful as a fence. The cereals are extremely abundant, quite different from ours of the temperate regions. The trees are very varied: many produce fruits and seeds, which, though not useful as human food, are excellent nutriment to the animals that sport among their branches. The graceful acacia is a pleasing object at all times, and especially when it forms a shady avenue to some princely abode. The Oriental palms in all their varied families have disappeared, the country being too far inland; but it was delightful to see for the first time the banyans, renowned in stories told us from early childhood. The fine grove of these noble trees which led from the city gate to the camp did not, however, realise our expectations. The long roots hung down indeed from the branches of the trees, but did not reach the ground, having been injured or destroyed by being in so public a thoroughfare of both men and beasts. The absence of beautiful flowers, however, greatly disappointed me. No splendid tropical plants adorned, as I had expected, the verandahs of the houses of the gentry; their ample compounds were not artistically laid out as in England, so as to screen the unsightly outbuildings of the mansion, and to gratify a taste for the beauties of nature; unless Nature herself had done something to adorn the spot, everything seemed left uncared for; a neglected road took the place of what would have been in England a fine carriage-drive. The dwellings of the poor were equally destitute of floral decoration. In the most narrow dismal streets of our crowded cities at home, pots of flowers may be seen in some upper windows, where the miserable tenants carefully cherish such plants as can bear the smoke and impure air, and thus obtain a small glimpse of the loveliness of nature. But here in a splendid climate, with every advantage that can be desired, a total apathy seems to pervade the population respecting flowers, or indeed anything which would require the bestowal of the very smallest trouble. The field flowers of England cannot of course grow in this torrid region, and there appear none to supply their places. The scorching rays of the midday sun, with a long dry season, during which the ground is not often moistened by a single drop of rain, are too powerful for tender roots which do not penetrate to any great depth. The chief flowers, I was informed, grow on trees or shrubs, and in some parts of the country on creepers hanging in festoons from lofty trees. These blossom at different parts of the year, but rarely at the particular time when I happened to visit any place. Except, therefore, in a few spots where special care and culture were bestowed, the six months I spent in India did not give me any very favourable impression of the native taste for flowers. They appeared to be chiefly sought after by the lower classes to make votive garlands and wreaths for their idols, for which a small yellow chrysanthemum and marigold are much in request; and by the higher, as complimentary offerings to guests.

But if the deficiency of flowers caused me some disappointment, the wild animals were a constant source of entertainment. No zoological gardens are needed here! The monkeys exhibited the most entertaining tricks and gymnastic exercises gratis for our amusement, and were neither feared nor regarded with much surprise as frequent visitors to the trees in our host's compound. The most charming little squirrels made themselves perfectly at home on the window-sills, and even ventured into the room if they had a chance of finding anything eatable. Beautiful green parrots were abundant in the trees, and especially appeared to delight in the large banyans, under whose shade we took our drive. Once the carriage was stopped in a narrow sandy road, bordered with cactuses, by a long string of camels, a sight which was too common in these parts to excite any alarm in the horses. As we were returning early one morning through the city from a visit to an institution, we observed in a narrow street a procession of bullock-carts, each containing something carefully covered; what was our amazement on beholding in each cart a fine young tiger standing firmly manacled down, and covered with a cloth as a sort of morning dress! His ferocity appeared entirely subdued by the sense of incapacity. It was impossible to divine the meaning of this strange spectacle, as there are no wild-beast shows here. We were informed, however, that they were for the barbaric native prince of Baroda, who places his special delight in collecting and keeping under his sway numbers of savage animals. Not long before, he had filled with horror the civilised portion of the community by trampling to death with elephants some unfortunate persons who had fallen under his displeasure. It is well that such a man lives in an age when public opinion has sufficient force to restrain him from further enormities of the kind. This was the only actual glimpse of the royal animal that I had in India; but tiger-hunting appears to be a favourite British sport in these parts. The prowess of the English in this daring amusement is much prized by the natives, as it is not unfrequently the means of rescuing a village, or even a whole district, from continual attacks of the savage beast. A tiger's skin is highly valued by the hunter as a trophy; I saw several adorning one gentleman's house. The claws are regarded by the natives as charms; they are worn as brooches by English ladies. Though I heard many snake stories while in India, yet I happily did not see one of these dreaded reptiles during my whole stay there; the nearest approach to one was at Ahmedabad, where I once saw the large trail of a snake across the dusty road. With respect to the insect portion of the animal kingdom, the less said the better. I did not see the gorgeous butterflies I expected, or indeed any that I admired,—but became acquainted with many whose presence I did not desire.

Ahmedabad may be regarded as a favourable specimen of a mofussil or provincial town. The general condition of a Hindoo city is much modified by the character of the English officials who are stationed there. In this respect, as in many others, Ahmedabad is fortunate, though not singular, in the advantages it possesses, as it has very long enjoyed the services of gentlemen of high culture and devoted energy. The results of these are very evident in the advanced tone of the more educated native inhabitants, in the enlightened development of many of the institutions, and the improvements which are continually going on in the city and its neighbourhood.

The privilege I enjoyed of being the guest of a Hindoo family enabled me to have far more friendly intercourse than I could have had under other circumstances with the native inhabitants, and the impressions formed in this city materially aided me in my subsequent judgments, both respecting society and the institutions of the country. The reader will not therefore, it is hoped, object to my giving in a journal form a somewhat detailed account of these.

Monday, Oct. 1.— Our host, the assistant-judge, kindly permitted us to accompany him to the court, to be present at the conclusion of the trial now pending. The case was a curious one. Several months before a large quantity of property was discovered in the possession of persons who could not give any account of it. Two men were apprehended as thieves, and these, when examined, stated that they were members of a large gang engaged in predatory excursions, and leading a wandering vagabond life. They gladly accepted the offer of being allowed to turn Queen's evidence, and proceeded to point out to the police various persons from different districts who were their accomplices. As many as thirty-two were thus apprehended, and thrown into prison together. Much time was occupied in taking depositions before the magistrates, searching for witnesses, and weighing their very loose and indefinite evidence. The prisoners themselves, although at first they made tolerably clear statements, after having been kept associated in prison for some time, gave such contradictory accounts, that little credit could be attached to them. Some of them greatly objected to take any form of an oath, or to make any solemn asseveration as required by law. The oath is very simple, requiring only that the Great God should be invoked as a witness that they 'speak the truth, the whole truth, and nothing but the truth.' 'What should I tell a lie for?' said one. A clever little fellow, about eight years old, was the son of one of the witnesses. He could not, of course, be expected to understand the nature of an oath, but was asked, 'Do you know the difference between truth and falsehood?' 'Who knows?' was the precocious reply. The young rogue was not, of course, aware that a certain Roman judge once showed the same scepticism when he asked, 'What is truth?' and did not wait for a reply.

The result of repeated examinations was, that the whole gang of thirty-two men and boys were committed for trial, but not before they had been four or five months in prison. The case for the prosecution was completed on the preceding Saturday, but, owing to the length and conflicting nature of the evidence, the trial was not concluded. Mr. Ghose, who had just been called to the English Bar, and was familiar with the proceedings of our courts of justice, was present on that occasion. The proceedings were in Guzerathi, the vernacular of this part of the country; but as this language, like all others of Northern India, is based on Sanscrit, and he was thoroughly acquainted with that magnificent language, as well as with Bengali and Hindostani, he found little difficulty in following the proceedings. He was much struck with the order and propriety with which the whole was managed, and felt an emotion of very natural pride that here, probably for the first time, an assize court was being conducted solely by natives of his country—the judge himself, necessarily a civil servant, being the first Hindoo who had obtained that honour. I myself felt perhaps no less proud that my country had been so successful in developing the native powers of self-government, and that she has infused her principles of justice into the nation for which she has so serious a responsibility.

We set off about noon—the judge, Mr. Ghose, and myself. Though the court was not a quarter of a mile from the house, we were obliged to go in a covered carriage, to protect ourselves from the powerful rays of a midday October sun. On arriving, we found the thirty-two prisoners sitting outside on the ground, chained together, or rather connected together by a rod uniting each pair of handcuffs, so as to compel them to walk in line. They were guarded by a small number of policemen, dressed in dark cloth, and evidently a superior set of men; their countenances and deportment indicated that energy, sagacity, and attention to duty which characterise our English police force. The court is a small simple unadorned building; the windows and doors being habitually open in these parts, publicity is obtained without much room within for spectators. Several persons were there to await the result of the trial; but their dress indicated that they belonged to the more respectable class, and not to the low vagabond people who infest our police courts.

We were ushered first into the justice's room, where I had great pleasure in seeing for the first time our friend arrayed in his official silk gown and bands—wigs are very mercifully dispensed with in these parts. The clerk of the court and other turbaned officials attended, and handed him very respectfully various documents, which he signed with as much dignity as our worthy Recorder at home. We then followed the judge into the court, and occupied chairs placed for us near him. The prisoners were brought in unmanacled, and stood in mournful array round the room. In ordinary cases there are no juries in these courts; it would indeed at present be a useless farce to introduce here our treasured English institution. In place of it there are two or more natives called 'assessors,' whose verdict the judge takes, and registers with his own. Not understanding the proceedings, I had leisure to observe the prisoners. There was great variety in their deportment and expression of countenance. Some were young men of an open and intelligent appearance, who spoke fluently and well—one might believe that they would maintain themselves honestly if placed in suitable circumstances; others were evidently low bad characters, who were getting their living dishonestly; some were elderly men, whom one regretted to see in such a position, when so near the close of life; worse than all, there were four or five miserable little boys, who had come from a great distance, and who had lost their mothers in their wanderings. The little witness again came up, and with cool effrontery pointed out the various prisoners whom he accused of being thieves. One of these was his own father, who indignantly repelled the charge, stating his conviction that the boy had been induced by the police to make these statements. I myself felt sure that no reliance could be placed in him.

The result of the trial was, that the judge and assessors did not consider the evidence sufficient to punish the prisoners; at the same time there was every reason to believe that the bulk of them were habitual thieves, forming part of large gangs which infest the country; these make annual predatory excursions to a distance from their homes, bringing back, to divide at the rendezvous, the plunder they have collected. The boys were probably being trained to a life of crime; some of them were known to have been living with a wicked-looking woman who was among the prisoners. They were acquitted of the theft, but required to give bail for future good conduct. When this announcement was made, a great lamentation arose among the prisoners. 'Where could they get bail?' they touchingly asked. In default they were led out one by one to be manacled again, submissively yielding themselves to the officer appointed to the duty. Law has evidently established a strong and mysterious sway over the minds of the population, however degraded. I was, indeed, informed that it is the awe and dread inspired by the paraphernalia of justice, which deters the common people from frequenting the courts.

The business of the court was terminated, and we left the poor prisoners sitting on the ground as we had first seen them, now piteously lamenting, and awaiting their return to gaol.

On the same evening we had an interesting visit from two native gentlemen, the Headmaster of the High School, and the Principal of the Normal Training School for male teachers. The latter of these, Mr. Mahiputram Rupram, had visited England to study the educational institutions, and returned full of admiration at our method of training teachers, which he endeavoured to introduce into his own Normal School. Both gentlemen gave me valuable information respecting the position and wants of the different classes of Hindoo society. The Government schools touch only the higher classes, among whom the desire for education is rapidly extending. No class exists here corresponding with our lower middle or mechanic class. The inferior portion of the population is quite untouched by any educational institutions; they do not feel the want of education for their children, and the higher classes do not appear to feel any sympathy for them, as in our country. A deep impassable gulf is between the different classes, arising chiefly from caste distinctions; never did I notice any friendly recognition of the lower by the higher, nor hear of any efforts being made to do them good or elevate their condition. When I urged upon a native gentleman the duty of trying to do something to diminish the ignorance of those who constitute the largest portion of the population, he replied, 'We have enough to do at present with the education of our own class, without thinking of these.' I endeavoured to explain to these gentlemen the kind of education which we consider adapted to meet the wants of this class, and the importance of endeavouring to elevate them; they appeared thoroughly to comprehend and appreciate the idea of our ragged schools. The subject of female education was one in which they were deeply interested. None but the higher classes attempt at present to obtain instruction for their daughters, and here great difficulties are experienced from the want of good female teachers. I promised to do all in my power to help them, but pointed out that it would be impossible to obtain the services of English ladies without proper arrangements being made for their residence in a strange land. Mr. Tagore suggested the establishment at Bombay of a Female Normal Training School, whence teachers might be sent out into the surrounding districts.

Tuesday, Oct. 3.—It was arranged for us to pay an early visit to the jail before the heat became oppressive. We therefore started between seven and eight in the morning, with the advantage of the escort of Dr. Wyllie, the superintendent. It is the custom in India to appoint a gentleman of the Civil Service to superintend the jails, most commonly the surgeon. Ahmedabad jail was originally a Mahometan college, and was converted to its present purpose in 1820. It is a fine-looking building, and near the citadel, but not of course well adapted to its present purpose, though the large space inclosed by the buildings gives it great capabilities of improvement. The first thing which struck us painfully was that the men had irons on their legs. This barbaric custom, which has long been exploded in our own country, is here preserved, and is indeed general in India in consequence of the usual insecurity of the premises. The prisoners were working in large open sheds with little appearance of confinement. A number were occupied in weaving strong cotton carpets, which appeared well calculated for wear. Others were making towelling of various kinds, very strong and good, from the cotton grown in the neighbourhood, while others were manufacturing pretty little cocoa mats and baskets. There was not in general a criminal look in the culprits; they were working with good will, and appeared interested in their occupation, as in an ordinary factory. Except the chains, there was nothing of a penal description in the scene around us; and though working in this cheerful open place at useful trades might not give the intended feeling of punishment, still it was to be hoped that training these men to useful labour, under good moral influences, must have a beneficial influence on their future lives. On remarking this with great satisfaction to Dr W., he informed me that the salutary influence of the day's work under proper supervision was completely neutralised, or even worse, by the corrupting influences of the night. There are 400 prisoners in this jail, for whom the number of sleeping-cells is totally inadequate, and three or four are consequently locked up together in the dark for twelve hours, viz. from sunset to sunrise. There is no possibility of preventing during this period communication of the most corrupting nature, both moral and physical. No man convicted of a first offence only can enter this place, which ought to be one of punishment and attempted reformation, without the greatest probability of contamination, and in gaining experience in evil from the adepts in crime who are confined with him; no young boy can enter without his fate being sealed for life! Juvenile delinquents, casual offenders, hardened thieves sentenced to a long term of imprisonment, are all herded together without any possibility of proper classification or separation. The condition of the thirty-two whom I had seen at the court on the day before was even worse than the others; they were all penned up together without work. There they had been for many months; and still they all were without any attempt being made to give them instruction, which might improve their moral and intellectual condition. This state of things was not owing to any neglect on the part of the superintendent, a man of enlightened benevolence, who devoted himself heart and soul to his work. The conditions of this jail are such that, though able and willing to remedy all these evils, if authority and means were given to him, under the existing circumstances he is powerless. There is ample room on the premises for him to construct separate cells for all the prisoners, with only the cost of material—this is not granted to him; he cannot therefore carry out the printed regulations that the prisoners are not to be made worse while in custody. The regulations direct that the juveniles shall be separated from the adults; this is now simply impossible. Rules are made that the prisoners shall receive instruction, but no salary is allowed for a schoolmaster; there is no place appropriated for instruction, and no time is granted for schooling; there are ten hours for labour, two hours are requisite for meals and rest, and during the remainder of the twenty-four hours the prisoners are locked up. It is indeed permitted by the regulations that some prisoners may be employed as instructors, but with the proviso that their hours of labour shall not be abridged for the purpose. Such instructors could not be expected to exercise any good moral influence on the other prisoners; yet to commence with these, if any educated men were among them, might lead to some better arrangement. The old college hall might possibly be employed as a schoolroom for a couple of hours after sunset; but light would then be required, and oil did not form a part of the authorised expenditure. There were, then, obstacles to any kind of instruction being imparted to the prisoners, which no amount of earnestness on the part of the officials or the superintendent could surmount.

On enquiring whether there were any females in the jail, we were conducted to a small separate court, where in a dismal ward there were some miserable women employed in drudgery work. There were no female attendants, and indeed no attempt appeared to be made to improve their wretched condition. I felt grieved and shocked that in any part of the British dominions, women who were rendered helpless by being deprived of liberty, and thus fell under our special responsibility, should be so utterly uncared for, as to be left under the superintendence of male warders, and without any means of improvement.

In all these observations I found that I had the full accordance of the superintendent; who, so far from being annoyed at the discovery of so many evils in this place, only rejoiced that some one should add force to his own representations by an independent testimony. He stated that he understood it to be in contemplation to build a large central jail for the long-sentenced prisoners; the removal of these from his own would of course remedy the overcrowding, though it would not enable each prisoner to have a separate cell. In the meantime the evils were very great in a sanitary as well as in a moral point of view. On one occasion more than 100 had died owing to a want of good sanitary arrangements. Immediate attention to the condition of this jail appeared therefore necessary.

Considering this as a common jail, without long-sentenced prisoners, the following points suggested themselves as necessary to carry out the intentions of Government :—

First.—A number of well-ventilated sleeping-cells should be constructed without delay, so as to enable every prisoner to have a separate cell for sleeping.

Secondly.—A trained and efficient teacher should be engaged to carry out instruction; arrangements should be made to provide a cheerful and well-lighted school-room. Educated prisoners may be employed as assistant teachers; these should be specially trained and instructed by the headmaster in their labour hours, so as to provide as efficient a staff as possible.

Thirdly.—The mark system and classification should be carried out.

Fourthly.—Prisoners awaiting trial should be kept in separation, but not under penal condition.

Fifthly.—The female department should be completely remodelled, under female warders. All the advantages provided for the men should be given to the women.

Wednesday, Oct. 3.—Our next visit was of a more agreeable description, viz. to the schools of Ahmedabad. Efforts have been made for the last fifteen years to introduce education among the little girls of the place. The result has been that, as those who had received some rudiments of instruction became themselves mothers, they knew the importance of opening the minds of their daughters, and not only were themselves more enlightened, but sent their children willingly to school. The school which we were about to visit was founded by a wealthy citizen of the place, since deceased; his widow, a superior woman, maintained it from respect to his memory; she placed its management under the care of a committee composed of English and native ladies; and though she did not wish to receive any pecuniary help from the public funds, yet she desired that it should have the advantage of Government inspection. The English ladies were much pleased to induce their native friends to act thus with them. How remarkable a step had here been quietly taken I did not fully appreciate until I had been in Calcutta, and other parts of the empire; then I found how very far behind Ahmedabad these other places were, in effort to promote female education among the leading Hindoos, —in emancipation of the ladies from the thraldom imposed by custom,—and in self-effort for improvement on their own part.

It was, then, with great pleasure that we set off soon after breakfast to visit this school for young ladies. Friends at home had bountifully supplied me with a variety of little presents—toys, beads, &c. Books would of course be useless, as English is an unknown tongue in India to the female portion of the inhabitants; but a number of pictures, tastefully mounted on fancy cards, we thought certain to prove attractive. Children in all parts of the world delight in gifts, especially from strangers; I received a welcome, therefore, by providing myself plentifully with these treasures. We were introduced into a large schoolroom, where about eighty little girls, whose ages ranged from six to eleven, were sitting in order on benches. The very slight clothing usual in this country did not conceal the profusion of jewels with which their persons were adorned—bracelets and anklets of every description, rings on the fingers and on the toes, pearl earrings and nose-rings, arranged according to the individual taste of each. The adornings were evidently special, in honour of the occasion, many wearing on their little persons two hundred pounds' worth of jewels. At all times, however, the habit of wearing ornaments of the precious metals, pearls, or other jewels, is so common that it is not safe for the children to go out alone, lest they should be murdered for the sake of them. This occurrence is by no means infrequent, and there are consequently arrangements always made for conducting the children to school, and sending them safely home. Having observed the children, we asked for the mistress of the school. There was none! Masters only, or pundits, were there, and also two or three inspectors of schools. The older classes were examined in our presence in some of the ordinary branches of education, and they seemed familiar with them; but all the younger classes, constituting nearly three-fourths of the school, were unable to take any share in what was going on. The infant system of education appears to be entirely unknown in these parts. I requested to hear the children sing, and they performed to the best of their power a kind of harsh intoning of the poetry they were learning. One of the pundits professed to teach needlework to the girls, and appeared somewhat proud of the specimens he produced; the attempt at fancy work was not bad, but the plain sewing would certainly excite much amusement in an ordinary needlewoman at home. When the examination was concluded, and the little presents distributed, we were informed that the lady-patroness of the school invited me to call on her. I was obliged, however, to decline the honour, as she could not admit the gentlemen of the party, and we were expected at the High School. She therefore politely sent in trays of flowers and pan-sooparee, with silver vases of rosewater to sprinkle on us, the usual mode of showing honour to guests. Pan-sooparee consists of bits of betelnut with a little lime to draw out the flavour, wrapt in leaves of the same tree. Spices are also freely distributed. The natives are much in the habit of chewing these. We were surprised to see four women there, observing the examination; they were widows who had come to present themselves as candidates for training to teach in the school. Their appearance did not excite in my mind any expectation that they could be qualified for such an office in any short period; still the fact was encouraging, that women were anxious to gain their livelihood in this manner.

We then proceeded to the High School. Schools of this kind hold an intermediate position between the branch schools, which are vernacular only, and the college where young men prepare to matriculate and take degrees. The branch schools may be considered as corresponding to some extent with our National and British schools, but the class of boys is higher, and there are not here pupil-teachers, but assistant-masters. The boys who are to be educated generally remain three or four years in the branch school, and five in the High School, whence they proceed to the college, if they succeed in passing their matriculation or entrance examination, as it is called. Hence these youths have a much longer period of school education than is usual in England, except in the higher classes of society. In the superior mission schools, it is not uncommon for the three kinds of schools to be combined in one institution, the scholars being received in a very rudimentary stage, and continuing in a superior class after matriculation, and until they had obtained the degree of Master of Arts. This I afterwards saw at Bombay. There was no mission school here, and the High School we were about to visit prepared the young men for university degrees.

It was indeed a remarkable sight. We passed from room to room, each one with its class of from twenty to thirty young men and a teacher, all absorbed in their lessons, and manifesting an attention and good conduct, as well as intelligence, rarely witnessed in England in a large school; the Eastern dress, with the bare legs and feet, made the spectacle very striking. Most of the students appeared to be between fourteen and twenty years of age; we little imagined then that a large proportion of them were probably married; we afterwards learned that an intelligent youth of eighteen, whom we saw there, had been married nine years! We were requested to question the elder classes, and as they were familiar with English, we had pleasure in doing so. We examined the three highest classes in our literature (both prose and poetry), Roman and English history, natural philosophy, and mathematics. The 'pons asinorum' did not appear to puzzle them, though, to satisfy ourselves that they thoroughly understood it, we requested the master to vary the figure and the letters as much as possible. In arithmetic the Hindoos are peculiar adepts. The students showed much proficiency in all the different subjects indicated. When asked to explain the eclipse which had recently taken place, they did so very clearly and accurately, and evidently saw the absurdity of the Hindoo superstition respecting such phenomena. I was surprised at a question put to them by Mr. G., 'What was their object in coming to school?' and still more astonished by the answer, 'To get a Government situation.' I asked the same question in almost every place I visited, and always received a similar reply. It is much to be regretted that these youths, evidently of fine powers and intellectual taste, are not incited to love knowledge for itself. They do not appear desirous of going beyond the routine which is necessary to prepare them for matriculation. Hence the knowledge of our literature is restricted to the extracts from celebrated authors in their class-books, and they cannot therefore become familiar with the spirit and characteristics of distinguished writers. Still, when we remembered that all the examination we had been giving them was in a language foreign to them, we could not but be astonished at their wonderful facility in it. The institution appeared admirably managed, and the instructors equal to their work. We regretted only that there was not a better supply of school apparatus, maps, diagrams, &c., which might have greatly facilitated the acquirement of real ideas. Altogether, the visit to this school was a most gratifying one, and we rejoiced to find so good a system of education introduced into India.

Thursday, Oct. 4.—The visit of a native lady was announced. She came attended by her son as interpreter, whom, in his genteel semi-English dress, I did not at first recognise as one of the students of the High School. It was he who had induced his mother to come and call on me. She remained some time, much pleased with inspecting all the presents, and with carrying away herself some tokens of friendship. It was impossible, of course, to interchange many ideas with her or with any other native ladies, but the sympathy and kindness which were reciprocated between us were valued on each side. This visit led the way to many others. On one occasion a Parsee and a Hindoo lady so far overcame their prejudices as to take tiffin with us. There seemed no reserve or jealousy among either gentlemen or ladies respecting these visits. I could not attribute this freedom from the conventional prejudices, of which I had heard so much, to any special favour shown to myself as a stranger; for I learnt to my surprise and pleasure that, not long before, my host had given a soirée to English and native gentlemen and ladies, when Mrs. Tagore well sustained her part as hostess, and especially entertained the ladies;—the evening was announced in the papers as 'a great success.' It is indeed little known in Lower Bengal how much advancement has been made in this part of Western India.

Friday, Oct. 5.—We visited this morning the Normal Training School, under the escort of the principal, Mr. Mahiputram Rupram. The building is not very commodious, but, until a better one can be provided, answers the purpose fairly. This, like many native houses, is built round a central square court. On entering we saw the windows of the second-floor filled with red turbans, the wearers of which were gazing at the strangers with that calm unimpassioned curiosity which was now becoming familiar to us. We proceeded to the schoolroom on the lower floor, where there were several classes of young boys, who were being instructed by students as an exercise of the lessons on teaching which had been given to themselves. The principal directed a student to give a gallery lesson to the first class, and though it was in the vernacular, and consequently unintelligible to me, I could perceive that the instruction was given well, and excited the intelligence and interest of the scholars. It was very strange in this distant part of the world, in the midst of a people differing so widely from our own in language, manners, and thought, to find the same system adopted which many years ago I had seen successfully carried out in the Home and Colonial Training School in London.

The principal had made a good use of the advantage he enjoyed in having visited the English training institutions. How much power does our country possess of disseminating wise and good principles over the world! In another class we noticed a lad of fourteen of peculiar intelligence, and were informed that he was a boy of low caste, his father being a shoemaker; it would seem as if the introduction of the industrial element into his education had stimulated his mental powers, for he far outstripped all his companions. The boys were then about to be dismissed to recreation, and I requested the master to discharge them, walking out in step, two and two; after various attempts, it was found impossible to accomplish this simple act. The difficulty which the native sailors found in pulling together, evidently arose from the same natural peculiarity which prevented these lads from stepping together: it can be overcome by proper training, for the sepoys go through military evolutions like other soldiers. I never heard any school, either of boys or of girls, sing together; not more than two or three ever attempted to do so, except in two of the Bombay girls' schools, and then the sound produced was very far from melodious or agreeable, but somewhat loud, rather resembling discordant shouting. The boys then left the school in 'Indian file,' and we went into a hall where a number of students were pursuing their studies; many did not look very promising instructors of youth, but the principal informed us that they were solely on probation, and that those who did not appear competent would be dismissed. We left the place much gratified with the institution, and with the efforts which are being made by the Government to secure a good supply of teachers for the boys' schools. Most of these students coming from a distance required to be boarded; they belong to different castes, but no difficulty is felt on this account, as they employ a Brahmin cook who can prepare food for anyone, and each adopts his own peculiar customs in taking his meals. It was on our return from this school that we saw the curious procession of tigers ignominiously carried along in bullock-carts.

There was still another important institution which remained to be seen, yet that was not very attractive to me. Accustomed as I have unhappily been to human nature in a state degraded by crime, it always has been still more dreadful to me to witness the painful spectacle of the light of reason obscured by disease. A lunatic asylum is one of the very last places which I should willingly visit. Learning, however, that the excellent superintendent of the jail, Dr. Wyllie, had established one with great effort and devotion of time and thought, I could not but accept his kind invitation to visit with him on another morning the hospital, dispensaries, and lunatic asylum.

The former of these institutions did not exhibit any peculiar features: they appeared established on the some general system as those in England, with adaptation to the peculiarities of the climate; everything exhibited the greatest care, businesslike accuracy, and thoughtful detail. The general appearance of the hospital wards is at first striking to a stranger, as, instead of the comfortable beds and other arrangements we see in England, there are hard mattresses, on which the patient usually lies in his clothes. There were several sick policemen, and I could not but suppose that their illness might be partly owing to the thick dark cloth clothing they are obliged to wear, and which in this hot country must be very oppressive.

We proceeded next to the asylum—it was in a large garden. The building was very plain and simple, but well contrived and airy. Dr. Wyllie had himself superintended the erection of it at a smaller expense than I could have imagined possible. His system was one of kind judicious physical and mental treatment, with full employment for the patients. They were occupied chiefly in cultivating the ground, which gave them great variety: some were digging, some drawing water from the well with the help of the bullock-cart, or manuring the ground with the aid of the dry-soil system;—others were preparing it for the reception of the seed. All were working steadily like any ordinary labourers, and the worthy doctor was not a little proud to show the produce of his garden, both in fruits and flowers. I could hardly believe myself among lunatics. There was very little, even with close observation, to indicate unsoundness of mind, either in manner or expression of countenance. Yet some were really very much affected. I saw a class of six or eight murderers. They were not placed in any strict confinement, though under more surveillance than the others. When there are suspicious appearances about the eyes, they receive medical treatment, and an attack of dangerous madness is thus averted. The benevolent spirit of the superintendent, which pervades the whole establishment, has probably much to do with its great success. This certainly might serve as a model for such institutions in the economical manner in which it is conducted, the comfort of the inmates, and their successful treatment. The only unsatisfactory part of the asylum is that allotted to women, and there, as in the jail, the great want was evident of well-trained, respectable *female* officials. However clever and well-qualified male officials may be—however devoted to their duty, and anxious to discharge it well,—they *cannot* understand, or do if comprehended, the work of a woman, any more than one of the other sex can take the place of a man. Our Heavenly Father has created the two sexes with different powers, and for different spheres of work, in His world. One cannot take the duties of the other without disturbing the order of His providence. A man cannot comprehend the proper work of the woman. The evils observable in the institutions of Ahmedabad, from the want of female officials in the departments appropriated to their sex, were evident in every part of India I visited.

There were many other schools which time did not permit me to visit. The various institutions, however, which have been thus briefly described, greatly impressed me, especially as they exist in a city in the Queen's dominions of which many of our countrymen here have not even heard. Without these, and deprived of the influence which, directly or indirectly, they have exercised on the native inhabitants, Ahmedabad would always be well worthy of a visit from a stranger; but its interest would consist rather in the relics of a departed alien race, than in any signs of life and improvement in the inhabitants. The dwellings of the lower classes appeared most dilapidated and miserable, and the streets, where any attempts of native ornamentation were observable, did not indicate any progress in civilisation. No institution did I observe or hear of but what had sprung up under British influence. All the native gentlemen whom I met were connected with government institutions of some kind, which had developed their powers, and given them that peculiar training which is the result of long experience. It was very gratifying to an Englishwoman to observe that all this beneficent action in the place was not the result merely of the necessity of carrying out business orders; they sprang from a direct and evident intention in officials to benefit as much as practicable the people among whom they were located. The railway and all its connected machinery may be regarded as simply necessary to the business proceedings of the country; but the establishment of an admirable and complete system of school-training, into which are introduced all the improvements of superior minds in England, the hospital, dispensaries, and lunatic asylum, and a large public library—all these are the result of many years of patient effort on the part of Government official gentlemen, who did not limit their exertions to the work which they were *required* to do, but had given their hearty voluntary labour to the improvement of the city. Ahmedabad is probably superior to most provincial or mofussil towns. It was certainly better and more enlightened in many ways than any other that I saw. It offers, however, an excellent example of how much may be done to raise India, by a judicious course pursued by those English gentlemen who are placed in office there.

It was not within the special scope of my enquiries to investigate many subjects of considerable interest, such as the tenure of land, the growth of cotton, and the municipal government. What I heard, however, led me to the conclusion that Guzerat is peculiarly favoured in these respects, and that these advantages, combined with great fertility of soil, give promise of much future improvement. This province appears in many respects to be a peculiarly interesting one, and would well reward the researches and investigations of intelligent persons who devoted time and attention to the subject, while the inhabitants, having felt the practical benefit of English administration, and having in many cases been long accustomed to friendly intercourse with resident official gentlemen, are quite prepared to receive in a good spirit any kind advances from the English. In all the intercourse I had myself with native gentlemen at Ahmedabad, and indeed generally throughout India, I was much struck with the readiness with which they seized and thoroughly comprehended new ideas, though presented to them in a foreign language, and with the courteousness and candour they exhibited in argument or discussion.

My first great subject was of course female education. I met with no exception in Bombay Presidency in the strong interest felt by native gentlemen on this subject. There was no need to point out to them the importance of obtaining female teachers for the schools. They felt it as strongly as I could do, or even more so, from having personally witnessed the evils arising from the want of them. But where could female teachers be obtained? No natives who can carry on such a work at present exist in India, nor can trained English teachers be procured. The few who are in the country are employed in the mission schools, and none can be spared from them, even if desired by the managers of the Hindoo girls' schools. To obtain teachers from England for each school would involve an enormous expense not to be thought of; and if one or two could be induced to come over to help to conduct a model school, with the assistance of teachers familiar with the vernacular, where could they take up their abode? It would be impossible to live as inmates of a native home. There are here no boarding-houses where any English lady could reside. There is no house for the accommodation of travellers in this ancient capital of a powerful race, except a 'travellers' bungalow,' which would not appear a very attractive or suitable place for the residence of a respectable Englishwoman. The missionary at Ahmedabad had not a home where he could receive any lady to board; and if he had, it would not be considered by the natives suitable for her to live there, as it would give to her work a proselytising character, which would entirely defeat its object. No guarantee on her part would remove the suspicion from the native ladies that her real intention was to convert them, and interference with their religion they would not tolerate. Should a house be taken for two ladies, where they might live independently? That plan did not appear to me feasible, for the expense of maintaining such an establishment, in which several menservants and a carriage of some sort would be essential, must be very great; and even if the cost of this could be met, it did not seem to me a position which I could recommend to any ladies, to come and live alone in a foreign city, in the midst of those of whose language and manners they were perfectly ignorant. Such were the conclusions at which we arrived after many long and interesting conversations. Besides, the introduction of a few English ladies here would not meet a general want. The Government had provided for a regular supply of teachers in boys' schools by the establishment of excellent normal training schools; why should not the same arrangement be made to insure a regular supply of female teachers? It is true that there would be far greater difficulties to be contended with, because a ready supply of students can be found for the male normal schools, from the young men who have received an excellent education; whereas there are no native young women in India who have received a similar education and preparation for becoming teachers;

besides, the national practice of very early marriages, and the seclusion of ladies, would for some time render it extremely difficult to find natives who would desire to become students. Still it was believed, not only by the native gentlemen, but also by many English gentlemen and ladies with whom I had the opportunity of conferring at various times, that there exist in the country a number of educated Englishwomen, who, through widowhood, orphanage, or other circumstances, have not at present the means of comfortable maintenance, and who would gladly avail themselves of the means of qualifying themselves to obtain a respectable livelihood as teachers. Such persons having been accustomed to the country, and probably somewhat acquainted with the language, would more easily be prepared for their future duties than new-comers, who would be obliged to occupy some time in studying the vernacular; still we might look forward also to obtaining lady-students from the mother-country;—a large number of young persons do not find a sufficient demand for their labour in our overstocked market, and we may hope to obtain some of these, who would devote themselves to the work. At any rate the experiment should be tried, and every effort made to commence what might lead to a proper supply of teachers for the girls' schools. Where would the funds come from? was our next consideration. On all accounts it appeared very desirable that the institution should be under the special care and sanction of the Government. 'But the Government does not care as much for girls as for boys,' urged my native friends in a tone of some reproach. I assured them that this was not the case, and that the cause of their hesitation and backwardness in taking any steps in this important matter, was from a fear of annoying them, by even apparent interference in their domestic affairs. It was therefore necessary for the natives themselves to ask Government to take the subject into consideration. They expressed their desire to co-operate in any way in their power, taking themselves part of the expense of the undertaking. Having requested some of the leading men to express their views in writing, the first record in my manuscript book was made by the principal of the Normal Training School, Mr. Mahiputram Rupram. The reader will, it is hoped, not regard the expressions used as less sincere, from their being tinged with Oriental enthusiasm :—' Be hopeful, O my heart, thy hovering doubts are past and gone; that which thou didst believe to be impossible will now be accomplished through the friendly exertions of Miss Carpenter, the famous philanthropist of Bristol. The grand object of her visit to this country is, I believe, to do what she can towards rescuing our women from their present degrading ignorance and superstition, and thereby elevate their moral and social position. May the Almighty and All-merciful God bless her efforts and grant her every success! Amen.'

Our host, who entered warmly into the subject of the female normal training schools, kindly invited the leading men of the city to a soirée for the discussion of it, and their feeling was unanimous and earnest. One of these, Mr. Premabhai Hemabhai, was a member of the Legislative Council of Bombay. Not understanding English, the subject was explained to him in his own language, and he wrote in Guzerathi what is thus translated :—

'I met Miss Carpenter this evening at nine at Mr. S. Tagore's house at Ahmedabad, along with several respectable gentlemen. She not being able to talk in Hindostani, Messrs. Tagore and Mahiputram interpreted between us. The great difficulty in the work of female education in this country is, that we cannot find competent female instructors among us. She has come here to observe the condition of women in this country, and to promote their education. I am of opinion that if we get an European (meaning English or any other foreigner) lady to teach them, it will be very well. Our women are very sharp, and quite able to learn what may be taught them. They easily learn our religious books taught them by male teachers. Secular learning is not more difficult. Secular education makes no progress because we have no female teachers. It is because they are ignorant that they (women of this country) do not understand in some respects what is right and good, and what is wrong and bad. They are not able to hear and read books containing good knowledge. Then, again, they are for the most part confined in their houses, which prevents the development of their faculties. I have much more to say. I have expressed my views very briefly. I conclude now. I very much thank Miss Carpenter for her coming over to this country to encourage education among our fair sex, and to improve their condition. It is very good of her to do so. I hope the social position and condition of our females will begin to improve from this time.

'P.S.—After writing the above I remembered one important circumstance which I write here. In this country, among some of the Hindoos on death occasions, the females beat their breasts, so much so that some of them lay bare part of their bodies, and beat their breasts with the palm of both their hands, and with such force that the beaten parts become very sore, and then some of them become sick, and some even die; some become dizzy, and immediately fall down on the ground. I have seen this with my own eyes. All this is the result of ignorance, the result of want of knowledge.'

This gentleman requested me to meet at his residence the following day a number of Hindoo ladies, whom he would assemble to visit me there. The ladies of the household and I went at the appointed time; the gentlemen were not of course invited. It was a most novel and remarkable sight. Between twenty and thirty ladies in native dress, and richly adorned with jewels, were assembled in the handsome drawing-room, which was fitted up in English style with sofas and couches, the walls being adorned with engravings and coloured prints. Many of the ladies brought their daughters, but the little creatures had no appearance of the vivacity of childhood, probably being somewhat impressed by the unusual assemblage, but still more by the consciousness of the splendour of their strings of pearls and varied ornaments. The master of the house received us with dignified courtesy, the youth who had brought his mother to call on me serving as interpreter. After the interchange of friendly greetings with the ladies, I was requested to address them on the subject of female education; my remarks were communicated to our host, who delivered them with great emphasis to the audience, in their own language. They appeared much interested, and on my expressing a desire to hear their views, one of them spoke with much energy and fluency, expressing the general accordance of her friends with the views I had expressed—their strong desire for the education of their daughters, and the earnest wish for female teachers. Should such a change be made, she said, they would be able to leave the young ladies at school much longer than was at present possible. The usual attention having been paid in the distribution of flowers and pan-sooparee, and the sprinkling of rosewater, we retired, much gratified with our reception, though I was at the time little aware how remarkable such a party is in that country, and how great an advance it indicated over the state of society in the capital of the Empire.

An evening party on the same day was hardly less remarkable, though at the time it did not strike me as being so. Mr. Tagore and his friend Mr. G., having been previously invited to dine at the house of one of the gentlemen of the Civil Service, desired to return the compliment, and the English gentleman accepted an invitation from him to dine at his house. Mrs. Tagore did the honours of the house with perfect propriety. Indian music was provided for us during dinner; some sweet but plaintive native melodies were played by two Hindoos on stringed instruments, and gave us some idea of the national music. Before this we had heard nothing worthy of the name, the festivals of the lower orders being celebrated by a repetition of discordant sounds without any attempt at tune. This dinner remained as a solitary incident in my visit to India. On no other occasion did I sit at table with Hindoo gentlemen and ladies. So great a change is gradually going on in Ahmedabad, through the insensible influence of British civilisation.

Our host did not wish that we should leave the neighbourhood without seeing some of the objects of interest it contains, and proposed taking us to the royal cemetery of Sirkhej. This is a famous place for excursions, and though not five miles from the city, a visit to it occupies a whole day. It was arranged for us all to start very early on Thursday the 11th Oct., and our expectations of enjoyment were raised somewhat high, having heard much of a picnic at Sirkhej as the greatest attraction to Ahmedabad. Knowing how such excursions are managed at home, we little imagined what preparations were considered necessary for one in India. At two in the morning the servants required to start under the conduct of the butler, and took with them, not baskets of cold provisions, but an entire cooking apparatus, chairs, tables, and everything necessary to prepare a regular breakfast and dinner, *comme il faut*. We did not witness the departure of the cavalcade, for such it must have been, but having been fortified by our 'early tea,' started about seven, to secure the cool of the morning. A bullock-cart was now to be our conveyance, for reasons which we soon perceived. On arriving at the bank of the river, we found that there was no bridge and no boat! Our only possibility of crossing was to submit to be dragged through the stream by the bullocks, who did not appear to regard this procedure with any surprise. We were warned that we might be upset in the water by their slipping into a hole; but no catastrophe occurred, and we were highly amused by the novel mode of transit. Our road, if such it could be called, lay through deep sand and over hillocks, so it proved somewhat wearisome; at length on an open plain two turrets or pillars appeared, which proved to be the entrance to this wonderful place. The first glance was not impressive. It is in the keeping of the Mahometans, and a considerable landed property is left for its proper maintenance; but here, as elsewhere, we saw interesting relics of the past—even those which are still deemed sacred—left in a very neglected and dilapidated condition, with many idle and low people lounging about, or pursuing their ordinary occupations there. We were, however, soon struck with a large domed edifice on the right of the entrance, the mausoleum of a saintly man, the spiritual adviser of Ahmed Shah, who died in 1445. It was a grand and solemn place within, evidently regarded as very sacred: the tomb itself was covered with rich cloths and tapestry, while much more was stored in a large receptacle, for use on state occasions. It was a very impressive feeling that goodness was so honoured, and after more than four centuries. To the west of the dome is a large square building with a mosque on one side, and on the other splendid colonnades. In the south colonnade are covered seats looking out on the tank, which is nearly a quarter of a mile square, and is itself surrounded with various small ruined buildings, probably intended for washing and bathing, or to be employed as pleasant summer-houses. There are other tombs; one is a chaste stone building, the mausoleum of Mahomed Begarha and two of his brothers, while a smaller one is that of his queen. Everywhere we saw beautiful specimens of architecture and lovely stone tracery for windows, though, except in the colonnades, there was a deficiency of grandeur of design. After a cursory glance, we found breakfast prepared for us with as much form and order as if at home. A kitchen is extemporised in these parts more easily than in England, and servants in India are less dependent, than with us, on what we are accustomed to consider the necessaries of civilised life. Ours was a singular position, invading with our modern usages this sacred relic of departed royalty. Shortly, there was another arrival: we greeted, to our great surprise, the assistant-magistrate, his intelligent son, our young interpreter, his wife, his son's wife, and other members of his family. They planned this excursion expressly to meet us here, and thereby added much to the pleasure of the day. They, too, came prepared to take their meals here, but according to their own native customs; and they therefore brought a carpet to spread on the ground, with the particular clothing which it is thought proper to adopt while eating—also their own Indian dishes. The party then strolled among the ruins, while I established myself in one of the shady recesses to sketch the tank and surrounding buildings, to which an unusual cloudy effect gave peculiar beauty. My work finished, I found myself quite alone, the two parties being dispersed, except three of the ladies and a young boy, who fortunately could speak a little English. They offered, through him, to accompany me round the tank, and I gladly accepted their escort. It was a very novel position, thus to be under the guidance of these Hindoo ladies in their picturesque native dress, quite at their ease, with their bare feet and toes with silver rings, which one of them took the opportunity of washing in the tank as we proceeded. The country round was very luxuriant, and I carried away as trophies splendid ears of grains entirely new to me. There was a deep well near our dining-place, to which the country people in picturesque dresses came to draw water. In remembrance of One of more than eighteen centuries ago, I asked them 'to give me to drink,' a request which was very kindly complied with. The mother of our young interpreter not being able to invite us to eat with her, sent us a present of some of their favourite dishes, and requested permission to come with her son and watch us at our meal, a request which, under the circumstances, we could not refuse. Everything connected with English manners is evidently as great a matter of curiosity among the native ladies, as their habits are to us. We again visited the tombs, and loitered among the porticoes, but left early that we may not be benighted in our perilous crossing of the river.*

On another day we made an afternoon excursion to the tomb of Shah Alum, at a little distance from the city, along a heavy dusty road, bordered with cactuses, where we met a long string of camels, which would have been somewhat alarming to European horses. This tomb was a very striking building, with a large mosque and minaret near. The buildings were beautiful and picturesque against the clear blue sky. We were fortunate in going on the festival of the New Moon, when the Mahometans from the country round assemble to enjoy the society of their friends, and to do homage to the Queen of Night in a manner little distinguishable from heathen ceremonies. The loud and discordant cries and clang of instruments were anything but agreeable or harmonious. Excepting when small parties went to recite their prayers to the priest, there was nothing which indicated reverence. Here, and on many other occasions afterwards, I was strongly impressed with the degree in which contact with Hindooism deteriorates a religion which professes spiritual purity, and freedom from anything bordering on idolatry. I could now fully sympathise with the prophet of old, who indignantly exclaimed, 'Your new moons and your appointed feasts my soul hateth: they are a trouble unto me; I am weary to bear them.'

A morning excursion took us to a remarkable well, covered over with galleries supported by ranges of columns. It was constructed in 1556 by Dada Harir,

---

* For a full description of Sirkhej and the tomb of Shah Alum, with beautiful photographs, see 'Architecture of Ahmedabad,' by T. C. Hope, Esq., C.S.

who built there also a mosque and mausoleum for himself. Much elaborate ornamentation was lavished to produce very little effect, the galleries not having even the semblance of a purpose, but Nature decorated the ruins with her own wild beauty. The inhabitants of the neighbourhood performed not only their ablutions, but the cleansing of their garments in it; the water has a dull leaden colour, and, being so covered over as to exclude the vivifying influence of the sun's rays, did not appear particularly inviting for personal use.

We did not visit any Hindoo temples; they do not appear numerous or important in these parts. The Jains are a leading sect here. They profess not to worship any God, but to reverence good men, whom they place in niches in their temples. There did not appear to be much to choose between their religion and Hindooism; the Jains seemed to be really quite as idolatrous. We went one morning to view a new and splendid Jain temple built by Hathi Singh, who died extremely rich in 1845; it is sustained by his family. We are accustomed to associate idolatry with barbarism, except among the ancient Greeks and Romans, who so marvellously blended with it the æsthetic element, and left the idols created by their own hand to be models for ever of masculine energy and feminine beauty. It was, therefore, singularly grating and indeed revolting to the feelings, to have it first brought forcibly to the mind, that here not only the low and ignorant cling to debasing superstition, which the advanced and enlightened of their nation discard, but that rich and influential men endeavour to gain popularity with their townsmen by giving position and splendour to the degradation of their so-called religion. This temple is most gorgeously adorned, built on a uniform plan, and decorated with multitudes of images. All of these are, however, to my taste extremely hideous; not one excited an idea which could elevate or inspire with a feeling of beauty, or of excellence of any kind. A priest, whose countenance was fraught with cunning and expressive of many bad feelings, forbad our entrance without an order from the proprietor; a small coin would probably have obtained admission for us, but I was glad that neither my friend nor I had one to offer him. The horror which I felt on seeing this Jain temple remained with me to the end of my journey, whenever I beheld an idol temple; for I increasingly perceived that the system perpetuated in these places degrades morally and intellectually a great people, and keeps woman bound in moral and spiritual thraldom. Until she is emancipated and brought to her true position in society, the Hindoo nation cannot become what they were intended to be by the Father of all.

The educated native gentlemen are becoming painfully alive to the evil of the present position of women, but do not yet venture openly to remonstrate. They present the singular phenomenon of the enlightened portion of a community being chained down by the ignorant and superstitious. One of the subjects now warmly agitated among them is the remarriage of widows. The present prohibition of this by Hindoo law is a cause of immense evil. If a child is betrothed, as we should call it, in infancy, and her *fiancé* dies, she is regarded as a widow, and subjected during the whole of her life to the privations and wretched neglected condition at present inseparable from widowhood. This state of things is the cause of great suffering and also immorality, in cases where the young widow is not favourably situated for support. A public meeting was held at Ahmedabad on the subject, while we were there, but ladies were of course not invited to be present. Polygamy does not now appear common among the superior classes. I heard of one case only at Ahmedabad. In some parts a singular custom prevails, that marriages may be celebrated only once in twelve years. This involves the necessity of performing the first marriage or betrothal when the child is an infant, if the appointed time then occurs. One gentleman considered that he should be awkwardly situated if his wife should die before the expiration of the twelve years, and thought it best to take another at once, to be ready for the emergency.

The subject of reformatory schools occupied much of our consideration. The native assistant-magistrate, as well as many others connected with the administration of justice, expressed considerable anxiety that provision should be made for the education of criminal boys. An existing clause in the law permits such to be sent to any duly authorised reformatory in the district. But none such existed here, nor was there any provision made for establishing one. The law appeared only as an isolated clause, and not as a complete Act forming part and parcel of the laws of the country, as in the case of our Industrial and Reformatory Schools Acts.

One more institution remained to be visited, and that, not the least interesting of the whole, was reserved for the last day of my abode in this ancient city. The missionary, Mr. Moore, had more than once called on me, and informed me respecting his proceedings. He had shown me his little school, which I regretted to see in so inconvenient and unattractive a building. This arose, he said, from the prejudices of the people, which made them unwilling to rent a house for the purpose. He told me that the parents of the children appeared grateful for the interest shown in their welfare, and that on the whole his work was encouraging. He had no chapel, as there was a station at a little distance connected with his mission, to which he devoted much time and attention. He kindly arranged to take me to visit this.

On Sunday morning, October 14, at half-past six, we mounted the bullock-cart, and, after passing through many of the low native streets, made our way slowly through sandy lanes. We passed several Mussulman antiquities and some pagan monuments, and at length stopped at a plain simple building, which was the mission schoolroom and chapel. A bright cheerful couple residing in an adjoining cottage greeted us with a pleasant cordial smile of welcome, the first I had seen in any native of the humbler classes. No sympathy appears ever to exist between the higher and lower classes in India among the natives themselves. Christianity has not yet taught them, 'All ye are brethren.' Being at home accustomed to exchange friendly smiles with any children who come in my way, it made me feel quite in a foreign country, to be unable to obtain anything but a vacant stare from any young persons whom I noticed. It was then most refreshing to the spirit on this Sabbath morning to be so greeted, and to receive a cup of new milk from the schoolmaster and his wife, as a token of hospitality. This station is somewhat isolated, and the inhabitants live together as a Christian community, without being annoyed by their heathen countrymen. They are all cultivators—that is, they rent small pieces of land from the Government, on the profits of which they live. These people are very poor, and there is no attempt to raise their condition from the mission funds; they dwell in small huts similar to those in ordinary use; but a striking difference between them and the heathen is at once perceptible in the sense of personal decency shown in their clothing and general demeanour. Among the lower orders whom I had hitherto seen, the men and children are usually devoid of any garment, except perhaps a cloth round their loins; at the same time they wear silver ornaments, and pearl or other earrings; the women are bedizened with any ornaments they can get hold of, with very miserable raiment, only partially covering the person. Here everyone was neatly and decently dressed, and I did not notice any ornaments in the place; though these are not forbidden by the missionary, they are not valued as they used to be. At the sound of a bell, the first I had heard in this heathen land, the congregation gradually dropped in, and took their places on the matting in an orderly manner. The service being in Guzerathi, I could not understand it, but I could warmly sympathise with the spirit which evidently pervaded this little congregation. Many looked intelligently attentive, and all joined in the worship in an orderly manner. A little Sunday-school was afterwards conducted by the schoolmaster and some of the elders: the Christian singing was sweet and refreshing, after the harsh meaningless tones I had heard in the schools elsewhere. After a short service for my benefit in English, and a simple but well-prepared breakfast, we departed, the members expressing a wish that some lady would often visit them, and take an interest in the improvement of the children. Truly it is strange that none do so!

This little colony appeared to me a striking instance of the natural effects of Christianity. An air of cheerful contentment pervaded the place. I was informed that the members generally live consistent lives, and endeavour to lead others to join them. Early marriages are entirely abolished, the young men not being married until they arrive at the age of eighteen, the girls at sixteen. Multitudes of such little stations all over the land would do incalculable good. 'Fear not, little flock,' I thought on leaving them, 'it is your Father's good pleasure to give you the kingdom.'

And now my visit was come to a close, and I had to bid adieu to my first home in India. My kind host wrote in my book the following passage, embodying thoughts he had offered in prayer at the family altar in our weekly service:

'It is not for nothing that India has been placed under the British rule. It is impossible to think that her destinies have been ruled by a blind unsparing Fate, or that it is for the glory and power of England alone that such a wonderful bond of connection has been established, by an inscrutable Providence, between the two countries, separated from each other by half the world, and a whole world of ideas and feelings. There is one hope, one intense conviction from which no true patriot can escape—that is, that England and India are to be a mutual blessing; that our country, once famous in the world's history, is destined to be helped out of her present degeneracy and utter stagnation. And is there no reason for this hope? and are there no data to base this conviction upon? What was India a few years ago, and what do we see around us? We see a marked progress, brought about by the influence of Western civilisation. We see a nation domineered over by caste and idolatry—a nation of which the men are completely enslaved to custom, and the women kept down and tyrannised over by the men by dint of sheer physical strength, which they cannot resist—a nation which has long ceased to be progressive, and of which inertia and stationariness is the natural condition. Even this nation, opening its eyes to the enormous evils around it, is gradually wakening to the influences of the bright light of thought and knowledge, before which millions of false stars are fading away. India sank down under the weight of the accumulated corruption of ages; foreign influences were requisite to rouse her. These are being felt through her length and breadth. A steady though slow progress is perceptible. The tyranny of society is slowly succumbing to the gaining force of individuality and intellect. Superstition is losing its strongholds one after another. Ceremonial observances are being replaced by true principles of morality. There are many things still wanting, hideous defects still to be remedied; but let us work each of us individually, and hope for a brighter future. May India be grateful to England for the blessings she has been enjoying under her benign rule! May England feel that India is a sacred trust and responsibility which cannot be thrown away!'

'Ahmedabad, October 14, 1866.'

CHAPTER III.

SURAT, BOMBAY, AND POONA.

It was with much regret that, on the morning of Oct. 15, 1866, I took leave of the native gentlemen, who accompanied me to the station at Ahmedabad to bid me farewell, for I had been treated by them as a friend, though a stranger in a strange land. Having exchanged greetings till the train carried me out of sight, and watched to the last the minarets near the station, which my young friend, the interpreter, had taken me to explore while waiting for departure, I experienced a little of the desolate feeling of being thrown completely among foreigners. It was, then, with much pleasure, that I recognised, at the station at Surat, the young Hindoo who had provided us with an abode on our journey from Bombay; the sight of a place one has visited before, when one is travelling in a foreign country, and the countenance of even a casual acquaintance, gives one almost a home-feeling. He was accompanied by an elderly gentleman, who had commenced a girls' school in Surat fifteen years before, and the principal of the Normal School, who was also the secretary of a society for promoting female education. With these gentlemen was the educational inspector of the district, who, with his lady, had kindly invited me to take up my abode at their house.

Surat is a remarkable old city. It has many of the same features as Ahmedabad, since it abounds in monuments of departed greatness; but it stands on much less ground, and is in a state of great dilapidation. Its situation on a river formerly navigable to Surat from its mouth for even large ships, rendered it naturally an object of attraction to European merchants, as well as a convenient place of departure for Mecca, for Mahometan pilgrims from all parts of Hindostan; this obtained for it the name of the Gate of Mecca. On the other side of the river are the remains of what was probably an ancient Hindoo city. About five centuries ago, probably, the Mahometans commenced to colonise Surat. The Portuguese found their way to the city soon after their arrival in India, and in 1512 sacked the then open town; it was afterwards fortified by the Mahometans. In the beginning of the seventeenth century the English visited the place; and in 1612 many conflicts occurred between them and the Portuguese, whose armaments were finally defeated; and the Mogul Emperor sent a firman authorising an English minister to reside at his court—thus opening trade to our nation. In 1615 a factory was established at Bharuch or Broach, the trade of which was so flourishing that in 1683, 55,000 pieces of cloth were sent from it to England. The Dutch commenced trade here in 1616, and for some years their factory competed successfully with that of the English at Surat. The French finally established another factory in this city in 1668, but all commercial prosperity was then sadly interrupted by the ravages of the Marathas, which led to the erection of walls of brick instead of mud. This warlike race still continued for some time its incursions. Continual troubles arose, and for a time the English left their factory; but in 1712 a new firman was granted to the English company, which was now thoroughly established in Surat, and the real government of the city was vested in presidents, a long series of whom ruled and passed away during the eighteenth century. The last titular Nawab died in 1842, and the flag of Delhi was removed from the citadel. This city has not only been a prey to the destructive attacks of its invaders, but has also been exposed to tremendous floods when the rains have swollen the stream of the Taptee; the waters have then risen to so tremendous a height that boats have sailed over the walls of the city. Great changes have also transformed buildings once famous. The noble pile, once the English factory, is now in part a lunatic asylum, in part a hospital for natives. The castle, once so important, can now boast of little but its historical associations. There is also an extensive asylum for diseased animals. A city with a history so remarkable, and with remains so interesting, would give scope for long researches to an antiquarian. But my object was the present, not the relics of the past—the condition of human beings, not of the brute creation. My short stay in the city did not allow of my devoting my attention to both, and I did not explore the curious records of departed splendour or power. A boating excursion in the evening was an agreeable termination of the day. On the left bank of the river we observed the house once occupied by the chief of the French factory, now the residence of a wealthy Banian. Farther on is a house called the Dutch Garden, where the chief of the Dutch factory resided. Most of the houses here have an air of dilapidation, and many parts show traces of the violence of the river, when swollen by rains. The banks, however, attracted our attention but little, for the exquisite beauty of the sunset on the water was so entrancing as to absorb all the thoughts and feelings. No one who has not witnessed it can comprehend the extraordinary richness and gorgeous red of a tropical sunset, reflected in the calm grey mirror of a broad stream. The landscape, even if uninteresting, when thrown into deep shadow against it, is invested with a solemn beauty. But the glory soon passes away—the pencil cannot portray it before one general gloom overshadows all. We might have felt some uneasiness in returning, if the moon had not given us the benefit of her silvery light.

Tuesday, Oct. 16.—A great confusion of tongues early broke my rest the next morning. The window of my sleeping-room overlooked the landing-place of the river. There, multitudes both of men and women assembled before sunrise to perform their ablutions, and for various household purposes, such as drawing water and washing clothes. Strange was the scene which was here every morning presented to an English eye; for the women appeared wholly devoid of any feeling akin to delicacy, and in this public place, to avoid wetting their garments, left the greater part of their bodies uncovered. It would seem as if the great seclusion of the women of the higher classes withdraws the refining influence of their sex from society;—those who are not so shielded are thus left in the rude position of barbaric life, where the weaker sex is oppressed by the stronger, and being degraded, is deprived of its special excellence. In India the voices and manners of the lower classes of women appeared to me more harsh and coarse than those of the men. I felt assured, however, that this did not arise from their nature being inferior, but from the condition in which they are placed.

It was necessary to be up betimes, since a very full programme for the day had been arranged by my friends. Our first visit was to the English cemetery, which is not far from the city on the road to Broach. It is thus spoken of in Murray's Guide: 'A mean wooden doorway opens upon a large expanse of broken ground, covered with weeds, trees, and mouldered tombs.' The present altered condition of the burying-ground proves how much devoted labour must have been bestowed upon it by the English clergyman of the place, who has made it one of his special cares, that his countrymen, whose remains are laid in a foreign land, shall not be forgotten or neglected. My attention was first drawn, not to the gorgeous sepulchral monuments, but to the extraordinary neatness and beauty of the place. While trees of English foliage were tastefully arranged to shade the walks and the tombs, lovely tropical plants and magnificent creepers, with their bright and splendid flowers, added a beauty to them which I had not witnessed elsewhere; the whole inspired into the spirit thoughts of the eternal spring, and the everlasting garden, while wandering among the abodes of the dead. Texts of Scripture recording heavenly aspirations, and a 'certain hope of a blissful resurrection,' were most refreshing to the mind in the midst of the surrounding joyless heathenism; they made me feel more intensely than ever the blessedness of that faith which survives the wrecks of time and the fall of empires, and calmly bears its testimony in the midst of a land of idolatry. He who has thus adorned with Nature's choicest treasures this abode of the dead, has not only shown pious reverence for the departed, but has soothed the wounded spirits of those who have been called to lay their beloved ones in a foreign land.

A number of costly sepulchral monuments are in this cemetery, of some antiquity; they carry one back to the time when the European factories vied with each other in Surat in gorgeousness of living, and the English presidents endeavoured to obtain the respect of the native princes and people by their magnificence. At the present day we understand better the true character of greatness, and the Hindoo nature is sufficiently enlightened to appreciate the moral grandeur of a railroad, as greater than external pomp. Though many of the tombs of the greatest pretensions are not such as to approve themselves highly to modern taste, and some remind one more of Mahometan than of Christian architecture, yet it is impossible to pass without notice the tomb of the Oxendens, those 'most brotherly of brothers,' as they have been called by Mr. Bellairs, in his 'Account of the Old Tombs of Surat,' which has been reprinted from the 'Journal of the Royal Asiatic Society' (vol. vi. p. 146), and gives an interesting description of these and other monuments. Christopher Oxenden died first, in 1659, and his brother erected over his grave a domed structure, with four pinnacles at the corners. On a small marble slab is a quaint inscription written by him in Latin, which may be thus rendered—

'Here lies buried Christopher Oxenden, by his life an example of probity; by his death, one of the perishable nature of life.

'He makes his entrance and his exit, and here he brought to a termination his undertakings and his life.

'He was able to enter in his accounts only days, not years, for Death suddenly called him to a reckoning.

'Do you ask, O my Masters, what profit you have gained, or what loss you have suffered?

'You have lost a servant, we a companion, he his life; but on the other side of the page he may write, Death to me is gain.'

Sir George Oxenden survived his brother ten years,

and then was laid near him, and a lofty mausoleum was erected in his honour, enclosing his brother's tomb. It is forty feet high, with two storeys, and massive pillars support two cupolas rising one above the other; round their interiors are galleries, reached by a flight of many steps. In the upper compartment is a marble slab with a laudatory Latin inscription, which is still legible. Sir George is styled 'Anglorum in India, Persia, Arabia præses,' but it is stated that the greatest glory of this noble mausoleum is that it covers 'generosos duos fratres fraterrimos.'

Many tombs most interesting to the antiquarian are found here—some displaying the armorial bearings of their families; but, as one author truly remarks, 'The devices of western heraldry quaintly contrast with the semi-Saracenic architecture of the tombs, and with the luxuriant tropical foliage in which they are entombed.'

Time did not allow of a visit to the Dutch cemetery, which is a little farther from the city; the tombs are fewer, but of more varied design, and overhung with luxuriant parasitical plants. The most splendid tomb is that of the Baron Van Reede, who was called the Mæccnas of Malabar, and who made and sent to Holland valuable collections of books and curiosities. He died in 1691. This tomb exceeds all others in size and magnificence; some idea may be formed of its costliness, from the fact that six thousand rupees were charged to the Dutch Company for mere repairs.

This reverence for the dead among Christians forms a striking contrast to the neglected manner in which at Ahmedabad the Mahometan tombs are left exposed by the wayside, without any wall or defence around them; it is strange that a people who show such peculiar and almost superstitious respect to the remains of their great men, as we saw at Sirkhej, should be so careless about those of their friends. It is also remarkable that the mode of disposal of the dead which is universally regarded with the utmost horror among Western civilised races, should be the approved custom of the Parsees, who are numerous at Surat. I had no desire to visit their tower of silence, where the dead are deposited, to be torn in pieces and devoured by vultures.

We turned from the dead to the living.

The boys' school, in which youths are prepared to pass their matriculation examination, and the Normal Training School, do not differ in general character from those at Ahmedabad. The girls' school, however, appeared superior, though exhibiting the same peculiar features. In the large schoolroom, containing from eighty to one hundred young girls, whose ages probably ranged from six to ten years, there was no female teacher, and the lower classes appeared inert and unoccupied. The first classes were intelligent, and answered the questions put to them by the inspector, who kindly accompanied us, with much quickness. The questions were of course in the vernacular, as in no Hindoo schools is English yet taught to girls. Being anxious to know how far the knowledge displayed by the girls was real, I requested that the class may be asked some questions respecting common objects. The nature of silk was that put to them, and a little girl, after giving a correct answer, at once ran for a lesson-book in which was a chapter on the silkworm, with a picture at the top; this she triumphantly brought, to demonstrate the correctness of the reply. The class wrote dictation in Guzerathi very correctly: at the head of every exercise each girl wrote an invocation to her deity for help.

Several native gentlemen were present, who took a

warm interest in female education; they wished for me to meet a number of the ladies themselves, and it was arranged for them to assemble in that room the same afternoon. A few English ladies were invited to accompany me, but of course no gentleman was to be present except those who were necessary as interpreters. At the appointed hour we went to the meeting, and found the room nearly filled with Hindoo ladies, chiefly the mothers of the young scholars. Seats of honour were appointed for the English strangers, whose dress and deportment were the subject of much criticism and comments among the native ladies. There were other arrivals after ours, and we were surprised to find that many had walked there unattended through the streets. One lady came escorted by her husband, who endeavoured to obtain admission with her, and who expressed much annoyance at being refused. I felt it then, as always, extremely tantalising to be unable to exchange any expressions of friendship with those ladies, otherwise than by dumb show; but I went among them, endeavouring to make my friendly feelings understood, and they readily reciprocated them. Some of the ladies had brought their young children with them, but on my attempting to take an infant in my arms, I was saluted with a loud scream, evidently being regarded with as much terror as is a black man by English children. I was in future cautious in my advances to creatures too young to comprehend the friendliness of my intentions. The pictures, toys, and ornaments which I had with me were objects of much curiosity not only to the children, but to the grown-up ladies, and I only regretted that I had not provided myself with more, to distribute as tokens of friendly interest. When the Hindoo and English ladies had surveyed each other sufficiently (I was becoming accustomed to have every article of my dress closely scrutinised), I was requested to address them; this was to be accomplished through two interpreters, as at Ahmedabad, since the elder gentleman who had summoned the meeting did not understand English.

Whether the sense of what I said was correctly conveyed to my audience I cannot of course say, but my remarks were certainly translated, and then delivered with full emphasis and considerable amplification, and appeared to be fully appreciated. At the conclusion, the young wife of the speaker came forward, and handed me an address, composed and beautifully written by herself in Guzerathi. The following translation was afterwards given me: the simplicity of the expressions guarantees the sincerity of the writer:—

To the very benevolent and virtuous woman,
Mary Carpenter.

'Dear Mother—A few days ago I learnt from my husband your name, and your object in coming here at such a great distance from your country. I was very anxious to see you. Now that you come here, and that you take so much pains to better our condition, I in behalf of these sisters here present feel very thankful to you. May God grant you long life, and may you continue to exert yourself in this laudable work!'

(Signed)

Surat, October 16, 1866.

These few words express the feeling which was everywhere manifested by native ladies in each Presidency, in connection with my visit. The fact of my coming from so great a distance to see them, unconnected with any society, and without any other motive than a desire to manifest friendly sympathy to them, was sufficient to elicit a warm response. 'She loves us for ourselves' has in it a touching significance to the heart, whether uttered by a poor dying Irish boy or felt by Hindoo ladies. A beautifully-carved sandalwood card-case was then presented to me from the ladies, a token of friendliness from Hindoo sisters which I greatly treasure, now that I am again in my native land.

This, we presumed, was the conclusion of our soirée, but on intimating our intention to bid farewell, we were requested to wait; garlands, bouquets, and pan-sooparee were distributed, and rosewater was sprinkled on the guests.

The next morning, October 17, my hosts kindly invited a party of about twenty-five English gentlemen and ladies to breakfast; and as the native gentlemen could not, in accordance with their national customs, sit at table with us, they joined us afterwards in the drawing-room, that we might discuss the subject of female education. It was a remarkable assemblage, and one which in itself indicated a great and most satisfactory progress. Every English gentleman or lady has very great means of doing good in India without any exertion or expense, by the simple exercise of kindly feeling towards those among whom it is their lot to live; every one who, in addition, occupies an official position in this country, confers a benefit if he discharges his duty with genuine hearty feeling, as well as conscientiously; not only does he valuable work, but is helping to draw the inhabitants of India into sympathy with England, and to infuse into them a true conception of the principles we adopt in our political and social economy. Such work must have been long going on in Surat, to have prepared the way for so much free expression of opinion and friendly intercourse between the two races, as I had the pleasure of witnessing on that morning.

The native gentlemen thoroughly entered into the importance of the scheme for a Female Normal School, and signified their approval in the following statement, which was signed by above twenty of the leading men of the city:—' We, the undersigned, think it most desirable and absolutely necessary for female education in Guzerat, to have a Normal Training School for female teachers opened in one of the principal towns in the province.'

A native deputy educational inspector thus inscribed his views in my book :—

'I have been engaged in the educational line since these last sixteen years, that is, as soon as I left my college studies in 1850. I think I was the first person who wrote a tract on the subject of female education in Guzerathi. The subject was fully discussed in several meetings of a literary society at Bombay, and it was finally decided that the female education ought to be commenced among Guzerathi people. I and several other brethren of mine undertook to establish girls' schools, and voluntarily devoted two hours every day to teach the girls. This was continued for some time, the taste for education increased, and after some time we found it absolutely necessary to appoint separate paid teachers. The taste for female education is still on an increase. The people are not so obstinate as they were fifteen years ago, in not sending their daughters to the schools. But the difficulty we now feel is that the girls, as soon as they reach the age of ten or eleven years, leave the school and cannot stay, owing to there being no female teachers. Hence I see that there is now a greater necessity for good female teachers; and I most fervently hope that female education, if carried on under good trained female teachers, will be beneficial in improving the general condition of the people.'

October 17, 1866.

It happened that Mr. Curtis, the educational inspector, had at this very time summoned many of his deputies to meet him at Surat on business. They conferred on the subject, and fully agreed in the importance of providing for a supply of female teachers, in the same manner as this had been done successfully for male teachers. In order to ascertain how far their views were practical, Mr. C. asked questions to elicit whether these gentlemen endeavoured to obtain education for their own families, and also whether they would like their wives to learn plain needlework—an art which in India is usurped by the male sex, tailors being employed to make even the clothes of English ladies. It was very satisfactory to hear a deputy sub-inspector say with some pride, 'My wife made all the clothes I have on; it was she who made this vest.' The native inspectors seemed all to feel their professional honour concerned in bringing forward their wives as much as possible in learning. One was proud to state that his wife had arrived at the fifth book. I afterwards learnt that one of these advanced ladies had made an application to enter as a student in the proposed Female Normal Training School. It would indeed be an immense advantage for a husband and wife to be both engaged in education, with mutual help in the different departments of a boys' and a girls' school under their respective care.

Wednesday, Oct. 18. — This morning early I went to attend the mission chapel, where there is worship in the vernacular every day at eight o'clock. It was a neat, large, airy room. There were very few present, but I remembered the Saviour's promise, 'Where two or three are gathered together in My name, there am I in the midst of you.' The few that were there evidently felt this, and there was a holy influence around. The singing was touchingly beautiful, led by the wife of the missionary. The master of the mission school and his wife were there, native converts. There was also a man of superior and intelligent air, who was employed to search out the most miserable and neglected children, and bring them into a little school which he taught. He said he loved the work, for he had been a poor miserable boy himself. Thus was our ragged school work practically developed in India. I learnt that this worthy man had been a servant in the household of the inspector, who had given him instruction, of which he had made good use. He was so earnest to help on others, that he accepted a lower stipend as schoolmaster than he would have gained in domestic service, to devote himself to his present work. There was also a young native Christian woman of very pleasing appearance, who invited me to her house. She was living with her parents. Her grandfather was the first convert made by the missionaries; her father, a very learned moonshee, is employed as a catechist, and is believed to do much good among his countrymen, the Mahometans. The house was particularly clean and neat; adorned with books, pictures, and beautiful needlework, it indicated everywhere the influence of Christianity on the household. No one who has not witnessed it can realise the marvellous change made in all the thoughts and feelings, habits and manners of Hindoos, by the reception of Christianity into the heart and life. Surely this young woman, now the third generation of believers, has a work to do for her people. The sister is already doing one as the wife of an excellent Parsee convert minister, and the mother of Christian children. Of that family I heard and saw much at Bombay. The first printing-press in Guzerat was established by this mission, and still occupies the original premises. They are airy and pleasant, very unlike such business establishments in England. Indeed, when seeing none but half-clad Hindoos, one can hardly fancy oneself in an office from which is to emanate knowledge over the whole province. Yet so it was, and in proof of it the missionary somewhat proudly handed me a copy of the Scriptures, on good paper, in a clear beautiful type, and a magazine in the vernacular, which is printed here and extensively circulated. The binding, too, was far from second-rate; indeed, some valuable copies of choice works were shown me, which were sent here to secure specially good workmanship. The mission committees at home, who reckon their success by the number of converts whose names can be enrolled in their reports, little comprehend how great and true a work is being steadily and unobtrusively done by the faithful men and women whom they send out to sow seed, which others may reap in this apparently unproductive field. Who can tell what good this mission in Guzerat has done?—Only the Lord of the Harvest, who will reckon up His fruits and His precious grain at the Last Day. It was gratifying to learn that the same Church clergyman who had shed so much beauty over the English burial-ground, showed his truly catholic spirit in working harmoniously with the Dissenting missionary. He himself specially devotes his efforts to preaching at the railway stations, where he welcomes all alike, of whatever creed or colour. In this heathen land, creeds and parties should be forgotten; Christians, of whatever sect, should strive only to bring all to accept the Lord whom we all love, as the wellbeloved Son, the sent of God, and to live in obedience to His laws. Every Christian, of whatever creed or Church, should strive to make his life consistent with his profession.

It was necessary to make a short visit suffice to the Public Library and the General Hospital. The former appears in progress to be a very good and complete one under native management, with European encouragement and help. It is astonishing what a new character these public institutions give to the portions of the city where they are situated. The municipal commissioners endeavour to keep space round them open, and improve the locality; sometimes a sacred tree is in the way which must not be cut down, sometimes mean miserable streets quite destroy the effect; but on the whole the ancient city seems to have a new life springing up within it, and a far better one than anything which could have been conceived in the days of its material wealth and magnificence. It is a happy thought that our nation has been the means of bringing this about; that our Government has, even with defects and shortcomings, conceived and executed so wise a system of ruling; that our people, with all their faults, have been the means of carrying it out, and of kindly giving a stimulus and aid to those who require it.

Many native gentlemen, and ladies also, came to visit me on this day. It was gratifying to observe the self-possession and yet modesty of the demeanour of the latter. They appeared anxious for improvement; this was evidenced by the fact that two young ladies attended a class which the missionary's wife held gratuitously at her own residence. In these parts, it appears impossible to obtain any female instruction except from the missionaries. A

Mahometan gentleman called, but did not bring his lady, though he invited me to visit her. He could not speak English, but made, through a gentleman who kindly acted as interpreter, many enquiries respecting my position and circumstances, feeling evidently astonished to see a lady thus venture forth alone. All the enquiries were probably not translated to me, for my Hindoo friends had too much innate sense of propriety ever to ask any question which might be regarded as ill-bred. At length our interpreter intimated that the Mahometan gentleman was desirous of putting the questions, 'How old are you?' and 'Have you any friends and relations?' On the first point I did not gratify his curiosity. Forty is here regarded as a great age, and fifty—which he suggested as my probable age—is reckoned almost superannuated. I satisfied his mind, however, on the second point, by showing him a photographic album well filled with friends and relations, which served to convince him that I did not come here from being without any friends at home to care for me. There are two newspapers, partly English and partly Guzerathi, belonging to the city; the editors called and assured me of their friendly co-operation, which they showed on more than one occasion.

Friday, Oct. 19.—This was my day of departure; but I must not leave without visiting the jail, which I did early in the morning. The shattered palisades round the surrounding enclosure by no means give an idea of a Government institution, still less of a jail. All the prisoners were in irons; this was indeed necessary for security in such premises. The same general features were observable here as in Ahmedabad: no instruction, and sleeping in association at night six or eight in a cell; by day weaving and other skilled labour, beautiful baskets, cane chairs, and other articles. The rattan was here ordered by the superintendent when he was not satisfied with the quality of the work. No attempt appeared to be made to carry out any system which would improve the moral condition of the prisoners. The wretched women were huddled together in a miserable place; they were said to be so bad that they could not be made worse. There did not appear to be any attempt to make them better.

And now again a departure from a place already become familiar, and farewell to many whom I had learnt to esteem. It is sad to leave friends just as one is beginning to know and value them; but such is the inevitable lot of travellers!

It was late in the evening when the lamps of Bombay sparkled in the distance; the sight of them was acceptable after a hot and dusty journey. One is compelled in India to be content to be covered with dust when travelling, as open windows are indispensable. I was truly thankful to find Mr. Scoble, that year sheriff, kindly waiting to receive me, and convey me to his hospitable abode, which he and his lady bade me regard as my home during my stay in the country. So I did think of it, in whatever part of India I was travelling, for I knew that there I had friends who sympathised in my work, and would be glad to see me again, and that in their house was one place which they permitted me to call my own. None can tell how much happiness they confer, or how much good they do, when they thus fulfil the apostolic injunction, 'Be not unmindful to entertain strangers.' Let me here offer them publicly, as I have often done privately, my grateful thanks.

It was one of those splendid moonlight nights so common in Bombay, when the open carriage drove through an avenue of cocoanut palm-trees to the large verandah of this pleasant Eastern abode. No one who has not visited tropical countries can imagine the exquisite loveliness of the long silvery branches, or rather leaves, of this beautiful tree, floating in a gentle breeze, and reflecting the light of the moon. The splendour of the Queen of Night, as she shines forth from her throne in the deep blue heavens, and sheds her rays on the waters, always entranced me; yet here she seemed invested with a fresh glory. My new home was at Breach Candy, so close to that rocky shore that during the rainy season the spray dashes against the windows of the house, and the incessant roaring of the waves is perfectly distracting to a person of weak nerves. Not very long before my arrival, a dreadful shipwreck had occurred near this spot, and my kind host and hostess had been called on for a large exercise of their hospitality, in succouring those who with difficulty were rescued from a watery grave. Now all was calm and peaceful. The large verandah terrace was always shady, and refreshed by the sea-breezes; this led directly into the spacious drawing-room, dining-room, library, and music and billiard-room, which all opened into each other and allowed a free circulation of air, venetian shutters carefully excluding the heat on the sunny side; punkahs are of course in every room, ready for use when required. There is no possibility of privacy or seclusion in the sitting-rooms of Indian houses; native servants appear everywhere unexpectedly, as the tread of their bare feet is noiseless; and indeed a tailor sitting cross-legged in the verandah, repairing house-linen or making female attire, is very commonly considered an essential part of the household. These, and the native servants generally, are not supposed to understand

English; the butler and valet frequently speak enough for common house purposes. It is, however, generally believed that the servants are acquainted with much more English than they profess, and hence the extraordinary knowledge possessed by them, and through them the public generally, of the affairs of their employers. Such a state of things appears inseparable from the present Anglo-Indian mode of life.

This house had a second-floor for sleeping apartments. Such is rarely the case in country houses or villas not actually in the city, as space is abundant, and it is certainly very agreeable in this hot climate to be spared the fatigue of mounting stairs. The rooms assigned to me were spacious and airy, overlooking the sea; and some of the windows were shaded by the tops of beautiful large cocoanut trees, one of which had actually nuts hanging from it in every stage of development. I learnt to feel quite a personal attachment to these trees, and did not wonder that they are held by some as sacred and worshipped—a far more innocent object of idolatry than the hideous images one sees everywhere. Every part of the tree—its fruit, sweet milk, fibre, shell, leaves, bark, and wood—is useful to man, and supplies the simple inhabitants of the southern coasts with most that they require in their primitive mode of life.

From the other windows of my room the sea presented a never-failing source of interest, whether in the morning light, glowing but calm, a soft warm grey in the zenith, against which the palms came out brilliantly; or in the rich deep red of the sun setting in the water; or when, in the middle of the darkness of night, I opened the shutter and beheld a flood of glory on the dark silent waves, which reminded me, 'Thy glorious eye pervadeth space,'—' The light of His countenance is over all His works.'

A morning sketch from those windows is now a treasured memorial of that sea-view: the distant hills of the bay, the extensive rocky beach, along which Parsees were generally wandering before sunrise to pay their morning orisons, and the palms bending towards the sea to escape from the unwelcome land-breezes.

Saturday, Oct. 20.—A delightful packet of home despatches was awaiting my arrival; for the first time also, since leaving England, was I able completely to unpack and arrange my affairs. Some rats had taken a fancy to the binding of a few of my books, but otherwise all were in excellent condition. Many friends, both native and English, came to welcome me, and gave me promise of many subjects for future observation. So much of interest had already presented itself in connection with the Bombay Presidency, that I was beginning seriously to think of not extending my journey farther, but of employing my six months' holiday in seeing and learning as much as possible in this part of Western India only. But the importance of taking some steps towards the establishment of a Female Normal Training School, as a first and essential step towards any improvement in female education, had now forced itself strongly on my mind. The various discussions of the subject with both English and natives, the careful consideration with them of every difficulty, the anxiety expressed by both Hindoo ladies and gentlemen that some such course should be soon adopted, and the necessity of having Government sanction before anything could be done—all these considerations led me to feel that I must make this subject my primary one, and that all other plans must be superseded by whatever seemed most likely to promote this. The subject of prison discipline was also one which I felt to be of the first importance to the welfare of India, and on which I was anxious to obtain some information which might be of some future service; —respecting this, I was peculiarly desirous of conferring with official gentlemen. The study of the subject in which I had engaged in the preparation of my work, 'Our Convicts,' and the close observation of the Irish convict system, under the direction of Sir Walter Crofton, the founder of it, made me wish to lose no opportunity of gleaning further information here. But the Court was likely to continue for some time longer at Poona, waiting for the approaching durbar, and few of those official gentlemen to whom I brought letters of introduction were now in Bombay. It seemed best, therefore, to accept the kind invitation of Lady Grant—to whose husband, Sir Alexander Grant, the Director of Public Instruction, I had brought an introduction from Lord Cranbourne—to pay her a visit at Poona during the durbar week, when I should have an opportunity of laying these subjects before the Government and the Educational Department. It was fixed, therefore, that I should take this journey on the following Wednesday, under the escort of Mr. Manockjee Cursetjee, who was himself going to attend the durbar.

Monday Oct. 22.—At an early hour my host, the sheriff, kindly undertook to accompany me to visit the jail, with his lady. A very different arrangement prevails here from what is adopted in the provincial towns. The jailer—or, as we in England should say, the governor—is here called the marshal, and has the responsible management of the place, under the supervision of the sheriff and magistrates. He was an Englishman, and very superior to the native officers I had seen elsewhere. I perceived at once the good effect of having an officer with full authority always on the premises and resident there. The sheriff had himself devoted much time and attention to it, and had made many improvements in the place. Leg-irons are now used only occasionally in extreme cases, and the marshal expressed his opinion that they need never be employed, if proper care is taken and a right discipline is maintained. A number of English sailors are here, for neglect of duty. It is strongly suspected that the captains provoke the men to misconduct while in port, if they do not require their services, in order to relieve themselves from their maintenance. A clergyman of the city kindly gives gratuitous services and conducts regular worship on Sundays, but there is no chapel or even schoolroom suitable within the jail where these can be held. The industrial work appeared excellent, and done with good will; indeed, the marshal said that he had never any need of the rattan: moral influence appeared to prevail here. There were, however, but few separate cells, and there is no instruction provided for the prisoners. The female prisoners had better premises than in the other jails I had visited, but morally their condition was equally dreadful. There are no female warders, and there is no instruction. Then there were five women locked up together, one of whom was a murderess. The poor creatures seemed pleased that they were sufficiently cared for to lead us even to look at them, and responded to our evident feelings of sympathy. I suggested that the visits of ladies would be valuable to the women confined in this and other jails; if unable to converse with them they would show them kindness, and even this would have a softening effect on them; they might also teach them needlework or other civilising feminine art. It was replied that this would be impossible, since there was no place here where ladies could sit down; and that, besides, these women were too low in their habits to be approached by any person of refinement. That such a state of things can exist in a country governed by Christians, filled me with horror. We cannot throw off the responsibility by the remark, 'Am I my brother's or sister's keeper?' These poor wretched creatures are in our hands, and cannot escape from us, or we from the duty imposed upon us by our relative positions. Surely the simple revelation of these things to the British public will stir up some to take up the cause of the Hindoo female prisoner, and never let the subject rest, until all is done for them that enlightened humanity can do. If we are debarred from giving them Christian teaching, let us at any rate exhibit to them the fruits of our holy religion, in our treatment of them, and let us discharge the solemn duty we owe to them.

Tuesday, Oct. 23.—The scenes I visited to-day were of a very different character. As I was anxious to see the girls' schools, under the management of the missionaries, a friend kindly accompanied me to-day to a school under her own management. It did not exhibit any features very different from those which I had already seen, the want of trained female teachers being there, as elsewhere, strongly felt.

A boarding-school for native Christian girls was, however, quite new to me, and an institution which I was desirous of observing closely, especially as I had for nearly forty years directed my attention to the education, physical, intellectual, moral, and religious, of the young of my own sex; the greater part of this period to young ladies, the last twelve years to the sole management of the first Reformatory established in England for criminal girls. I wished, then, to study how far the same principle might be applicable in this country. The school I was about to visit is a boarding institution, under the care of Mrs. Nesbit, who, animated with Christian love for these children, devotes herself in her widowhood to them, and to other good works among the natives. She occupies rooms in the premises, which she makes her home, thus shedding her influence and refinement into the school. The building is a very simple and unostentatious one, and its deficiencies and inconvenience of arrangement had decided the supporters on providing a better one, to which the school was about to be removed. The teachers are women, except a pundit, who is engaged to give grammatical lessons in the vernacular, in the presence of a female official. The scholars are chiefly orphans, and of different nationalities—Hindoos, Armenians, half-castes—but all associating without the slightest distinction. Their ages varied considerably, some being very young, others probably fifteen or sixteen. The deportment of all was pleasing, and when they sung their voices blended sweetly and harmoniously. In England, such girls would be generally intended for domestic service, and prepared for its duties while at school. I was informed, however, that such can rarely be the case in India, owing to the universal employment of men in the household occupations, with us exclusively appropriated to women; it would not, therefore, be safe for a young girl to be placed as servant in a family. The girls are usually married when about fifteen or sixteen to native converts, and it is of importance that they should be prepared to be good wives and mothers of families. Mrs. Nesbit has them trained, therefore, to do all kinds of housework; this is not only in itself very useful, but is valuable in strengthening the muscles. Laundry-work is at home an excellent occupation in these respects, and is besides often very remunerative; it appears, however, that this is never carried on in school. Attention is, however, paid to needlework, and some is even taken in for customers. The singing was sweet, and in other respects this school gave me satisfactory proof that, under good female instruction, Hindoo girls are quite equal to their English sisters.

Wednesday, Oct. 24.—The railway journey to Poona is one of no ordinary interest, for it is on the famous Bhore Ghaut Incline, which rivals the wonderful Alpine road. The first part of the journey is by Salsette to Tanna, whence the celebrated caves may be visited; the distant hills and sea, with the fertility of the country, make the route interesting to a stranger. When the ascent of the mountain commences, the train divides, and the speed is greatly diminished; this is a considerable advantage, as it enables the traveller to enjoy the marvellous beauty of the scenery. The road is not one simple ascent, but has to be carried backward and forward along the brow of different ridges; hence there is a perpetual change of scene—stupendous precipices, deep gorges, extensive plains, and overhanging mountains, presenting every possible variety. A month before, there were also magnificent waterfalls, from the effect of the rains, but now there were only a few traces of these. The day was sultry, but as we rose we reached a fresher atmosphere, and at last arrived at Khandalla, near which is a sanatorium for soldiers. The scene was now entirely changed. On reaching the top of a steep ascent one usually expects to find a corresponding descent the other side. There, however, we were on the top of the high table-land which forms the Deccan. The face of the country was now strikingly altered, though in the distance were mountains, and we could trace on the steep face of one some famous sacred caves; yet around us the country became increasingly barren, and the regular and well-made roads indicated that we were approaching a large military encampment. We passed an engineering college and residences of official gentlemen. The strange mingling of civilisation and barbarism is nowhere more striking than at Poona. It had been very observable on the road, for the inferior carriages were filled with men and women, probably going to the approaching durbar, whose nude condition and rough unregulated deportment, especially in the case of the women, were particularly repulsive. Poona itself is still a stronghold of Brahminism, and having been a capital of the Marathas, is particularly filled with the insignia of idolatry, displayed in hideous images and paintings, and in remains of ancient palaces and very narrow streets and staircases. These contrast strangely with the comparatively new encampment, and with the houses of the English resident gentry, and all the state consequent on the Court being there.

Thursday, Oct. 25.—This morning was devoted to the schools, which are particularly good at Poona. It is very striking to see the anxiety for learning in the young men. It appears, however, that this arises from the fact of successful application being the means of obtaining scholarships, which more than suffice for the maintenance of a young Hindoo, and also Government employment. If those are not procurable, still there is considerable demand for clerks and writers in various offices; and this, if not always a very lucrative mode of living, is more in accordance with native taste, and deemed more honourable, than employments involving more physical labour. Hence very great efforts are often made by parents to keep young men at the High School, and then at college, considering this a good investment for their future benefit. This is a step in advance. A gentleman at Surat, who had received all his education gratuitously from benevolent persons, told me that his father had spent 30,000 his rupees for marriage, but would not have spent 3,000 rupees for his education. We visited four educational institutions for youths—a Branch School, a High School, a Mission School, and a Normal Training School.

In the Branch School, as English is not taught, the masters are inferior and worse paid, but they appeared to teach with great care and skill. The building had probably been a large dwelling-house surrounding a court, and with porticoes: in some of these the classes are held, while families occupy other portions of the house. This has a remarkably picturesque effect, though not very convenient for tuition. The scholars are, however, more tractable than our young English boys, and we did not notice any tendency to disorder, even under the excitement of the presence of strangers. It was strange to see the little fellows sitting on the ground with a reed pen, tracing out, at first rudely, then with beautiful neatness, the Marathi characters. The writing produced in the school was remarkably good. On our asking for a specimen, the schoolmaster kindly sent me a number of exercises which far surpassed any that could be shown in our ordinary National or British schools; some of them were even illuminated;—he sent with them some verses of his own composition addressed to Sir A. Grant, which were an exquisite specimen of ornamental chirography.

The High School we visited had in the higher classes young men who had attained a very superior degree of education. Their acquaintance with the structure and genius of the English language was remarkable, as was evinced by the facility with which they not only translated at first sight correctly into the vernacular very difficult passages from our literature, but rendered passages of their own language into good English. In geometry and the higher branches of arithmetic, they showed great proficiency. The following tables will have considerable interest:—

Castes of Pupils attending the School in the Poona Subdivision on April 30, 1866.

	Number of schools	Hindoos	Mahometans	Parsees	Others	Total
Boys'	137	6758	292	1	—	7051
Girls'	3	131	1	—	22	154

Period of Attendance of Pupils of Schools in the Poona Subdivision up to April 1866.

	Number of schools	Under 3 months	3 to 6 months	6 to 9 months	9 months to 1 year	1 to 2 years	2 to 3 years	3 to 4 years	4 to 5 years	5 to 6 years	6 to 7 years	7 to 8 years	8 to 9 years	9 to 10 years	10 to 11 years	11 to 12 years	Total
Boys'	137	1641	1278	957	767	1055	515	391	214	140	62	21	9	1	—	—	7051
Girls'	3	49	35	22	19	15	7	5	2	—	—	—	—	—	—	—	154

We here see that while in Poona there are 137 boys' schools, containing 7,051 scholars, there are only three for girls, containing 154, and of this small number only 29 have had a year's instruction, only two having been from four to five years at school; while of the boys more than a third of the whole number have had from one year to nine years' teaching. Two of these girls' schools I visited; they were in small and very unsuitable buildings, and with very inefficient teachers—a striking contrast to what I had seen in Ahmedabad and Surat, and what I afterwards saw in Bombay. So little can a judgment be formed of even one Presidency from the condition of a part of it.

The Mission Day School is a large one, containing from 600 to 700 youths. It is in what appears to have been an ancient palace, judging from the size of the halls and the richness of the dark wood-carving.

The scholars are all assembled once a day for Scripture reading, and they presented a very striking spectacle when so gathered together in the grand old hall, though their minds did not appear to be much occupied with what was going on. The large library and class-room are also very striking, and for the first time I saw objects of natural history displayed to awaken the curiosity and stimulate the intellect of the scholars.

There and elsewhere the superintendent or missionary candidly owned that their schools are not sought after for the sake of Scripture instruction, as has been sometimes represented, but to obtain instruction at a cheaper rate. They have generally, however, expressed the hope and belief that though at first the scholars show repugnance to Scripture instruction, yet that good effects do eventually show themselves, both in direct conversions, and in a diminution of prejudice; there cannot but be a good influence arising from hearing the simple teaching of our holy religion, even if the hearers do not receive them as divinely inspired. Here also the exercises were very beautifully written, and I carried away some specimens of these, and also of maps drawn by the young people, which did the highest credit both to teachers and scholars, and are highly prized by friends at home.

The Normal Training School did not appear as good as those which I had seen elsewhere. Many young men apply for admission into it without any special gift for teaching, but in order to obtain a gratuitous education, afterwards employing this to procure situations. This of course has to be discouraged; it appeared to me, however, a matter of regret that with a view to this, English is not as thoroughly taught as in the High Schools. Even if young men are intended only to be teachers in vernacular schools, it is very desirable that they should have their minds enlarged, and their power increased of improving through English civilisation, to enable them to improve their scholars.

Many of the students attending the High School as well as the Normal School come from a distance, and a boarding-house is provided for them. This we were invited to visit, and were escorted there early one morning by the Director of Public Instruction. It appeared well situated for the convenience of the students, with a garden, tank, &c. On our arrival, many of them had not left their sleeping apartments—others were reclining, looking at their class-books, in preparation for the examination; studying it could hardly be called, so listless was their air. At this inert manner I was not surprised, when I learnt that it is quite unusual for them to take any exercise in the evening after their six hours of study are completed, nor do they ever think of rising early to take any exercise in the morning. After surveying the premises, before our departure we were informed that the students were assembled for breakfast, and invited to see them. What was the consternation of us ladies, when the door was thrown open, to behold seventy young men sitting on the floor with their food before them, stripped to the waist! We speedily withdrew.

After this, we had a more agreeable visit to the Mission Boarding School for young girls. It was a pleasant house in the outskirts with a large garden, a sort of home school. About twenty-five little Brahmin girls attend as day-scholars, and share in all the benefit of the instruction. The general features of the school are much the same as at Mrs. Nesbit's, the girls learning to cook and do housework, in the same manner as they may be expected to do in their future homes. Their native style of dress is not altered except as far as to cover the person decently, and they do not wear shoes and stockings. The strictest economy is observed; indeed, I noticed that the little cotton jackets of some of the girls were somewhat in the fashion of Joseph's 'coat of many colours'—manufactured out of pieces of print sent from England, as we have seen done at home in our ragged schools. The lessons we heard indicated good teachers and intelligent scholars. Their singing was peculiarly sweet and beautiful. It was indeed very pleasant to hear our favourite hymn—

There is a happy land, far, far away!

sung with feeling by these little Hindoo girls. Some of them wrote for me a verse in English very neatly, as well as some lines in their own language. Who can tell how many precious seeds are thus being sown in these little hearts, or what fruit will be brought forth from them! We learnt that, beside the regular instruction in singing, an English lady gives the most advanced lessons at her own home, accompanying them with the piano. She finds them apt scholars. One thing more I was desirous of ascertaining, viz., whether Hindoo girls can play actively, or whether it is impossible to surmount the listlessness of their natures. I therefore requested the lady superintendent to release the children, and let them have a good game. My friends thought that it was unreasonable to expect that they could show any animation in the presence of strangers. I had, however, a better opinion of the nature of young girls who have not been subjected to unnatural pressure, and was right. There was a large graceful tamarind-tree in the garden with overhanging branches; under this the scholars danced and played with as much life and animation as any English girls.

There is in Poona another small orphanage for native girls, supported by resident ladies.

English girls are not forgotten in India; indeed, especial care appears to be taken that they shall be properly educated and provided for. In Bombay there are large boarding-schools for both the sons and the daughters of soldiers. As the climate there is considered relaxing for children of European birth, an establishment is provided at Poona for the very young ones. This appears admirably situated and well managed, the children being happy and healthful.

The jail at Poona presents the same unsatisfactory features as elsewhere; and, as at Ahmedabad, the evils of the present arrangements are strongly felt by the superintendent, a gentleman who, though only temporarily filling the post, throws himself heart and soul into his work, without being able to prevent the injurious effects he perceives. He exerts a strong moral influence on the prisoners, and thus avoids the necessity of punishment. The female department was even worse than elsewhere, for between forty and fifty women were locked up together without any attempt to improve them. Among them were some murderesses and very hardened abandoned-looking women, while others were young and with agreeable countenances. What must these become from such contact, and without any attempt to infuse better influences! All sense of shame is lost, for on asking a young woman what her caste was, she replied that she was of the 'thief caste.'

The superintendent has carried out, with much success, a ticket-of-leave system in favour of some prisoners who have been a length of time in the jail, and who have given reason to hope that they purpose living an honest life. Labour, if skilled, is very high here, and in much demand. Hence he experiences no difficulty in getting good employment for any whom he can recommend, and these report themselves regularly to him. The Chinamen are very good gardeners, and particularly neat and persevering in their work. When a piece of ground is given them to live on, they cultivate it admirably, and obtain from it abundant produce. This I had afterwards an opportunity of witnessing at Matheran, near Bombay. The superintendent was at that time employing as a gardener, on his own grounds, a Chinaman who had been a pirate and a murderer, and who is doing very well. This is the only experiment of the kind which I heard of in India. Its success encourages to an extension of the plan with long-sentenced prisoners.

A Central Jail, or (as we should say) Convict Prison,

is in course of erection, the director, Dr. Wiehe, having secured for the purpose fifty acres of land; this would give him an opportunity of carrying out in its entirety the Irish convict system, which has had such remarkable success. But, most unfortunately, while the gentlemen who have the practical management of these Indian prisons are fully alive to the immense importance of the separate sleeping-cells, and other matters essential to reformation, the Government of each Presidency has not the power of making the needed alterations. As the first outlay is larger for a prison constructed with separate cells, only a small percentage of them is allowed, and thus in the new jail the old bad system is to be perpetuated. Would that in India the same interest could be excited on the subject of prison discipline, as of late has been the case in our country! Would that some Howard or Mrs. Fry would arise there, deeply sensible of our grave responsibility in that country, who, with the knowledge of the subject acquired during the last twenty years, would not rest till an improved system is inaugurated!

There are, indeed, I was already beginning to learn, difficulties in the way of reform in India which do not exist in England. At home the felt necessity for a reform in any department is brought forward by the press; a public opinion is created, the matter is laid before Government, and the necessary steps are taken to obtain fresh legislation if needed. But in India there are few to know or to feel the necessity of a change in such matters as prison discipline, except the gentlemen who are immediately concerned in the management of the jails;—these are fully occupied with their official duties, and unable to engage in any movement, even if that were the right course to adopt to effect improvement. There are indeed great difficulties here.

My friends did not allow me to be exclusively occupied with subjects of this kind, but desired that I should see some of the lions of Poona. A heathen temple, however picturesque, was no great attraction to me; but the Parbati Hill is considered so very remarkable a spot, that I gladly accepted an invitation from my kind hostess to make an excursion to it. The drive there is well-wooded and beautiful, and near the foot of the hill is a fine tank reflecting the surrounding scenery. Large elephants properly caparisoned for riding, and palanquins with bearers, were waiting at the bottom of the hill, evidently for visitors, and to my surprise I learnt that the long flight of low steps leading to the temple at the top was to be mounted on these animals. This was indeed a new and extraordinary experience, but it was an opportunity too peculiar to be lost. So the animal knelt, and Lady G. and I mounted by a ladder to our seat, holding firmly as he rose. One has certainly a good view of the country round, and feels in an elevated position on an elephant's back; but the sensation of going up steps on it was not very agreeable, and one had a feeling that he might tip over and bury his burden under him. Of that, however, there was no real danger, for the creature never placed down his foot, without having carefully examined with his trunk whether all was quite safe for his heavy body. It appeared that he had never ascended these steps before, and his driver continually addressed him in a low, musical, and confidential tone. I learnt that it was to this effect: 'Go on, my lord, I entreat you! Many other elephants have taken this journey before—there is no danger—go on, my lord. You are my father, my father's brother,' &c. This was not a very enjoyable position, and we were thankful when we were safe on terra firma. The temple is certainly very curious, and worth seeing as a specimen of idolatrous worship. The largest temple is dedicated to Shiva, and in it is a silver image of the god, with two images, said to be of gold, representing Parvati and Ganesh sitting on Shiva's knees. Everything around reminded us of an idolatrous and degraded worship, containing nothing to elevate or refine the mind. It appeared to have been a special festival, many of the native princes having visited the place and made large offerings to the Brahmins, whom we saw counting over their heaps of rupees. A gentleman once met with an old scholar in that position, who offered him to become a Christian if he would procure for him a government post! The knowledge that such deceptions are attempted is probably one cause of the great dislike usually felt by the Hindoos for 'native converts.' A palace was built near this temple by the last Peishwa; it is now in ruins. We looked through the broken framework of the window, whence he watched the final overthrow of his troops by the British in 1817. The landscape now looked singularly rich and beautiful. May it never again be desolated by war!

Oct. 28.—The next day was Sunday, and it was a most refreshing change to attend the Christian worship of the Mission Chapel, even though it was in an unknown tongue. We had to be up betimes, for this was a very special occasion. Lady G.'s ayah was to be baptised, and her master and mistress wished to be present on the occasion. This young native woman had struck me at first sight by her superiority in mind and manners to any other I had seen. Her demeanour indicated great refinement and intelligence, and she was able to speak sufficient English for ordinary communication. Lady G. said that she had no share in her conversion, which appeared to have taken place through her own deep earnest thought. She had been with her mistress at the house of a gentleman, who had regularly a Marathi service for any of the servants to attend who desired it. She had been deeply impressed by what she had heard, and, on afterwards accompanying her mistress to England, was so struck with the very different condition of a Christian country from her own, that she wished to be baptised, considering that Christianity was proved by its fruits to be the best religion. To this precipitate course her mistress did not give her sanction; but on the ayah's return to India she learnt to read, placed herself under the instruction of a missionary, and now her heart's desire was to be accomplished of becoming a member of a Christian church.

There is no rest from labour in India on the Christian Sabbath. It is indeed the day particularly employed by many to accomplish their own special work. We observed many women at hard drudgery occupations as we rode along. Such a fact alone indicates the radical difference between a Christian and a heathen country. The ayah had been much struck in England at not seeing any 'women coolies.' She said that she had heard the reason was that the sovereign being a woman did not allow her own sex to be degraded.

The approach to the little mission station was in harmony with the feelings which a bright Sunday morning inspires at home. 'Beauty shall spring up out of ashes.' What had been a wilderness was converted into a lovely garden by a few months' care from the missionary; beautiful tropical creepers were overhanging the entrance. All was simple, but neat and clean. How unlike what we had witnessed the day before! The elder school-girls led the singing most sweetly, and after the introductory service in Marathi, the young convert modestly presented herself for baptism;—having answered satisfactorily the ordinary questions, she received the sacred symbol. Again there was an offering of a heart to the Lord—a father came to present his little one for admission to the Church. The service was now in English; after the conclusion I learnt that this infant was the child of a second marriage, the mother being present, a respectable-looking young woman, and a former pupil of Mrs. Nesbit's. He had several children by the first marriage. Two pleasant-looking girls were about to be married on the following Tuesday, and I much regretted not being able to stay to be present at the ceremony. Conversing with these worthy people, and hearing their simple histories, impressed me with the conviction that they felt Christianity to be a blessed reality, and that in their humble way they were helping to promote the coming of the kingdom of God.

The great subject of Female Education occupied, of course, a large share of my attention. This city appeared far behind those which I had hitherto visited, in the elevation of the female sex. No native lady visited me, nor was I invited to the homes of any. The girls' schools were small and poorly conducted; but as they were established comparatively recently, only through the zealous efforts of some of the native school inspectors, it was evident that a desire was springing up in the same direction. This indeed was proved by the earnest conversation I had with several of these gentlemen. One of them thus stated his views in my book. All of these written expressions I regarded as very valuable, because they were the spontaneous effusions of their own minds:—

'We have watched the progress of female education in the Bombay Presidency from its very beginning, and have contributed to promote its interest both by personal exertions and pecuniary assistance. Since the last eighteen or twenty years, female education has made a steady progress on this side of India; and all the prejudices which the people showed, and all the obstacles which they raised when female schools were first opened, have gradually disappeared, except those which the constitution of Hindoo society still presents. One of these is the early age at which young females have to go to their husbands, and assist in the performance of domestic work. This will be seen from the fact that no girls of more than twelve years of age are to be found in our girls' schools. Before the age of twelve, children can master but very little beyond the mere elements of reading and writing, and after that age our females cannot by their social observances mingle with men. Among the pupils of our female schools, there are many who possess means and opportunities of prosecuting their studies longer; but for want of competent teachers, with whom they can freely associate, they are obliged to stop, with great reluctance, just at the point where a desire for useful knowledge and higher education springs up. To assist them at such a time, schools entirely conducted by competent females would be very useful, and for establishing such schools a staff of female teachers must be trained up. To do this, we must have a female training-school, superintended by an educated and experienced lady. *India at present cannot supply such superintendents from amongst its own females, and therefore we must have them from*

England. From Miss Carpenter's account of the female teachers in England, and of the means they adopt to make an insensible, and even a depraved creature, a good wife and a kind and prudent mother, we are led to hope that the *advent to India of such teachers would be a great blessing to the future generations of the country.*'

Poona, October 27, 1866.

It was in accordance with the similar wishes expressed by intelligent native gentlemen at Ahmedabad that I had first drawn out a simple scheme for a Female Normal Training School; I had discussed it fully in every point at Surat, and here I availed myself gladly of the opportunity presented by the presence of the Director of Public Instruction in this Presidency to consider the scheme thoroughly; it then received his general approval. The pressing want in the country is female teachers for girls' schools. When the rapid progress of male education gave rise to the need of a speedy supply of male teachers, there were already a number of young natives who had received considerable education, and who, with special training for the duties of a teacher, might soon be prepared to be schoolmasters. Simple arrangements for boarding these young men, and suitable instructors, were all that were required to establish a normal training school; and as the office of schoolmaster was considered more honourable than others involving manual labour, there was no difficulty in obtaining candidates, and the schools are now well supplied with native teachers.

But with regard to female teachers the case is totally different. It is evident that as the children leave school at so early an age, and then usually are too much occupied in household affairs to improve their minds, very few could be trained to be teachers except by a long course of instruction. But their position as wives, either by betrothal or in reality, prevents them from being able, if they were willing, to prepare to become teachers; this is also prevented by the social habits of the higher classes. Widows who cannot be easily maintained by their families are at present, unless in very exceptional cases, the only natives who can be enlisted as students. We must, then, look for others now in India—whether English, Eurasians, or any others—who may supply this want, to train as teachers. There may also be many of the superfluous governesses in England who will be glad to come out, learn the vernacular, and be trained, if there are proper arrangements; thus a commencement will be made, and several of these, being already educated women, would be very soon able to throw their influence into the schools now existing, and improve them considerably. But what is to be the position of these Christian students? A proper house must be provided for them, with all needful appliances in this foreign country. They cannot have the protection of the missionaries; they must have that of the Government. It is also necessary that this school should be a Government institution, not only to give the necessary feeling of permanency, but as a guarantee to the natives that it is *not* a proselytising institution. It must be an essential condition that no one while in the institution should, under any circumstances, be allowed in *religious interference of any kind*. These being the conclusions fully accepted by all with whom I conferred, I drew out, in accordance with them, the following sketch of such an institution, as would supply the want felt by all the enlightened natives:—

First.—A house should be procured, adapted to furnish a comfortable residence for about a dozen Christian students, with a lady superintendent. Arrangements should be made for the separate boarding of non-Christian native students, when required. Arrangements for necessary furniture, board, and attendance, to be made by the Inspector of Schools.

Secondly.—A lady superintendent, who should be responsible to Government for the entire management of the institution, should be obtained from England; also a superior mistress for training. In each case the passage-money to be paid under certain conditions.

Thirdly.—Persons who wish to become students in training must apply to the inspector, and must satisfy him that it is their intention to study and faithfully to prepare to be teachers. They will receive board and instruction while in the institution. All English students must learn the vernacular, and all native students English.

Fourthly.—Any girls' schools existing in the neighbourhood may be employed for the training of teachers, and the students may thus be exercising a beneficial influence in the schools now taught by men, before they are prepared to take charge of schools themselves.

Such a plan would, it seemed to the intelligent natives, as well as to myself, be likely, if well worked out, to meet a great and general want.

I found, however, to my sorrow, that this important plan, and the improvement in prison discipline which was so greatly needed, could not, as I had then hoped, be effected by the Presidential Government. I resolved therefore to remain no longer in Bombay, but to proceed at once to Calcutta, to lay the whole before the Supreme Government.

The next day the grand ceremonial took place—the durbar, which had so long excited the expectations of so many. The native princes had been during the preceding week flocking into Poona. On one occasion we saw a considerable crowd in the street; it appeared to be caused by a procession, headed by native guards in very grotesque attire, which was partly native and partly English. Then followed an elephant, gorgeously decked out, on which was seated a native prince, and beside him we were amazed to recognise an English gentleman, who had probably been appointed to do him the honours of the occasion. To the great regret of all, this was the last durbar which would be held by the present Governor, Sir Bartle Frere, who was universally beloved; and many therefore made a special point of attending to do him honour. It is unfortunate that there is no suitable building for such an occasion, and some ordinary tents placed lengthwise formed by no means a place of reception befitting the dignity of the British nation. Thus, though one end of the tent was specially reserved for English ladies, immediately behind the Governor, we were greatly disappointed at not having an opportunity of surveying the dignified persons and their bejewelled dresses, who came to pay their homage to the representative of British power. The accounts given in the local papers convey, therefore, more idea of what took place than what we saw.

CHAPTER IV.

MADRAS.

On arriving at Bombay, I found that the Ahmedabad party had preceded me there. Shortly after my departure, Mr. Tagore had been prostrated with fever; and as this did not appear likely to yield to medical treatment there, he had obtained a three months' leave of absence, and was proceeding, with his lady and friends, to Calcutta.

During our voyage out we had endeavoured to ascertain, from various experienced travellers, some information respecting the different routes. One official gentleman, resident in Calcutta, informed us that he was then returning from a journey to England on a three months' leave of absence. He had travelled from Calcutta to Bombay by land viâ Lahore, the mail route, with a view to save time, as the railway was not completed; this was, however, a very difficult and unpleasant journey, and he assured me that the fact of his having accomplished it, led him to warn me not to attempt it. Subsequent testimony was to the same effect. Every one who had practical knowledge on the subject informed us that the best, and indeed the only satisfactory route, was by steamer to Calicut, by rail across the country from Beypoor to Madras, and thence by steamer to Calcutta. A gentleman who was about to proceed with his family to Lahore from Bombay, considered the direct course to be fraught with so much difficulty, that he meant to travel viâ Madras and Calcutta. A glance at the map of India will show how very circuitous a course this is, and how enormous a saving of time, money, and fatigue will be effected, when the railway is completed which will connect the two most important Presidency capitals, Calcutta and Bombay.

My friends and I determined again to join parties, and to proceed by the 1st of November coasting steamer.

Before our departure, however, our Parsee friend, Mr. Manockjee Cursetjee, insisted on our all dining at his house à l'Anglaise. This gentleman's father had been a reformer among his people; to his memory a beautiful drinking-fountain has been erected in Bombay by his son. About thirty years ago Mr. Cursetjee first visited England, and he was warmly received and hospitably welcomed by distinguished persons in our country. He has in his own family led the way to the elevation of the female sex, by giving his daughters a superior education, bringing them to England, and leading to the establishment in Bombay of a superior Parsee ladies' school. In every possible way, Judge Manockjee Cursetjee endeavours to promote, both by precept and by example, the social improvement of his people and of society at large, especially by the elevation of the female sex. It was no small triumph over conventional customs, that an English lady was invited to dine with Parsee and also with Hindoo gentlemen and ladies, and the fact of such an entertainment having been actually given is worthy of a distinct record.

The sail from Bombay is very beautiful. It is only necessary to fancy oneself on a pleasure excursion instead of a business voyage, thoroughly to enjoy the glorious harbour, the receding city, the distant mountains, the ever-shifting islands, the blue sea, and the cloudless azure of the sky. Our invalid seemed to improve with the sea-air, and the days passed quickly by, till on the 4th Nov. (Sunday), after morning service performed by the captain, we found ourselves off Calicut. Numerous boats soon surrounded the ship, and we gladly engaged two to convey us straight to Beypoor, as soon as the midday heat was somewhat abated, thus saving our invalid a carriage journey of about ten miles.

It was a glorious afternoon—the Sabbath sheds a brightness over nature even here. For some distance we had observed the coast covered up to the hills with forests, which, by the aid of a glass, we discovered to consist of cocoanut palms.

We were now completely in the region of this valuable and interesting tree, and rowing along near the shore, we saw the graceful forms of these feathery palms, which almost encroached on the sea-sands; the little native cottages under them, and the half-savage inhabitants, occasionally strolling along. Our boatmen were strange, uncouth, half-clad beings, who made considerable display of their rows of regular white teeth, as they kept some degree of time by the aid of a rude song, in the chorus of which all joined. Never had I been so completely cut off from all civilised life, the only traces of which now were my companions and the ship, which was gradually disappearing in the distance. It was one of those wonderful scenes which inspire the mind with thoughts that cannot be uttered.

At length, as the sun was setting, our boatmen landed us safely near the large new hotel at Beypoor, which is kept by a Parsee. This place was a wonderful contrast to that we had just quitted. We were able to get some of the comforts of civilised life, which were very refreshing after our voyage, and necessary to prepare us for our long journey. Beypoor appears likely to become an important place, and we were told that this large and well-situated hotel is often the resort of pleasure parties.

We started early in the morning. We were now in the Madras Presidency; the whole face of the country, and the manners of the inhabitants, were greatly changed. When we had with some difficulty secured our luggage, and established ourselves and our belongings in the comfortable saloon railway-carriage, we found ourselves surrounded by numbers of boys pressing us to buy cocoanuts. These were in a soft milky state, very different from what we ever see them in England. So we obtained some, that we might quench our thirst with the pleasant milk, and be reminded of Mrs. Barbauld's hymns, beloved in childhood. The notices at the railway stations were in new languages, which were unintelligible to my Hindoo friends. I could perceive a great difference between the square forms of the written tongues derived from Sanscrit, and the rounded letters with flourishes of the languages of the tribes we were now among. All the groups of natives we saw at the stations had, however, so very low and barbaric an aspect, that I wondered what could be the utility of writing railway notices and the names of the stations in two distinct characters besides English, such uncivilised-looking beings not being likely to be able to read. My native friends informed me, however, that many of those we saw were Brahmins—that all Brahmins are educated, and therefore could read the notices.

The country was in most parts rich and well cultivated. It appeared to consist principally of rice-fields; these were carefully irrigated, and were then generally under water. As we proceeded, the hills which bounded the horizon gradually increased in height, until they assumed the form of precipitous mountain ranges, apparently the outcrop of the high table-land which forms the Deccan. Rolling clouds threw shadows over them, and the mist rising revealed new beauties. On each side the view was splendid. We were approaching the Neilgherries, a fine mountain range, where is a climate perfectly English in temperature. Many resort there when oppressed with the heat, and at different heights the productions of both tropical and temperate climates are found in great perfection. The Neilgherries were continually spoken of to me during the whole of my stay in India as a sort of land of promise, where might be found the most splendid scenery, wild mountains, wooded dells, cascades rivalling those of Tivoli, creepers with gorgeous flowers hanging from the trees in graceful festoons, an unrivalled climate, English comforts and society. These, however, I was not destined to enjoy, except in imagination and in distant vision.

Night journeys in India are often preferred to day travelling, as they are cooler, and the carriages are so arranged, like the berths in a ship, as to afford some comfortable rest. We lost some grand scenery during the night, but enjoyed repose, and found ourselves in the morning approaching Madras. Again there was a considerable change, and it was curious to observe, in the fields we passed, the primitive modes of procedure among the people, in drawing water and in agricultural work. Labour here is of little value—the cost of living is very small to the uneducated peasant, and it seems as if the trouble of learning new and better plans is so great, that it more than counterbalances any advantage that would arise from the introduction of them.

The city of Madras at once impressed us with its size and imposing appearance, and it had evidently made rapid progress during the last twenty years. It appeared at first sight worthy to be a Presidency capital. Formerly travellers were obliged chiefly to depend on the hospitality of the residents, but now there are numerous large hotels, both in the city and in the environs. We therefore drove along the beautiful bay surrounded with large official buildings, and then a broad well-made road, superior to anything we had before seen in India. Indeed, we thought the way very long before we reached the large hotel which had been recommended to us, and then found to our dismay that it was full. Being anxious to obtain rest and refreshment for our invalid, who, though he had borne the journey wonderfully well, was becoming quite exhausted, we availed ourselves of the accommodation of the next that offered, as we were perfect strangers in the place. Unfortunately for us, this hotel was not complete in its arrangements, and the head of the establishment not residing on the premises, being a Hindoo, the varied miseries we had to endure may be better imagined than described, left, as we were, to the mercy of a number of male native servants. The steamer was, however, daily expected from Ceylon, which would convey us to Calcutta; we therefore determined to practise, as best we might, the virtue of endurance, since no remonstrances appeared likely to better our condition, or to procure for us a proper supply of well-cooked food at the appointed hours.

Though I had no intention before leaving England of

visiting Madras, yet, having been favoured by the Secretary of State for India with an introduction to the Director of Public Instruction there, as well as elsewhere, I was thankful to feel that there was some one in Madras who might show us a little sympathy. The delivery of my note was promptly followed by a kind visit from that gentleman, Mr. Eyre Powell, who arranged at once to show me as many of the lions as could be seen the next day. These proved so interesting and attractive, that I gladly accepted the kind invitation of Mrs. Powell to take up my residence at her house, until another steamer should touch here. My friends proceeded without me to their homes in Calcutta.

Madras is a striking and interesting city, perfectly different indeed from any others which I had hitherto seen. It has always been a stronghold of the missionaries, who have probably done more here, in the establishment of good schools and in general work, than in most other places. There is a large number of professed Christians among the lower orders, many being Roman Catholics; but it is a general complaint that these are even less principled than the avowed heathens; they have thrown off the restraints imposed by the faith of their fathers, without being imbued with the principles of Christianity, or the ordinary morality taught in civilised life. English is more commonly understood here than elsewhere by the native servants, a very great convenience to strangers. I had far less difficulty in consequence here, for the servants whom I met with were obliging and civil. The general costume somewhat differs from what I had seen in other parts of the country, being generally a simple white dress without shoes and stockings, and a turban folded in a peculiar manner. The head is usually shaved, leaving a long tuft of hair on the top or back of the head. There is sufficient difference in the ordinary air and deportment of the natives from that of the inhabitants of Bombay, to enable them to be easily recognised when in the public schools. Madras is everywhere called the 'benighted Presidency.' I cannot speak of the exact amount of education in general in it, though that appeared very satisfactory; but I can say that I saw more advancement in female improvement than I witnessed in Calcutta and many other parts, while the general tone of native society appears educated and intelligent. Madras certainly no longer deserves this epithet, if it ever did.

The work of the missionaries has been particularly vigorous and successful in Madras in the promotion of education. My attention was first directed to the schools of the Free Scotch Church Mission. That for boys is situated near the sea, and appeared very extensive and complete; it shows most strikingly what can be effected by one man, who, with devoted heart and single aim, devotes himself to the welfare of his fellow-creatures. In 1837, the Rev. John Anderson founded this school. On occasion of the distribution of prizes to the scholars in the Evangelistic Hall (Dec. 22, 1864), the chairman, Col. Rowlandson, said: 'When this school was first founded, it was soon recognised and spoken of as a remarkable era in the history of missions in Madras, destined to exercise a mighty influence upon the future of this Presidency; and well I remember the sensation awakened throughout all classes of society by the bold, uncompromising, undisguised, and till then unheard-of declaration, upon which Mr. Anderson based all his hopes and plans, of one supreme aim and object, viz., to win souls to Christ! And truly one had only to enter their schools, and following on from class to class, listen to the way in which they taught and opened out the Book of Life, not merely in the letter to the understanding, but closely applying its truths to the hearts and consciences of their pupils, to feel persuaded that as their eye was single, and their aim true to God's glory, so assuredly would God own and bless their labours. And not long had we to wait for proofs; for soon the whole society of Madras was heaving with excitement and profound interest in the great battle, then for the first time in this school unflinchingly fought with caste exclusiveness, in which they nobly triumphed; followed soon with the thorough heart-conversion and baptism, in the face of the extremest opposition, of first one, and then another, and many others in quick succession amongst their pupils, given to them by God thus early to encourage their faith and perseverance, and to become living witnesses to their labour and devotion, as faithful, zealous, and efficient fellow-labourers in the work, long after their first teachers and spiritual fathers were called to their rest.

'To ascertain the precise extent to which these schools have influenced native society, is not so easy; but it may help us to form some adequate idea of how great and how real that influence for good must have been, to consider the many thousands of the sons and daughters of India whose minds, hearts, and characters, during the most impressible years of life, for the long period of now nearly twenty-eight years, have been brought under the teaching of these schools, to carry back with them into the private and familiar intercourse of family and social life the daily lessons of light and truth here learnt, in vivid and irresistible contrast with the prevailing ignorance and error around them! Nor must we overlook the powerful impulse for good communicated to other feebler schemes of education previously existing, in the faithful and open avowal of the one only true principle of a Christian mission, as also in the admirable system of instruction here first introduced, and soon after taken up and adopted by many others.'

Mr. Anderson has passed away from his sphere of labour here, but his spirit and influence remain. He is remembered with much interest, and the school is still called among the natives 'Anderson's School.'

On going through the various classes of the school with the worthy superintendent, the Rev. Mr. Miller, I quite agreed with him that the boys are attracted to the school, not only because the fees are lower; but because they feel the happy influence of the Christian sympathy and kindness they here receive. When hearing a Scripture lesson given by Mr. Miller, and seeing the lively interest which was felt in the lesson by both teacher and scholars, it was evident that a permanent influence was established of the most valuable kind, and indeed one which I was informed did not cease with school-days. Such agency does more than any other to remove the barrier which exists between the races. It is much to be regretted that personal records of such schools as these are not given to the public at home, instead of the somewhat dry and brief statements too often found in official reports.

In 1843, Mr. Anderson established the first girls' school in Madras, into which he with difficulty collected four or five little girls, by the promise of a reward. Many girls' schools have since then been established by this mission, as well as by other agencies, and by the natives themselves. For some time it was found necessary to give the children a small daily payment for attendance; then this ceased, and now the anxiety for education has become so great that the scholars pay a trifling fee. These payments are of course small, but they testify to the value attached to the schools by the parents. The last report mentions that they amounted in the year, from all the girls' schools, to 320 rupees. One of the schools which I visited was in excellent order, and was presided over by a native minister—Rev. R. M. Bamboo. He devotes much time and effort to make the school known and understood by the educated natives, and edits a magazine for the benefit of the young girls who have left the school, and who desire to keep up the education they have received. It is an interesting circumstance that the writers in this periodical are chiefly native Christians, many of whom were educated in the schools of the mission. The school in Blacktown is taught by a native Christian woman, and on Sunday the classes meet for purely religious instruction. It is a remarkable fact that the attendance then is not greatly below that of other days. In all the mission schools, caste is of course entirely disregarded, as Christians recognise no such distinctions. Scripture instruction is also given at one part of every day. Though there may be some objection shown at first, yet this soon wears away: as the attendance is voluntary, one of the great difficulties arising from caste is thus overcome without a struggle. There are many young ladies of Brahmin caste in these schools. Some of the little girls struck me as remarkably bright and intelligent, and there can be no doubt that Hindoo girls would generally be so, if properly educated.

The widow of the excellent Mr. Anderson conducts a girls' boarding-school, in which there are now between fifty and sixty scholars. These young persons, remaining longer under tuition than non-Christian girls would do, show greater results. This school is also pleasantly situated near the sea, and a home spirit is infused into it. The excellent lady at the head of the establishment, makes it her great aim to prepare the girls for their future duties in life. They do the greater part of the domestic work, and much of the practical management of the house is entrusted to the elder of them. The economy practised in the household makes the expenditure very moderate, the cost of the support of each girl being only 5 rupees a month, or 6*l.* per annum.

The Wesleyan Methodists have also excellent mission schools here, which I visited with much pleasure. It was gratifying to hear one who had laboured in this field for thirty years, state his happy conviction of the very great changes which he was permitted to witness in the state of feeling in the natives towards Christians. If the conversions are not numerous, still there is no longer the hostility towards missionaries which once existed, and the ground is being prepared for future harvests. There is an excellent boarding-school connected with this mission also. It was very interesting to observe the demeanour and intelligence of the girls, and peculiarly so to find here young native girls employed as monitors, to instruct the younger classes. One teacher, a native Christian, is the wife of one of the masters in the boys' school.

One Hindoo girls' school deserves special mention, as it is carried on in the house of the native gentleman who is the chief patron. His own daughters assist in teaching, but on the occasion of our visit they withdrew from the presence of gentlemen. Here, as elsewhere, there were only male teachers, and the children are withdrawn when between ten and eleven years of age, if not earlier.

A system of a 'grant-in-aid' from Government has been laid down in the Madras Presidency, with a view to help the mission schools. This requires that all teachers in the schools receiving it shall have obtained a certificate of competency. This regulation is very possible and advisable in the school for boys, but with the girls' schools this cannot be accomplished; and instead of receiving nearly half the outlay, as is contemplated by Government, the grant is necessarily small for the girls' schools—not exceeding one-tenth. If a good normal female training-school were established, teachers might obtain a certificate from it which would enable the schools to receive a larger grant.

The Government schools appear much the same as elsewhere. They have the peculiar advantage of being under the special observation of the Director, who was himself for fifteen years principal of the Presidency College. He gained the love and gratitude of his students by the warm sympathy he showed them, and the sacrifice of time and strength he voluntarily made to advance their intellectual culture, not only in the regular hours allotted to study, but early and late beyond them. Being himself enthusiastically fond of astronomy, he admitted the students to his observatory, and revealed to them the glories of the heavens. No one can tell what influences he has thus diffused. The native gentlemen in Madras, with whom I conversed, repeatedly assured me that they still regarded him as a father, and they so fully confided in him that they never hesitated to express their opinions frankly to him, even though differing from him. A native gentleman on the other side of the peninsula, who had received his instruction, assured me that, as students resorted to the college from every part of the Presidency, there is no district in it where his influence is not still felt. On being obliged to resign his post in consequence of the new appointment, an address was presented to him by the students, and money was raised by them to establish a scholarship in his name. It is probable that the Director does not value this warm spontaneous tribute of gratitude from those among whom he has so long worked, less than the well-merited imperial recognition of his services which he has recently received from his Excellency the Governor. On the occasion of the visit of the Maharajah of Travancore to Madras, Lord Napier conferred on Mr. Powell the Order of Companion of the Star of India.

A visit to the Presidency College was interesting, even though the time at which I went was unseasonable. It was very striking to see in the hands of these young Hindoos, the works of the highest minds which were formed and fostered under the influence of our Western culture. The acuteness, metaphysical subtlety, and patient research of the Hindoo are well known. The union of these with the vigorous intellect of the Saxon, the rich imagination and deep philosophy of the ancient Greek, and the combination of all in our first-rate English classics, which bring the highest thoughts, embued with Christian ethics, to bear on the present phase of the world's life—all this culture, wisely given, with due regard to the actual wants of the Hindoo race, cannot but be of the highest value. Here, as elsewhere, I was struck with observing the large number of young men under tuition; many of whom, in England, would be in the counting-house, or otherwise entering on the real business of life. A considerable portion of the students were also evidently more anxious to obtain university honours and Government employment than to improve their minds; and to grasp a certain amount of book knowledge, than really to master the thoughts of the author they studied. Still, the sight of this and similar institutions was gratifying, and made me feel proud of my country. Finding one class engaged on a Shakspeare lesson, I had the opportunity of hearing a scene of Hamlet analysed by the students. It was rather strange to hear our grand English classic treated as we unmercifully treat in our schools the noble tragedies of the ancients, and subjected to verbal criticism after the fashion in which our schoolboys construe, scan, and parse Homer or Euripides; yet it was interesting to perceive how thorough a knowledge of our very difficult language is imparted to the natives, and how they are consequently prepared to share our thoughts, and somewhat understand our actions.

A Mahometan school presented very different features. This is established by Government in a quarter of the city chiefly inhabited by these people, of whom there are many here. They are chiefly very low and ignorant, and live an idle life, in consequence of many of them being pensioners. When any rich Mahometan is unable or unwilling to perform the pilgrimage required by his religion to the shrine of the prophet, he may be absolved, by giving a sum in charity, somewhat equivalent to the expense he would have incurred in the expedition, to poor persons. Many cases of this kind occurring, in the course of time a pauperised race is created, in the pensioners thus selected to atone for the omission of their superiors. Nothing more degrades a man than thus subsisting on charity, and yielding to the inertness of body and mind, which takes possession of those who have no stimulus to exertion. The Director wisely thought that the only mode of cutting off the entail of degradation, so to speak, would be to educate the rising generation; and he therefore established a large school here, putting at the head of it a superior and intelligent Englishman. It was at first very difficult work for the superintendent to obtain anything like regular attendance. We, who have had twenty years of ragged school experience, can quite understand how little can be done with even quick and intelligent children, if the habits of the families are low, and there is consequently a want of appreciation of the importance of education. But with energy and perseverance,—a determination to raise the scholars, even at the risk of losing a few,—and setting a high standard before them and himself, he has succeeded in making attendance at the school regarded as a privilege as well as a duty, and has now a tolerably regular set of boys there. The youths in the highest class did not equal those whom I had seen elsewhere, and it was doubtful to our minds whether any of them would succeed in matriculating. The boys of the lower classes were of an inferior-looking type to those whom I had observed in other schools. Still the enterprise must be regarded as a great success, and the progress of the scholars had evidently produced an effect on their families. One portion of the school routine appeared to present a great barrier to improvement—the number of different languages taught in it. There were actually six masters of different languages engaged in different rooms instructing their respective classes. Hindostani is considered the vernacular of the Mahometans, and all have to learn that grammatically.

English is the *lingua franca* in all parts of the country for professions and clerkships—that is, of course, everywhere an essential. The vernaculars of the natives of Madras are Tamil and Telugu; one of these must be acquired for communication with their fellow-citizens. The Mahometan parents wish their children to learn either Persian or Arabic; every boy is expected to acquire one of these two languages. These boys come usually *quite* ignorant, and with untrained minds; every language has its own peculiar genius and mode of thought; it would certainly appear, then, that for each boy to be learning four languages at a time must not only prevent his acquiring any one correctly, but must engender a confusion of thought, which is very injurious to the moral as well as to the intellectual development. At home, in our British and National Schools, a second language is never attempted, in the lower middle-class schools it is rarely taught, and in our public schools it is beginning to be understood that the almost exclusive study of two dead languages, however valuable themselves, is injurious to the general development of the mind, and to due preparation for the work of life. What, then, must be the effect on these ignorant lads of the enforced study of four languages?

There is a large boys' school for Hindoos managed by themselves only. Some time ago a rich native bequeathed on his decease a large sum of money for benevolent purposes. The executors let it remain many years unappropriated, and it was at last suggested that it might be employed for educational purposes. Legal proceedings were necessary to put it on a sure foundation; but, with the help of some influential English gentlemen, this was accomplished, and very extensive premises are devoted to an excellent Hindoo school. Patcheappah Hall, so named after the native gentleman through whose benevolence it was established, stands as a monument of what the natives can do for themselves when once they have a real desire to accomplish anything.

There is another portion of the community which has a strong claim on the English, and this is fully acknowledged—orphans who, on one side at least, are of English descent. In Madras are very many families of mixed race—half-castes, generally termed East Indians, or, as they prefer being called, Eurasians. A large proportion of the orphans are of this race, though others are the children of English soldiers or artisans who have died in the country. There are at Madras two sets of asylums. That for civil orphans, both boys and girls, I had not an opportunity of studying, as the day on which I visited it happened to be a holiday. To the Military Male Orphan Asylum I paid an interesting visit. We arrived just as dinner was ended. It had been laid in a pleasant verandah, and the crows were busily performing the part of scavengers, devouring all the fragments that remained. The institution is pleasantly situated, with large airy rooms, and considerable space around. The three hundred boys marched to the schoolroom in excellent order, and formed in classes. They appeared very attentive and fairly advanced in their lessons, answering well any questions put to them. Much apathy and dependent spirit seemed to pervade these boys, however, as to their work in life, and preparation for it; none of those whom we asked respecting their wishes for the future, seemed to have entertained any desire to exert themselves, or thought beyond the present. In this respect they formed a striking contrast to our industrial school boys at home, who are full of energy and vigour; many there are ready to hold up their hands when the question is put, 'What boys wish to go to sea?'—an enquiry which elicits no response in these regions. This kind of listlessness and apathy may be traceable in part to the inherent inaptitude for exertion existing in the East Indians, and partly to the natural tendency of institutions to engender such a spirit, unless it is counteracted by the system adopted. Everything appears to be here done which is possible to promote a healthy physical and mental development. Active recreations are provided for the boys, who practise gymnastic exercises; the elder ones give considerable attention to cricket. They are besides taught to do part of the housework, and to make their clothes. The last report thus speaks on this point: 'One point requires further notice. A very large portion of the ordinary school-work was formerly performed by native servants. This in itself was a great evil, since it was too frequently found that these servants were dishonest, untruthful, and generally of a character whose influence and example could not but have an injurious effect upon the boys. On the other hand, their employment prevented the lads from learning the great lesson of self-help, while a further evil was the resulting idea that manual labour was degrading and suitable only for natives. Notwithstanding a considerable increase of work, caused by improved sanitary and other arrangements, the services of ten servants have been dispensed with, their work being performed by the boys at a saving of .75 rupees per mensem. In addition to this, the introduction of sewing-machines, worked by selected boys, permitted the whole work of preparing the clothing of the orphans to be done within the walls, at a saving of at least 25 rupees per mensem.' The expense of ten servants was saved by this management, the health of the boys was improved by the exercise, and the 100 rupees per month thus economised were added to the dietary, and produced a perceptible improvement in the physique of the boys. As the children are often received very young, there is an infant or nursery department, presided over by a matron and her daughter, where the infant system is developed. Perhaps the presence of strangers prevented the sports of these little ones from being quite as spontaneous as could be desired. Still, everything appeared to be arranged to make this institution, what it may certainly be regarded, a model one.

The Society for the Propagation of the Gospel in Foreign Parts has here a station, which diffuses its influence in the country round; and has, besides the common schools which it has established, an institution to train young native converts for the ministry. This seminary is presided over by the secretary of the Society, the Rev. Alfred Symonds, who exercises a truly paternal influence over the students. I had a sort of ancestral claim on his kind attentions; his father and mine were friends in childhood, and to his brother, an eminent physician of Clifton, I owe, under God, restoration from a dangerous illness some years ago. This was one of the strange and unexpected meetings, of which I had many in that country. He therefore invited me to come and hear the young men receive a Greek Testament lesson before their morning meal. About sixteen native students surrounded the study-table, with the reverend secretary, their instructor. The sight of a number of young men, who have seriously devoted themselves to go out, heart and soul, to preach the Gospel, and to help on their fellow-creatures to travel heavenward, is always an interesting one: in the present case it was peculiarly so, as facts declared, more clearly than words could do, that they courageously abjured the idolatry of their nation, that they loved Christ better than country or kindred, and that they earnestly desired to lead their people in the same blessed way. It may of course be attributed to prejudice on my part, but there always appeared to me a peculiar openness of expression in genuine native converts; they rejoiced in the liberty with which Christ has made His servants free, and felt that a sympathy existed between them and other followers of the same Master, of a totally different kind from what can be shared by such as have not the same glorious hopes. Such were certainly my feelings as I sat amongst those students at Vepery College. Though no peculiar dress is assumed by Christian converts—who do not desire to denationalise themselves, and who do not forget, or wish to do so, that they are Hindoos by race,—yet they are careful generally to adopt a simple and neat attire, and wear on the head nature's beautiful covering instead of the turban: this alone imparts a different expression to the countenance.

The subject selected for the lesson was the first chapter of the Epistle to the Galatians. They had previously studied it with their instructor, and now showed the accuracy and care with which they had been taught, and had learnt; scarcely a single correction required to be made, though they were expected not only to translate accurately, but to explain the meaning and bearing of each verse, and to show that they thoroughly understood the various inflections of the

Greek verbs, and their value. It was a lesson full of the deepest interest to the listener, who was carried back, not only to days long past, when a beloved teacher and father gave such lessons to those who have been for many years ministers of the Word, and have even passed their prime,—but to the early period of the Christian Church, when, in the peculiar circumstances of the new converts, many exhortations were given which are probably now very imperfectly understood in their true bearing. These students were not new converts, I was informed, but from childhood had been taught to know those Scriptures which are able to make us wise unto salvation, and having been selected from many others in the southern Christian districts of the Presidency, were preparing to go out and teach. I gladly availed myself of permission to say a few words of encouragement to them, expressing the deep interest I felt in their future welfare. We then all adjourned to family worship, a refreshment and privilege in this heathen land. It was indeed delightful to see these young men join a real family circle at prayer, where they were received as brethren, and saw what a true English family really is. They then retired to their domiciles, small houses in the compound, where those who had families of their own lived separately with them, and after the morning meal returned to their daily studies. I was happy to be able to leave some books for their library, which would be a memorial of my visit, and to receive from them afterwards a friendly acknowledgment of them.

Sunday, Nov. 11.—I attended a native church service. The edifice is well constructed and attractive-looking, but it seemed to stand quite isolated in the midst of the population. The passers-by looked askance at it, as a thing with which they had no concern, and which they regarded with something worse than apathy. But one listener after another dropped in, and looked reverent as they quietly took their places. The church music was well performed, and though the service was in Tamil, yet the earnestness and feeling with which it was conducted by the native clergyman made it interesting.

In the afternoon Mr. Powell, my host, had kindly assembled a number of the most enlightened native gentlemen at his house, to consider the subject of the Normal School. There was little difficulty in making them understand the object and bearing of the proposed institution, because a few of them had already been planning something of the kind; they had, however, perceived that the scheme was beyond their powers, as the co-operation and aid of English ladies were essential to it. They all spoke warmly of the kindness and sympathy Mr. Powell had shown them, but lamented the general want of friendly intercourse between them and the English. 'A great gulf,' they remarked, 'was between the two races, and nothing would be so calculated to bridge it over as such visits as mine.' I had often been puzzled by the great unwillingness evinced to the girls learning English; at first I presumed that the language was considered too difficult, but this could not be the reason, as in the mission schools the elder girls can speak it, and the young native ladies who greeted me on my first arrival at Bombay were familiar with it. At last, on investigating from these gentlemen the cause of their evident objection, one answered, 'We do not want our ladies to be made humble Christians.' It is indeed much to be regretted that there should be any ground for fear that the possession of our language, which would so much facilitate friendly intercourse, should be connected in the minds of these gentlemen with a fear of improper interference in their homes! It is to be hoped that this fear will soon cease. These gentlemen were much interested in hearing of the work going on in England, and the knowledge of my engagement in it appeared to inspire them with confidence in my present intentions. They all readily signed the following statement, written by one of them in my manuscript book:—

'We, the undersigned, being deeply interested in the cause of female education, feel it absolutely necessary for its promotion to have an institution established for the training of female teachers.'

I told them that the next step to be taken, if they were anxious to obtain such an institution, was to memorialise the Government, praying that it might be established. I clearly perceived that under the existing condition of India, this work, to be permanent and effective, must be undertaken by Government, with the sympathy and co-operation of the natives.

There were other institutions in Madras besides those directly educational, which I was anxious to see and understand.

I visited the hospital, which appeared an admirable one, and the result of much skill and effort on the part of the official gentlemen who had the direction of it. There is a very striking difference between such institutions here and in England. The wards we are accustomed to at home are well warmed and full of comfortable beds, with patients carefully covered up, and attended on by respectable trained nurses; they are changed in this hot climate into dormitories as open and airy as possible, with punkahs to give the sufferers some refreshing movement of the atmosphere; the patients lie on hard mattresses in their ordinary dress, generally without any other covering over them, and there is a sad dearth of any suitable attendance on the sufferers. Trained nurses are almost unknown in India. How can this want be supplied? The services of trained officials from England it would be impossible to procure in sufficient numbers; and, unfortunately, the many Englishwomen who must exist in the country as the widows or other relatives of soldiers or mechanics, appear to lose all desire to exert themselves, or to undertake any service which has the least appearance of being menial. The East Indians manifest little desire to make efforts, and generally exhibit a species of pride which is most unbecoming, and which prevents their endeavouring to gain an honest livelihood. The native women, the class of persons who ought to supply this want, are perfectly ignorant in their ideas, and uncultivated in their manners: a long training would be necessary to prepare them for what ought to be their special avocation, and for which they would be probably well fitted. Two patients in this hospital particularly attracted my attention—one was a young Christian Brahmin, who appeared to be in a decline, and who, through attending the mission schools, had his attention drawn to the truths of Christianity, which had deeply affected his mind. Without any solicitation on their part, he determined to join the Christians, and left his home in the country to come to Madras. His parents followed him, and instituted legal proceedings against the missionaries, under whose protection he had placed himself, in order forcibly to take him back. As, however, he was above sixteen, and gave evidence that he had acted solely on his own free choice, the verdict was given against the parents. He seemed very happy. I afterwards sent him some books, and was glad to learn that he was better, and able to leave the hospital. The other was a poor Christian woman, not a Hindoo. She was in a melancholy state, having lost her relatives, and feeling solitary and deserted as well as ill; she was so desponding and depressed in spirit, that she was supposed by the officials to be deranged in mind. I believed that it was Christian sympathy which she required; the poor woman appeared thankful to receive a few words of this, and I promised her to endeavour to procure for her the visits of some Christian lady. This was afterwards done. There is a wide sphere of Christian work open in India for all who will devote themselves to it, quite independently of that which now appears too exclusively to absorb the attention of English ladies—the conversion of the heathen. This work, somewhat beyond the pale of the Church, can be carried on without distinction of sect; it has not been entirely neglected in Madras. The ladies here have formed a society for giving work to poor destitute women, as there is no workhouse. It is very necessary that Christians should exert themselves to care for the poor connected with them, and not in this respect be behind the natives, who are not deficient in kind charity towards their own poor. Many English ladies appeared to be giving much time and effort to this institution, and had established there a small girls' school, for the children of their poor applicants.

A large museum bids fair to become a very admirable one. Time did not permit me to examine carefully the different departments, which were all arranged with remarkable care and neatness; the institution appeared to excite some attention and interest in the town, as the entrance is free, and there are sufficient officials to protect the specimens. The most remarkable object—indeed it is probably a unique one—is a collection of the bones of the gigantic dinornis, which had been brought from New Zealand, and presented to the institution. Madras appears to possess, from its maritime position, peculiar facilities for obtaining rich and curious specimens of natural history; such a museum ought also to be the depository of objects illustrating the productions of the country, and the habits and skill of the natives throughout the Presidency. Such will doubtless be formed here, whenever an interest in natural science, and a thirst for knowledge *for its own sake*, are excited among the natives.

On Monday, Nov. 12, precisely at 7 A.M., the carriage was at the door to convey me to the School of Industrial Arts. This institution owes its very existence, as well as its present flourishing condition, to the zeal and energy of Dr. Alexander Hunter, M.D., a surgeon of the Madras Army. This gentleman was stationed in the Black Town, or that part of Madras occupied by the native population. Being himself a great lover of art as well as of nature, and of a benevolent disposition, he offered to give young native boys some instruction in drawing in their leisure hours. They seized the opportunity eagerly, and improved so rapidly, that it was evident that natural genius exists in the native mind, which only wants development. For some years the kind-hearted doctor devoted his leisure hours to the gratuitous instruction of these young boys. The Government eventually perceived the importance of fostering native genius, and of availing itself of the services of so enthusiastic and able a gentleman as Dr. Hunter. He was permitted to change his duties, into those of superintendent of a School of Industrial

Arts. Some valuable information, derived from the reports, will be found in a subsequent part of this work; it will be interesting to trace the process by which Dr. Hunter, at first himself the sole instructor, gradually transformed students into masters, and thus, at comparatively little cost, perpetuated his great work, and developed native powers. I was introduced into a large room, where the drawing and engraving on copper were being carried on. At one end were a number of native students, copying under the direction of a native master; at the other a class of thirty or forty boys, who had come under the escort of an official from the Military Orphan School, to receive drawing lessons. They looked much more animated and interested than when I saw them in the institution. Outlines of beautiful natural objects are usually the studies from which they copy; the more advanced take the objects themselves, and form designs from them for various useful things, such as lamps, vases, knife-handles, picture-frames, &c. Though these designs are very beautiful, and most delicately executed, indicating patient work and a well-trained hand, yet I did not observe the indications of much original genius. The students did not appear to commune with nature for herself, and to catch the inspiration which she only can impart; they only copy what may be turned to some practical use. I expressed surprise that they did not make studies of the various picturesque objects which they might see everywhere around them. A mere shed adorned with some luxuriant creeper, with the bright lights and dark defined shadows cast by a tropical sun, such as might be seen from the window of that very room, would make a sketch that an English artist would search for in vain in our dull climate; while the human figure in its natural state is always at hand for study. Dr. Hunter informed me, however, that these youths care for nothing which cannot be turned to pecuniary account: there is as yet in India no love of pure art, or demand for its production. In colour, however, some original genius developes itself. The natives have not yet attempted to colour landscapes or other natural objects, but in ornamenting their houses, and making designs for textile fabrics, they exhibit a peculiar and beautiful taste. Some specimens of their arrangement of colours I saw in an adjoining room, where there were beautiful specimens of varied art. The women in Madras are in the habit of drawing coloured patterns on their floors and before their doors, with great skill and care in the selection of colours: copies of some of these were in this museum. Various workshops to teach special trades and arts have been gradually added; these are in some degree remunerative, and many youths are here instructed, and enabled to gain an honest livelihood. A kindly feeling pervades the whole institution, inspired almost insensibly by the benevolent spirit of the superintendent. Europeans, Eurasians, and Hindoos of every caste, are here on precisely the same footing. At first youths of high caste objected to the introduction of those of low caste; but on the intimation that this school was intended for the benefit of all equally, and that those who objected need not enter it, the desire of obtaining instruction overcame prejudice, and there is now no distinction of colour or caste in the institution. The 'dignity of labour' makes all equal, and teaches the grand doctrine of universal brotherhood.

The next day I received a visit from one of the native gentlemen who had come to the conference, and who had written the day before, requesting permission to bring his wife to call on me, as she took a warm interest in my work. It was indeed a most interesting visit, and the first of the kind I had received since my first evening in Bombay. On entering, the lady asked her husband 'whether I were a descendant of Sarah Martin?' He repeated the question to me, and informed me that he always communicated to her any accounts of excellent women which he met with; that she was well educated, and herself wrote articles in a magazine for ladies. It was a touching thought, that the unobtrusive work of the pious humble sempstress of Norwich had produced an influence in this remote and heathen country, and touched the heart of this gentle young Hindoo lady! She showed the fruits of the kind and sympathising influence she had been under, and her deportment was not only refined and modest, but confiding and open. She manifested a warmth of affection which was quite refreshing to my spirit here among strangers, and called forth a true response. Her husband informed me that he and some others had made a decided move away from idolatry. They had received a visit from Keshub Chunder Sen, the leader of the most advanced party of the Brahmins at Calcutta, whose recent lecture, 'Jesus Christ, Europe, and Asia,' had excited warm discussion among both Christians and natives. His eloquence and glowing words had kindled among them the religious enthusiasm, which had been previously pent up in their hearts. They had determined to open a place for the worship of the one and only true God, and an opulent native gentleman had placed his large drawing-room at their disposal; there they held regular religious meetings every Wednesday at six o'clock. While thus abandoning idolatry, they did not desire to give offence to their countrymen by relinquishing customs which were not directly immoral, while they set their faces decidedly against what they deemed absolutely wrong. As they still held to their ancient sacred books, while departing from idol-worship, they called their congregation the Veda Somaj, or the assembly of those holding the Vedas. Perceiving the religious tone of my visitor, I placed before him a small volume of my own.* On glancing at it, he said that it would be very useful to him in the preparation of a volume of prayers which he was compiling, and requested permission to carry it away with him. This gentleman was the secretary of the Veda Somaj, and he promised to communicate to the president my desire to be present at their service.

Wednesday, Nov. 14.—I received a kind invitation from the president of the Veda Somaj, with the rules which they had drawn up for the guidance of the society. These present a singular combination of enlightened moral feeling, and a high religious view of the absolute unity of the Deity, with a clinging to old national customs, and a desire, if possible, not to offend their countrymen, or to separate from them. I believe that they are attempting what is impossible, for the Master has said, 'Ye cannot serve God and mammon,' and 'The Son only can make us truly free.' The attempt, however, to obtain religious freedom, and to bring back Hindoos from idolatry to a true faith, is worthy of honour, and deserves our warmest sympathy. None can tell what this first attempt, such as it is, has cost those who made it—how much moral torture, how much loss of friendship, how much persecution from

---

* *Morning and Evening Meditations, with Prayers.* By Mary Carpenter: 1 vol. 12mo. price 4s. Longmans: Paternoster Row, London.

their native friends. 'Indeed,' said one of them to me, 'they think us worse than Christians,' a remark painfully significant. The rules of the Veda Somaj are as follows:—

COVENANTS OF THE VEDA SOMAJ.

1. I shall worship, through love of Him and the performance of the work He loveth, the Supreme Being, the Creator, the Preserver, the Destroyer, the Giver of Salvation, the Omniscient, the Omnipotent, the Blissful, the Good, the Formless, the one only without a second; and none of the created objects, subject to the following conditions.

2. I shall labour to compose and gradually bring into practice a Ritual agreeable to the spirit of pure Theism, and free from the superstitions and absurdities which at present characterise Hindoo ceremonies.

3. In the meantime I shall observe the ceremonies now in use, but only in cases where ceremonies are indispensable, as in marriages and funerals; or where their omission will do more violence to the feelings of the Hindoo community than is consistent with the proper interests of the Veda Somaj, as in Sradhas. And I shall go through such ceremonies, where they are not conformable to pure Theism, as mere matters of routine, destitute of all religious significance—as the lifeless remains of a superstition which has passed away.

4. This sacrifice, and this only, shall I make to existing prejudices. But I shall never endeavour to deceive anyone as to my religious opinions, and never stoop to equivocation or hypocrisy, in order to avoid unpopularity.

5. I shall discard all sectarian views and animosities, and never offer any encouragement to them.

6. I shall, as a first step, gradually give up all distinctions, and amalgamate the different branches of the same caste.

7. Rigidly as I shall adhere to all these rules, I shall be perfectly tolerant to the views of strangers, and never intentionally give offence to their feelings.

8. I shall never violate the duties and virtues of humanity, justice, veracity, temperance, and chastity.

9. I shall never hold, or attend, or pay for nautches, or otherwise hold out encouragement for prostitution.

10. I shall encourage and promote to the best of my power the remarriage of widows, and discourage early marriages.

11. I shall never be guilty of bigamy or polygamy.

12. I shall grant my aid towards the issue, in the vernaculars, of elementary prayer-books and religious tracts; and also of a monthly journal, whose chief object shall be to improve the social and moral condition of the community.

13. I shall advance the cause of general and female education and enlightenment, and particularly in my own family circle.

14. I shall study the Sanscrit language and its literature (especially theological), and promote the cultivation of it by means not calculated to promote superstition.

To-day being the —— day of the month of ——— of the Kalyabda ——————— I hereby embrace the faith of the Veda Somaj, and in witness whereof set my hand to this.

My host accompanied me to this native worship, and his presence was gladly welcomed. The place of meeting was well filled with native gentlemen, the president occupying the chair; near him was my friend, the secretary of the society. To my great surprise and confusion, he commenced by reading an address introducing me to the meeting, expressing the warmest sympathy with my work in England, and high appreciation of the motives which prompted my friendly visit to my fellow-subjects in India, and my desire to promote female education there. It thus concluded. 'Our sister does not understand our language, but we do hers. Let us therefore for her satisfaction, and to the satisfaction of our Common Father, offer up in His holy presence our heartfelt prayer in our sister's own language, before we commence our usual service.' Then he offered with deep reverence one of the prayers in my 'Meditations,' omitting only the allusions to Our Saviour. Their ordinary service followed, with a discourse from the president. In conclusion, that same prayer of mine, which had been translated into Tamil and printed, was handed round to the audience, and offered up in the vernacular. Need I say that this evening was one of the most treasured ones of my whole delightful sojourn in the country? It was then laid among my sacred memories; it is now enshrined with holy and sorrowful thoughts of the departed, for he who uttered that prayer has since been called to the Father's house above.

Nov. 15.— Symptoms had appeared of the approaching monsoon, which on this side of India is at a different time from the rains on the western coast. This probably delayed the expected steamer which was to convey me to Calcutta. Two objects of interest were near at hand, and these I visited, for once, on foot! These were the Horticultural Garden, and the Cathedral. The present time was not the season of the year to expect many flowers, but the tropical trees and plants were most interesting. The chief object of attraction in the cathedral is a beautiful monument to the lamented Reginald Heber, one of those whose names will not die in India.

I received also a farewell visit from the secretary and his sweet young wife, who brought me some of her needlework as a remembrance. I requested her to write a few words in my book. Without hesitation she sat down at the table, and inscribed the following passage in Telugu, neatly and evenly written. It is translated by her husband: 'I am extremely delighted to see you. All our females should feel extremely obliged to you for the pains you take in their behalf. I believe that education, and intercourse with English ladies like yourself will be of the greatest possible advantage to my countrywomen. I do further hope very much that everyone coming in contact with you will acquire some of that excellent wisdom of yours which has been the result of your good education.

   (Signed)   'THAYARAMMAL.
       'P. SUBROYALU CHETTY,
  '*Secretary to the Veda Somaj, Madras.*'

November 15, 1866.

During the following night I was awakened by a tremendous sound, as of abundance of rain, as well as of a rushing furious wind. I hastened to the open windows and the venetian shutters; with difficulty could I close, in the violence of the storm, the eight large windows on three sides of my spacious room. Even when they were firmly fastened the sound of the storm was overpowering; the thought of the raging of the sea could not be dispelled from my mind, and sleep was effectually banished. The monsoon was now beginning in right earnest, and the trenches and reservoirs which my hostess had been making in anticipation of it as a future supply for her garden, to which she devoted much attention, were becoming rapidly filled. There was no longer for us the delightful drive through the government park and along the beach, which every evening had so refreshed both body and spirit. Nothing but necessity induced anyone to expose carriage, horses, and driver to such incessant torrents; and had it not been for the long verandah, we should in vain have desired to enjoy any of the outer air.

The steamer happily did not arrive that day, but there was an announcement by telegram of her approach from Ceylon. The next morning the weather was somewhat calmer, and the distant booming of cannon, before the day dawned, informed us of its approach on the morning of the 17th. Had I not secured and paid for my berth, I should have been unable to proceed, for this was the time of the year when Calcutta gentlemen were returning with their families from their much-needed annual excursions, and this French vessel was very crowded. In Madras roadstead, ships cannot approach near the shore, or even the pier. Passengers have to be lowered from it into a boat to be conveyed to the steamer. The sight of these apparently slight native conveyances, guided over the rolling waves by the half-clad, strange-looking beings, gabbling a foreign language, to one unaccustomed to the sea was not a very pleasing spectacle, and somewhat calculated to excite alarm; but my course was onward, my present goal Calcutta. Without contemplating the danger, therefore, I boldly trusted myself to them, and after a little difficulty, caused by the constant lurching of the boat, found myself safe in my new abode. The considerate office-keeper had told me that he had secured 'a good home for me;' the steward had arranged for me to share the cabin of a young English lady, who was going out to join her fortunes to those of a missionary who had been long settled at Delhi; and she proved a very kind friend to me during a most disagreeable voyage through the Bay of Bengal.

The shores of the beautiful bay, and the distant hills surrounding Madras, soon receded from view; I had begun to love the city, for there was much to interest in its various institutions, and I perceived a wide field of usefulness prepared for any who would work it; I had found there kind hearts, and had been received not as a stranger, but as one with whom true sympathy already existed. It was with sorrow, therefore, that I bade farewell to its shores, and for the first time prepared to go forth *alone* among strangers!

CHAPTER V.

CALCUTTA.

THE banks of the Ganges greeted our longing sight on the morning of November 20.

It is a very strange feeling to find oneself for the first time actually in the very spot which one has looked at on the map from one's earliest childhood, and of which one has heard so much and talked so much all one's life. I had not been long enough a traveller to lose the vividness of novelty; and though still very weak, and somewhat miserable after the tossing of the vessel in the Bay of Bengal, yet it was impossible to be insensible to the fact that we were now floating on the waters which for thousands and thousands of years had been held sacred by countless millions of the inhabitants of this marvellous land. This broad majestic stream does not require any historic memories to invest it with intense interest. These very waters, which we were cutting through as unconcernedly as if they belonged to any ordinary estuary, had taken a marvellous course ere they reached us. Their first origin on the snow-clad Himalayas is grand and mysterious; to penetrate to the very source of the sacred river is worthy of a life pilgrimage. When the weary devotee, or the ardent lover of nature, has painfully attained a height which would seem the highest point he is to reach, peak beyond peak appears beyond him. At length he discovers in the midst of wild and grand displays of nature's most rugged and majestic wonders, the young stream dashing fearlessly down, joyous, pure, and free, which is to become the sacred stream of an empire! Who can describe, who has ever attempted to tell the course of those waters? Who could venture to enumerate the scenes of sorow and of death which they have witnessed, —how many mourners they have soothed by imparting not only a refreshing coolness, but a holy calm? In its course onward to the ocean, what noble cities it has passed, bearing onward their merchandise, purifying their atmosphere; what fine tributaries it has received to swell its flood; and now, after dividing its waters into the numerous streams which form the delta, it is still grand and beautiful, terminating its course in a way worthy of its progress to the ocean!

The banks are low, presenting no peculiar features; but as we approached the capital, those acquainted with it recognised and pointed out to the other passengers many well-known residences or institutions. The excitement of anticipation began to spread among all the passengers. I was probably the only one in the vessel who had no great expectation of meeting anyone, or even of finding a home on landing. On the departure of my party from Madras, I had expressed the intention of proceeding by the next steamer; but they might not be aware that a French vessel would be the first arrival, and not being one of the regular British steamers, its approach was heralded by no cannon; my friends would therefore probably not be aware of my actual arrival. I had of course written to them as soon as I had arranged my plans, but letters take a slow and weary course of about thirteen days in their transit from Madras to

Calcutta, and my unfortunate missive did not reach its destination until long after my own arrival. The telegraph of course would be deemed the natural and certain mode of speedy communication, but I was informed that it was out of order, and consequently useless. This is not a very unusual condition of things. When at Ahmedabad the wire snapped over our heads as we were taking a morning excursion, and some days after, a missionary, riding quickly along, was seriously injured by a stroke from the still hanging wire against his chest. A gentleman told me that he once received a telegram after a letter which was despatched at the same time;—I had therefore thought it useless to telegraph. I did not know the address of the friend who would receive me, having trusted my letter to the general direction of Calcutta. Experience had inspired me with a dread of Indian hotels. In this rather disagreeable emergency, I found kind friends in my fellow-passengers, Mr. and Mrs. G., who were returning home with their little girl. This lovely child was one of the very few I saw in India who had not suffered morally from the surrounding influences of the country; her parents had taken care that she should have no communication with native servants, but if not actually with her mother, was under the charge of a respectable young Englishwoman, who was what we should call a nursery governess. My new friends expected to meet their carriage on shore, and did not hurry from the vessel on her arrival, but waited until the crowd had somewhat dispersed. What was our dismay, when we at last effected a landing with our luggage, on finding, not only that there were no servants and carriage waiting, but that no conveyance of any sort was within sight or hearing! The landing-place was at some distance from the city itself. Everyone had gone his or her own way, and there was nothing we could do but sit by the wayside on our boxes, while Mr. G. went to procure carriages; this we expected would involve a walk of nearly three miles, and an absence of at least two hours. Such was my first introduction to the capital of all India! I certainly was not much impressed with the excellence of its arrangements, or with the approach it had made to the common conveniences of civilised life! The sun was not far from its decline, and we were anxiously calculating the flight of time, and fearing the night dews for the little darling; we watched the few passers-by, hoping that some one might act the part of a good Samaritan to us, and succour us in our distress; the few who did go that way passed by on the other side, evidently bent, very naturally, on securing accommodation for themselves, or enjoying some festivity after their long voyage. At length Mr. G. arrived, just as the shades were beginning to close in around us, his early return having been facilitated by having met a friend who had given him a lift. He insisted on my accompanying them to their home, and I thankfully yielded to his hospitable sway.

The road from thence to Alipore, a pleasant suburb of Calcutta, was not very prepossessing. It had formerly given promise of being an agreeable residence for those who desired to escape from the close air of the city; but the property had been purchased within a few years by a native prince, whose retainers and surroundings were not in accordance with English ideas, and the district was left in his hands. Hence there were none of those indications of affluence and refinement which we always see in the vicinity of large and important cities of Europe. Native huts, intended simply for protection from the elements, not as residences, take the place of our well-built comfortable homes; and a cottage garden filled with useful vegetables and gay flowers is here unknown. Indications of the ravages of the long-remembered cyclone still remain, in trees bereft of their branches, and bending, as if in terror, to escape from its fury. Many parts have a devastated air; no renovating spirit appeared to animate the residents. At length, after what seemed a long and tedious ride, we reached a commodious villa, built in the style which Anglo-Indians find so well adapted to the country, and surrounded by beautiful grounds and a well-arranged garden. The kind attentions of my host and hostess dispelled the thought of past troubles, and at a very early hour the next morning my friend, Dr. Chuckerbutty, arrived to convey me to his house, which for the present he begged me to consider my home.

The part of the city (Chowringhee) where I was now located is in the immediate vicinity of Government House. This is a fine mass of buildings, presenting an imposing effect, and is worthy of being the viceregal residence; a large open space surrounds it, and near it are the chief business streets, with the handsome-looking square now called after Lord Dalhousie. The regular evening drive is on the strand. Passing by Government House, with the adjutant birds standing in quiet dignity on its lofty roof, or taking their posts as sentinels on the pillars of the entrance-gates, we soon reach the banks of the Ganges, which is in that part crowded with vessels from all nations. The scene is very animated at the time of the usual evening promenade: carriages of every description, from that of the Governor-General with his brilliant equipage, to the humble gharry; English gentlemen and ladies in light and gay attire; East Indians, and native gentlemen of different ranks, and of a great variety of costumes. The carriages of these last contained no ladies. It was impossible to repress a painful consciousness that while we were enjoying the cool air, and admiring the setting of a tropical sun, reflecting his dazzling rays of gold and crimson in the glorious stream of the Ganges, they were sitting within dreary walls, deprived of the society of those who might have called out their highest powers, and to whose pure enjoyments they might have imparted the highest zest.

My earliest visitor on that first day was the very one with whom I most desired to make acquaintance. Before we had risen from our evening meal, Baboo Keshub Chunder Sen was announced. Before leaving England I had formed a high opinion of this Hindoo reformer, from various religious writings of his which had reached friends and correspondents there; and a testimony was borne by those personally acquainted with him to his private character as being quite in accordance with his public teachings. In India I had frequently heard him spoken of as the chief religious leader of the age, indeed the only one whose zeal led him to make public efforts to rouse his countrymen from idolatry. The party of the Brahmos, or pure theists, had been roused to take a distinct position some years ago by Debendernath Tagore, the son of Dwarkanath Tagore, who was the intimate friend of Rammohun Roy. Mr. Sen had, however, seceded from them, and headed a party of his own. This gave rise to much controversy and acrimonious writing in the party papers, and I had determined to suspend all judgment until I should be on the spot, and see and hear for myself. The result of a long and interesting conversation that evening was, that I felt greatly impressed with the candour, spirituality, and religious feeling of my new friend; he gladly carried away with him several religious books which I brought for him, together with an engraving of Rubens's affecting picture of the 'Descent from the Cross,' which he hung in his study.

The religious movement among the educated Hindoos of Bengal is so closely connected with their social progress, and through them that of the population generally, that it is necessary here to take a brief review of its origin and present position. It is a remarkable fact, and one of deep significance, that the origin of this reformation was from within, not from without;—that it was commenced by no excited enthusiast, no devotee absorbed in spiritual contemplation;—that there was no attempt, or even desire in its author, to form a sect or to lead a movement; and that it is only after the slumber of a quarter of a century that the spirit of one of the noblest men whom India or the world has ever seen, is beginning to rouse his benighted countrymen.

The Rajah Rammohun Roy was born more than twenty years before the close of the last century. The enlightenment and civilisation which are now inseparable attendants on the British rule, had then scarcely dawned on India. English education, opening the way to literature fraught with Christian feeling and founded on Christian priniciples, had not then been introduced into every Presidency, preparing the natives for posts of emolument and honour, and penetrating to regions at that time sunk in barbarism. Rammohun Roy does not appear to have learnt the English language until he was advanced in life, and then he acquired it rather through intercourse with official gentlemen than with a view to the study of literature. He was the son of an influential Brahmin, and consequently well instructed in the national sacred literature; his foreign education and early influences were derived from Mahometans. His biographer and friend, the late Rev. Dr. Lant Carpenter, the father of the present writer, thus speaks* of his early life:—

'Under his father's roof he received the elements of native education, and also acquired the Persian language. He was afterwards sent to Patna to learn Arabic; and lastly to Benares to obtain a knowledge of the Sanscrit, the sacred language of the Hindoos. His masters at Patna set him to study Arabic translations of some of the writings of Aristotle and Euclid, and it is probable that the training thus given to his mind in acuteness and close reasoning, and the knowledge which he acquired of the Mahometan religion from Mussulmen whom he esteemed, contributed to cause that searching examination of the faith in which he was educated, which led him eventually to the important efforts he made to restore it to its simplicity.

'His family was Brahminical, of high respectability, and of course he was a Brahmin by birth. After his death the thread of his caste was seen round him, passing over his left shoulder and under his right. His father trained him in the doctrine of his sect, but he very early observed the diversities of opinion existing even among the idolaters; and that while some exalted Brahma, the creator, others gave the ascendancy to Vishnu, the preserver, and others again to Shiva, the destroyer. It is scarcely possible, too, but that his mind must have been struck by the simplicity of the Mahometan faith and worship; and, at any rate, it

* *Vide* 'The Last Days in England of the Rajah Rammohun Roy,' by Mary Carpenter. London: Trübner, 1 vol. 8vo.; price, 7s. 6d.

early revolted from the frivolous or disgusting rites and ceremonies of the Hindoo idolatry. Without disputing the authority of his father, he often sought from him information as to the reasons of his faith. He obtained no satisfaction, and he at last determined, at the early age of fifteen, to leave the paternal home, and to sojourn for a time in Thibet, that he might see another form of religious faith. He spent two or three years in that country, and often excited the anger of the worshippers of the Llama by his rejection of their doctrine that this pretended deity—a living man—was the creator and preserver of the world.'

When Rammohun Roy was between twenty and thirty years of age, he became a collector at Burdwan, in the East India Company's civil service, and in that position acquired fluency both in speaking and writing the English language. By the death of his father and brothers early in the century, he became possessed of considerable property, which enabled him to carry out the plan he had conceived of reforming the religion of his countrymen. He removed to Moorshedabad, where he published in Persian, with a preface in Arabic, a work entitled 'Against the Idolatry of all Nations.' The book raised against him a host of enemies, though no one undertook to refute it. In 1814 he retired to Calcutta, and gradually gathered around him, as early as 1818, some intelligent and influential Hindoos, who united with him in a species of monotheistic worship. Very small progress has this small band of worshippers made in these fifty years! Not many of the rich and influential of his people are yet prepared courageously to emancipate themselves from the bondage which still holds them.

It is evident that at this period Rammohun Roy not

only laid no claim to being an inspired teacher—indeed he never did—but he did not base his teachings on any existing revelation; he had also no sympathy with Hindooism itself. The light of his own grand mind, which had come in contact through literature with the finest minds of antiquity, distinctly revealed to him one only God, one sole spirituality, as the object of religious worship. The best mode of converting his countrymen, he conceived, was to prove to them that 'the most celebrated and revered work of Brahminical theology,' as he himself expresses it, 'establishes the unity of the Supreme Being, and that He alone is the object of propitiation and worship.' These writings (the Vedas) are in Sanscrit, a language which is still jealously guarded from the study or even the simple hearing of the lower castes. He brought the Vedanta, or resolution of the Vedas, within the reach of all castes of his countrymen by translating it into Bengali and Hindostani, and afterwards publishing an abridgment of it with an English translation. Towards the close of his paper he says: 'My constant reflection on the inconvenient or rather injurious rites introduced by the peculiar practice of Hindoo idolatry, which more than any other pagan worship destroys the texture of society, together with compassion for my countrymen, have compelled me to use every possible effort to awaken them from their dream of error. . . Whatever men may say, I cannot be deprived of this consolation—my motives are acceptable to that Being who beholds in secret and compensates openly.'

The publication of this and other similar works of course attracted the attention of the English, especially of missionaries. The first notice we find of him is in 1814, when he is spoken of as 'acquainted with the

New Testament, and disposed to hear anything which can be enforced by the authority of Christ.' He was willing to converse with missionaries and even visit them, and offered Eustace Carey a piece of ground for a school. In 1817 he wrote to an English gentleman:—

'The consequence of my long and uninterrupted researches into religious truth has been that I have found the doctrines of Christ more conducive to moral principles, and better adapted for the use of rational beings, than any other which have come to my knowledge; and have also found Hindoos in general more superstitious and miserable, both in performance of their religious rites and in their domestic concerns, than the rest of the known nations of the earth.' *

In order to satisfy his mind as to the teaching of the Old and New Testament respecting the absolute unity of the Deity, he devoted himself to the critical study of the original languages in which they were written; and in 1820 published a series of selections from the Gospels in English, Sanscrit, and Bengali, which he entitled 'The Precepts of Jesus, the Guide to Peace and Happiness.' At that time the impression he produced is thus spoken of by a writer in the 'Calcutta Review':—

'Here we observe an individual, born and bred in a country benighted under the most gross idolatry and superstition, who, by a just use of that understanding which our gracious Creator has given to mankind to guide them to all truths, having discovered the falsehood of that system of idolatry, and the absurdity of those superstitions, conscientiously abandoned both; and thereby subjected himself to inconveniences and dangers of which persons living in more enlightened

* *Vide* 'Last Days,' &c. pp. 46-47.

societies can hardly form an idea. Next he directed his attention to the Christian religion, and that same just and honest use of his understanding, which discovered the falsehood and absurdity of idolatry and superstition, satisfied him that *Jesus* was the Messiah—that He was employed by God to reveal His will to men, and to make known to them the only true religion. He observed the internal and historical evidence of Christianity to be such as demonstrated its truth. Blessed with the light of Christianity, he dedicates his time and his money, not only to release his countrymen from the state of degradation in which they exist, but also to diffuse among the European masters of his country the sole true religion, as it was promulgated by Christ, His apostles, and His disciples.

'A Firm Believer in Christ.'

Calcutta, July 12, 1821.

Unfortunately, the missionaries did not welcome the steady advance which the noble Brahmin reformer was thus making towards Christianity. They attacked his book, and he was drawn into a controversy with them, while at the same time his countrymen opposed him in every possible way. He pursued his onward course, however, earnestly and steadily, established a Unitarian Christian place of worship, in co-operation with the Rev. William Adams and other friends; and having vindicated his right to retain his social position as a Brahmin, he undertook a voyage to England, hoping thereby to promote many social reforms, and to return to his country enriched with the treasures of Western civilisation, and more prepared to improve his countrymen. This was not permitted him. After remaining little more than two years in our country, and gaining the high esteem of all who knew him, he was removed from this world by rapid disease, in September 1833. The reader is referred, for what information could be collected respecting the Rajah's residence in England, to the work already referred to—the 'Last Days.' It will there be evident that his value for Christianity continually increased, that he distinctly declared his belief in the divine mission of Christ, in the miracles, and the resurrection, and that though he never was baptised, he was in the habit of attending Christian worship, and he was regarded at the time as being in full sympathy with the Christian religion.

Though the personal influence of Rammohun Roy had drawn many intelligent Hindoos round him while he was living in their midst, yet it does not appear that he so greatly inspired others with his own elevated views as to induce them to make any sacrifices, or any great efforts to promulgate them. He had not presented to them an absolute religious faith, obedience to which would remove the grand obstacles in the way of the progress of his countrymen: their hearts were not touched, and their moral nature was not sufficiently elevated, to make them accept, from an intuitive sense of fitness, a code of morality which was entirely separated from the living spirit of the author of it. He had exposed the national vices, and the horrible practices which had received the sanction of religion; he had denounced caste as the root of innumerable evils; and yet he had presented to them no higher authority for the abolition of their cruel and wicked practices than arguments drawn from their own sacred books, which, their priests pretended, taught them; and motives of expediency led him to preserve his own caste, while perceiving the evils which the institution caused.

He was greatly before his age, and though his teaching and example laid the foundation of a movement against idolatry which ought to embrace all its attendant social evils, his countrymen were not sufficiently advanced to comprehend him, or to second his efforts. For a time, then, his influence and teaching appeared to have produced little effect.

Various indications, which had recently reached us in the West, had excited a hope that the period was now come when the spirit of the Hindoo reformer was leading on his countrymen to a purer religion and a higher civilisation. My present visit to the scene of his labours, however, did not enable me to realise these hopes. One place of worship only—that which he had himself founded and dedicated to the worship of one true God—was pointed out to me as the house where the Brahmos assembled for worship once a week, on Wednesday evenings. This had been recently renovated by Debendernath Tagore, the leader of the sect, the son of his personal friend. There I joined in their Bengalee worship, in memory of him whom I so highly venerated; but I did not see the leader of the sect, nor even had I a personal interview with him, as he left the city shortly after my arrival. No interest appeared to exist in hearing anything respecting a man who had conferred such honour on his country. I could not even learn where was his house in the Circular Road, formerly the resort of enlightened Hindoos and friendly Europeans; nor where was the site of that printing-press which he had established in Dhurmtollah, to defend himself to the public against the attacks of his opponents. The absence of any cenotaph, record on marble tablet of his very existence, or statue, as an enduring memento of his grand and noble presence, was rendered more remarkable by the fact that a finely executed bust of his friend Dwarkanath stands in the public library to testify to the respect of his fellow-citizens. Nor did I discover any trace of his spirit among his professed followers. Instead of that earnest and candid search after truth which was so characteristic of Rammohun Roy—that devoted study of the Christian Scriptures, because he perceived that they were 'a universal guide to truth and happiness'—I found among the Brahmos an extreme prejudice against Christianity, combined with ignorance of the contents of the New Testament, which they were unwilling to study, having satisfied their minds, by a perusal of deistical works, of the antecedent impossibility of revelation or miracles. Even the 'Precepts of Jesus' with its various translations, is out of print, and its very existence appears generally unknown. In social progress they were in many respects beyond what are called the 'orthodox Hindoos,' or those who most tenaciously adhere to their religious rites and ancient idolatrous social customs; but at the same time further progress is discountenanced by them, and it was on this ground particularly that Keshub Chunder Sen and the advance party had separated from them.

Yet with all these discouraging facts before me, I gradually discovered that the character of the great reformer had produced a deep impression on many hearts, and one which is slowly but surely preparing for future improvement. One Hindoo gentleman, and one only, did I meet with who had personally known Rammohun Roy, and he dwelt with intense interest on everything connected with him. The following passage, in which he wrote for me some of his reminiscences, will be interesting to the reader :—

'My father and Rajah Rammohun Roy were friends. The friendship arose from the circumstance of their mofussil residence being in the same part of the district of Hooghly. My father was an orthodox Brahmin, but this did not interrupt his friendship with the Rajah, when his heterodoxy came to light; for, though of the old class, my father was liberal, and had a great respect for the Rajah. So great was his attachment to his noble friend that he wellnigh suffered excommunication for it, when the abolition of suttee brought upon the Rajah, as the author of this outrage, that social misfortune.

'I was introduced to the Rajah at a very early age by my father, and the friendship of the fathers soon led to the establishment of a friendship between the sons. The Rajah's youngest son, the late Rana Persaud Roy, and I being nearly of the same age, and being constantly thrown into each other's society, we soon began to find a pleasure in being together, and our intimacy grew up with our years. We lived like brothers, and the friendly relations between our families were generally firmly cemented.

'Not long after I had been established in the family of the Rajah, the Rev. Dr. Duff, whose memory I cannot recall without a thrill of gratitude passing through my frame, came to India, and formed a project in concert with the Rajah of establishing a school for giving English education to native children. At that time missionaries and missionary institutions were regarded by natives with great mistrust, and the Doctor and the Rajah with great difficulty could obtain but five pupils for their projected new school. I was one of these five, and I am now the only survivor out of this lot. The good Doctor has mentioned this fact with great complacency in many of his recent discourses, both here and in Edinburgh.

'My friend Rana Persaud and I formed, as far back as 1860, a scheme for giving instruction to the females of respectable Hindoo families. The system of zenana teaching, which then came into existence, was to our minds not suited to this end; and we arranged for instructing our females in some respectable school, to be established in the heart of the native town, and presided over and managed by some respectable mistress—respectable not only in attainments, but also in social position. We broached our scheme to Dr. Duff, who approved of it fully, and engaged the services of a clergyman's wife for this purpose in Scotland. But before we could carry our scheme into operation, I was deputed by Government to Lahore on public duty, and during my absence there my friend was gathered to his fathers, and our cherished scheme fell to the ground.

'The untimely death of my lamented friend rendered abortive several other schemes that we fondly cherished. Among other things we had an idea of going to England together, there to visit the place where his illustrious father sojourned and breathed his last, and ultimately to erect a marble statue on the spot to preserve his memory. But the hand of death anticipated us, and the regret is that we fell short of our duty to the illustrious deceased; not that his memory will be lost, for it requires no artificial monument to preserve it; and even if it does, there is a more substantial monument which will last so long as the English literature endureth.

(Signed)   W. M. CHATTERJEE.'

The new religious movement of Keshub Chunder Sen excited my warm interest, especially as it is carried out with much zeal by those who have associated themselves with him, and is accompanied with decided advance in the social position of women. They have no recognised religious teacher, and though Mr. Sen is confessedly their head, yet any who feel a desire to preach, or conduct religious worship, are allowed to do so; and they also go out as missionaries with their leader, to endeavour to arouse the spiritual nature of their countrymen. Women have not yet been admitted to join in worship with their husbands, but a separate prayer-meeting has been established for them, and this I was allowed to attend.

On Saturday evening, November 24, I was conducted to a small house, which was rented for the purpose, in the native part of the town. The rooms surround a small court, over which on special occasions a canopy may be drawn. This had been done on a recent occasion, when a marriage had been performed there by the Brahmos without idolatrous rites. On entering the central room with a lady who understood Bengali, and served as interpreter, I was agreeably surprised at being at once most affectionately greeted by the assembled ladies, who warmly expressed to me their pleasure at my thus visiting them. After some friendly communication, they seated themselves on the carpet, and reverently covered their faces to engage in prayer. Mr. Sen then entered with his assistant, and placing himself on the dais, solemnly offered up prayer in their native tongue; the ladies at times joined in a kind of chant in a low melodious tone. I was afterwards informed by my friend, that they had been supplicating for blessings to be bestowed on her who had come from a distant land to greet her Eastern sisters. How many whispered blessings may be near us, how many hearts may be beating in unison with us, of which we are little conscious! The service concluded, the ladies invited me into an inner room, where refreshment was provided, consisting of sweets, fruits, &c. They seemed particularly pleased by my assisting in handing them round, and we all partook; with Eastern hospitality, they insisted on my carrying some of these delicacies with me to my home. The husbands of the ladies had brought them in palanquins or carriages to the place of meeting, and remained waiting outside. The Hindoo customs forbid a married couple from holding any communication in the presence of others; it is even regarded as improper for a husband in any way to notice his wife. A father ought not even to see his daughter-in-law, or an older brother a sister-in-law. These rules are not always strictly enforced, but all who profess to be orthodox must obey them; the extent to which they are disregarded may be considered as a pretty correct indication of the degree in which any family is liberal or the contrary. It was then a matter of great surprise to the lady who accompanied me, and who was fully conversant with the Hindoo customs, when an invitation was gladly accepted by both ladies and gentlemen to meet together at tea at Dr. Chuckerbutty's house on the following Monday. Mr. Sen kindly undertook the office of sending special invitations, himself accompanying them.

The house of our meeting is situated in one of the least agreeable native districts of the city—Mirzapore Street. A stranger to India cannot imagine the condition of these low streets, inhabited by natives pursuing various humble callings, and apparently in a state of entire isolation from the superior grades. This part of the city seemed a perfect network of streets, and on a subsequent occasion, when I required to wend my way in a carriage alone to this place, with a native driver who could not speak English, my situation was perplexing in the extreme;—after traversing in vain street after street, I should have given myself up for lost, had I not fortunately discerned some passers-by, whose dress indicated that they probably understood English, and who directed the driver. Yet in the midst of such a district we find the residence of a millionaire; turning up a narrow lane with an open sewer on each side, I saw an opulent native gentleman alight at his home from a genteel carriage; and our driver took us on to a dirty courtyard, leading to the large family mansion of a gentleman of position. Shortly after my arrival, I drove through the busiest part of the native town, Chidpore Road. It was dirty and narrow; indeed, the low shops seemed placed one before another to make the most of the room. The naked salesmen here wear their long black hair instead of the turban. A variety of races may be seen, many having come from distant parts to dispose of their produce. The odours arising from this district are indescribable; it would appear that the native gentry who reside in this locality, must have had their sense of smell blunted by long habitude, and thus are not aware of the exteme unhealthiness of such a condition. Here, to my surprise, I found that the Brahmo Somaj is situated, and that in a lane turning out of it is the once sumptuous mansion which still bears the name of Dwarkanath Tagore. There he gave splendid entertainments to distinguished English guests. On the occasion above alluded to, there was a stoppage in the way; we soon perceived that this proceeded from an idol procession. A number of trumpery-looking stands were being carried along, on which were hung a great variety of broken toys, flags, or anything that came to hand to make a display—such as one might fancy our ragged-school children might have collected together for a procession; these stands were carried by the most grotesque-looking men and boys, generally in a state of nudity, but in many cases adorned with some one article of clothing, which might have been procured from a ragshop. One wore a cocked hat, with nothing else upon his body; another, a soldier's jacket; these articles were evidently regarded with considerable pride by the wearers. As the procession moved along, no entertainment or enthusiasm was excited in the spectators; reverence there was none, and solemnity was evidently not the intention of the procession. A few women were at the windows, or at any opening where they could see what was going on, but there was no excitement or joyous shouts, which show the exuberance of life in our English boys. At all times I saw the same apathy pervading the population. I was told that the Hindoos were the most contented of people; what I saw of the lower orders led me to think their existence a joyless one, devoid of any desire to ameliorate their condition.

On Monday evening, our party of Hindoo ladies and gentlemen arrived at 7, punctual to the appointed hour. Two English ladies only had been invited as interpreters. Our host himself would not have appeared, had it not been the wish of all present. The dress of the ladies, while in native style, was close and neat, perfectly suitable to this their first entrance into a mixed company. Dr. C. had kindly wished that refreshments should be provided in accordance with the tastes of his guests, but they desired that no departure should be made from ordinary English customs; they partook of tea and coffee with evident pleasure, much gratified with what they considered the great condescension of their English friends, in assisting to hand these refreshments to them. The entertainment of the ladies during the evening was a greater difficulty. I had relied on various albums and scrap-books which I had brought with me; but when I observed a lady look at one upside down, without any possibility on my part to make her understand its meaning, a different mode of proceeding was evidently necessary. I therefore explained a portfolio of prints and drawings to a circle of gentlemen, and then requested one of them to do the same to the ladies. This was accomplished satisfactorily. Music varied the evening; and Dr. C.'s daughter gave them much pleasure by playing and singing to her guests. The evening passed thus agreeably; there was no painful shyness or reserve, and yet at the same time there was throughout a propriety of demeanour which was very remarkable, when it is remembered that such an assembly was probably the first of the kind ever held. At 9, we saw our guests safely into their carriages, each lady under the care of her own protector, all having been greatly gratified with the evening. We little realised at the time how important a step was thus being made in social progress, and how much steady effort at emancipation from prejudices must have been previously accomplished, to enable these native gentlemen to take it. This evening awakened in the minds of many of those present higher aspirations, which led to further improvements. The importance of the step was shown by the indignant comments of some of the native papers, which were opposed to progress.

The Court had not yet returned to Calcutta, having been detained in the North by the great durbar. I could not therefore deliver my introductions to various official gentlemen, and determined to avail myself of the present leisure to take an early opportunity of visiting the schools. The first I saw was an excellent specimen of the Calcutta schools, being those belonging to the Free Scotch Presbyterians, originally established by the Rev. Dr. Duff. This gentleman may indeed be considered the founder of the mission school system in India. I was informed that there was at first considerable opposition, especially from home committees, to this direction of missionary effort. The excellent Doctor, however, persevered, being fully convinced of the importance of early directing in a right course the minds of the rising generation, and his example has been generally followed. The series of schools which are usually associated with his name will ever be a monument to his enlightened benevolence. In addition to excellent schools, there is a college and a large library. Several of the teachers are native converts; it appeared to me, indeed, that I could generally detect which were so by a more open and happy expression of countenance. Whenever I had an opportunity of conversing with such, they expressed to me their true satisfaction at having obtained, at any cost, the blessedness which those only can feel who have received the heavenly message from the Saviour Himself. They had practically learnt the duty of leaving even father and mother at the call of their Master, and they had experienced a rich reward in giving all up for Him. There was nothing peculiar in the management of this or other schools which I saw in Calcutta and the neighbourhood; the necessity of preparing the young men for a degree guided everywhere the course of instruction. Dr. Duff's girls' school is the best I saw in this city except the Bethune School, which possesses peculiar advantages removing it from comparison with any other. Dr. Duff's is indeed the only good day-school for girls that I saw or heard of, and in this respect Calcutta fell very far behind Madras, Bombay, or even Ahmedabad. Though the premises are not as good as might be desired, the school seemed well filled and in excellent order. In one class a female native convert, a widow, was teaching with evident success; in another class, a young Hindoo widow was receiving instruction with a view to train as a teacher; she received a small gratuity weekly to provide her food, being thus debarred from obtaining a livelihood. The Mission Orphan Boarding School is an excellent one. There are from 50 to 60 girls, their ages varying from 6 years old to 16. Here, as elsewhere, the missionary and his wife reside on the premises, and give a tone to the school. For the first time since I had been in India, I saw a gallery lesson given to the younger department of the school by a young woman, who had been trained in the Church Female Normal School. She had married, and was now a widow. The animation and interest displayed by the children, and the agreeable and lively manner in which the lesson was given, formed a striking contrast to the ordinary teaching of the younger classes in the ordinary Hindoo girls' school. I was requested to examine the older class, and somewhat hesitated to do so, knowing how easily young people are perplexed by the questions of a stranger. I found, however, that they were perfectly at home; though the examination was conducted in English, they answered admirably, both on geography and on Scripture subjects. In comparing these girls with those in the native day-schools, it is necessary to bear in mind not only that these are the whole day under care and influence, but that they remain at school later than is possible, according to existing customs among the Hindoos. Yet with these deductions, it is evident that young native girls are quite equal in intelligence and quickness in learning to their Western sisters, if properly instructed and trained. The same fact is particularly striking also in the small boarding-school of Hindoo girls in connection with the Normal School. Not only did the little girls show much animation when receiving a lesson from one of the female teachers, but when work was over, and they were permitted to go to play, they had as active and joyous a game in the midday heat, as our children at home would indulge in on a bracing October morning. The Female Normal School is supported by the Indian Society for Promoting Female Instruction, and is in connection with the Church of England. There are (as stated in the Report for 1866, which is the fourteenth) ten students, who are most carefully instructed in Bengali, as well as Scripture, the ordinary branches of female education, singing, drawing, and fancy work—these last being found useful and attractive in the zenana-visiting. They are expected to remain three years in the institution, and afterwards to engage in teaching, for at least two years, in schools or zenanas. The students appeared interested in their work, and gave promise of being intelligent and earnest in their future duties. Every arrangement was made conducive to their health and comfort, and a comfortable home is also provided for zenana teachers. This society has also branch schools in various parts of the country in connection with the central one in Calcutta; these contain about 350 children. I visited also a benevolent institution for poor boys and girls, of whom, by a fundamental rule, three-fourths must be Christians. There are about 140 boys and 80 girls, chiefly East Indians. A school for Jewish girls, chiefly Armenians, is taught by an English certificated teacher, the only one I met with in India.

The instruction given in zenanas by private teachers forms an important feature in the female education of Calcutta. Some years ago there was extreme reluctance to admit these teachers into families; at present there is a great demand for them, and it is difficult for sufficient funds to be raised to supply the demand. It is obvious that in the case of young married ladies this is the only means by which education can be given. It certainly appears extraordinary that native gentlemen of affluence do not show a willingness to pay liberally for such advantages; as in England suitable payment would be made for the services of daily governesses. Hence the difficulty of obtaining funds, though the Government contributes to these in lieu of schools. The zenana teachers speak encouragingly of the effects of their instructions. Having accompanied a lady who takes an active part in this work, it was interesting to observe the warm and affectionate greeting given to the visitors by the Hindoo ladies; in the seclusion of the female apartments, which are frequently very dull and devoid of any object of interest, it must indeed be very gratifying to these native ladies to receive kind instruction, and to have intercourse with sympathising strangers.

However valuable the zenana-visiting is in cases where it is impossible under existing circumstances to attend a school, yet it is obviously far preferable for young girls to have their minds expanded by seeing something beyond the walls in which they are afterwards to be immured. The excellent Mr. Bethune, who will ever be remembered as having given the first great stimulus to female education, left a large sum to be devoted especially to the promotion of that of the higher classes. A splendid and commodious building has been erected bearing his name, and placed under the care of Government, which also contributed largely to the support of the school which is carried on there for the daughters of native gentlemen;—in order to meet their wishes as far as possible, it is placed under the care of a native committee. It has the advantage of a trained female teacher as superintendent, and all the appointments are calculated to meet the wants of a large institution. Unfortunately, the school is at present small in comparison with the number which it might accommodate. It is much to be regretted that the excellent instruction provided is not made available for private classes of married ladies who are permitted by their husbands to have such advantages, and for the training of teachers on the Government system. With but a small addition to the present staff, the presence of male officials might thus be entirely dispensed with, and a good training institution established at very little additional expense, and to the great advantage of the young ladies who attend the schools. It is to be hoped that the earnest desires of the advanced party may ere long be fulfilled, and that enlightened native gentlemen may have the happiness of obtaining for their wives, the mothers of their children, such instruction as may enable them better to discharge their duties.

A day spent in a country missionary excursion was a pleasant variety, after devoting so much attention to the institutions of the city. The name of the Rev. Mr. Long is well known throughout all India; among the enlightened natives he is regarded as a martyr to his anxiety to protect the weak in the indigo troubles, which led to his imprisonment for libel. Whether his course was wise or not on that particular occasion it would be useless here to enquire; but no one can hesitate to esteem the devoted earnestness with which he has for twenty-five years directed his energies to the improvement of the lower class of natives, and endeavour to draw public attention to their real wants. I gladly accepted his invitation to accompany him to a station some miles from the city, which would give me an insight into the mofussil mode of life. The regular residents in Calcutta seldom go beyond the sight of streets and houses. It was delightful to change these for wild jungle and the long graceful bamboo. After a time a little hedge-school appeared, of a very primitive nature, being held in an open shed with the ordinary surroundings of cottage life. The children were sitting with palm-leaves in their hands, inscribing unknown characters on them with bits of stick, dipped in some sooty composition to serve as a pen. This primitive mode of writing is in great favour in these parts, having the advantage of cheapness, and also of obliging the scholar to write his lesson correctly at once, as no erasure is possible. A specimen of this writing I carried away with me. I was much surprised at the advance in learning which was indicated by the questions put to them by Mr. Long; their answers showed much intelligence and mastery of ideas. Among other subjects he questioned them on natural history, with the leading divisions of the animal kingdom and many scientific terms; they answered admirably, and proved, by the illustrations they gave from familiar animals, that they thoroughly understood what they were saying, and that this was no word-knowledge. Mr. Long has adopted the excellent plan of dividing the time of one thoroughly trained teacher among a number of these village schools, giving a day to each; he thus instructs the teacher, and introduces a higher standard into the schools, especially as he himself not unfrequently visits them. He cannot adopt the same plan in a small girls' school which we afterwards visited, because there is extreme fear among the Hindoos of their daughters being converted; they would consent to sewing only being taught by a native convert teacher. Mr. Long justly thought that it was doing good to the young scholars to have the silent and softening influence of a young woman who is a convert, and I was struck with the evident effect of her presence on the school, while the master conducted the education.

A zemindar had expressed his desire for a visit, and I was happy to embrace the opportunity of visiting a native gentleman's mofussil residence. He appeared to occupy the position of a country squire in England, residing on an extensive estate. There was a large tank before the mansion, with steps leading down to the water; but the general aspect of the outer premises indicated some degree of dilapidation. My companion, Mr. Long, could not go further than the entrance court; but a young gentleman of the family introduced me to the interior, where I was received very courteously by the host, who summoned the ladies to the drawing-room. One after another they appeared; his mother, wife, daughters, and innumerable aunts, nieces, and ladies of every degree of female relationship, numbering altogether nearly forty. The younger ladies brought their books in their hands, and seemed pleased to show their advancement in education by reading some Bengali lessons to me. The ladies are fully occupied with domestic employments, of which the size of the establishment must furnish an ample supply. The young gentleman held a Government office, but otherwise the burden of the maintenance of the family appeared to fall chiefly on the head of the house, as some of the ladies were married to Kulin Brahmins, who consider themselves merely visitors in any family they honour by their alliance, leaving the maintenance of the wife and children on the father of the lady. They hospitably invited me to partake of some refreshment; but as Mr. Long could not be admitted, they kindly offered to place some fruit in the carriage that I might share it with him. I thankfully accepted some fine Cabul grapes (packed carefully in small boxes embedded in cotton), pomegranates, and other tropical fruits. Mr. Long was no stranger there; he had on a former occasion exhibited the magic lantern to the delight of the neighbourhood, the court being thronged, and the ladies of the family enjoying the spectacle from the housetop. I found him negotiating for a repetition of the entertainment, to the great pleasure of the family. How marvellously are means now multiplied of instruction and recreation combined, and how friendly a feeling must be excited in such a district towards a gentleman who would thus devote himself to promote the pleasure of native families! As we were walking down a woody lane to our conveyance, I observed with admiration some fine living specimens of a large tropical bulimus, a land shell of the snail kind, and was informed that they had appeared in that district since the famine. No explanation was given of the connection between the famine and the advent of the bulimus, the difference between *post hoc* and *propter hoc* not appearing to be understood. I was promised that a few specimens should be prepared for me, and on our return in the evening we found some obliging youths watching for our carriage to give me several fine shells, which they had collected; unlike English boys, they regarded thanks a sufficient return for their courtesy, and declined to accept a few silver coins. This visit to the zemindar left a most agreeable impression on the mind, and showed what friendly intercourse might take place between the two races, when it is animated by so truly Christian a spirit as Mr. Long's. At length we reached the mission station, which is in the midst of an extensive rural district. A pretty country house surrounded by a well-arranged garden, was well calculated to give the natives an idea of English comfort and simple elegance. The missionary's wife delights to come here and stay a few days, diffusing around that influence which a true Christian woman can always give. Near it are various native cottages and the school-house. Mr. Long is a firm believer, as I am myself, in the possibility of elevating young children of apparently the most degraded nature, by the adoption of proper means; he also does not appear to be convinced, as most people are, of the great natural superiority of the Brahmin caste. My own experience was not sufficiently great to entitle me to give a decided opinion on the subject, though I was certainly inclined to agree with him; and never during my stay in India could I intuitively discriminate different castes, or distinguish Brahmins. On the present occasion, Mr. Long examined the classes in which different castes were mingled without distinction, and afterwards, on telling the Brahmin boys to rise, we were struck with observing that some of the most refined and intelligent-looking boys were of an inferior caste, thus confirming his theory.

In order to give some idea of the surrounding country, Mr. Long had arranged for a row along a canal which was a useful medium of communication for the produce of the district. We entered a most primitive canoe-like boat, with an awning so low that a seat on a hassock was almost too high; in some parts we could occasionally pick the flowers on the banks, and in others we could hardly make our way between the sedges. At length, when I was beginning to fear that we were so far from our starting-point that we ran a risk of being benighted on our return, we reached a little homestead looking very much like England with its cattle and children at play, and found that we had made a circuit, and had returned to the cottage of the native Christian family who resided at the station. It was pleasant to be greeted by them with that feeling of fraternity which springs up spontaneously between Christians in this heathen land, and strange to enter an ordinary-looking little Hindoo house, and find familiar English books, and hear uttered with loving respect the name of a devoted Christian lady which I knew well. I bade adieu to this peaceful hamlet with regret, and with a strong feeling of the good which was here being done so unostentatiously. The missionary gains much influence by these quiet visitations to the homes of the natives, where he is received with openness and confidence, and he is thus preparing for more extensive and effective action in future.

Before arriving at my Calcutta home, I paid another visit of a less agreeable nature. I had not been in an idol temple during their so-called worship, and, repugnant as it was to my feelings, this was an experience I ought to have; and Mr. Long kindly agreed to conduct me to one, a temple of the goddess Kali, which was much frequented. We drove through a thickly populated suburb, and alighted at the entrance of a narrow lane, lined on each side with low shops or stalls, which were hung with quantities of garlands of yellow chrysanthemums or African marigolds, for the votaries of the goddess. I had often seen some semi-nude labourer wearing such a garland, and was informed that this was in token of the wearer having been performing his devotions. The pictures which are sold in such places are of the most hideous kind, not calculated to inspire any emotions of virtue or reverence. On arriving at the temple, an educated young man volunteered to escort us, and led us to a gloomy courtyard, where he showed us the block on which the victims are immolated to the goddess, who rejoices in the shedding of blood; we then entered the inner temple, where the priests and others were making a dreadful din—music it could not be called—and a number of natives were standing with bent heads, but without any appearance of solemnity. All was noise and confusion. I begged my friend to withdraw from this scene. The young man followed us, asking for something for Kali, and assuring us that Europeans did not generally object to make an offering. We were of course inexorable, and pursued our way to the carriage, followed by the young man. At last, thinking apparently that he was making an irresistible appeal, he exclaimed, 'I have read Matthew, Mark, Luke, and John, and the Revelations!' —'You found nothing about Kali there,' rejoined Mr. Long. 'Good afternoon.'—'Good afternoon,' he civilly answered, and departed, perceiving, doubtless, that we were shocked, rather than otherwise, with what sounded to us somewhat like blasphemy.

There is much that is distressing to meet one at every turn in this city of Calcutta, and everywhere in India. We see heathenism assuming a daring front in the midst of Christian civilisation—instruction affording only subject to the scorner—determined opposition to improvement, and blind submission to the tyranny of custom. Then, again, we meet with the most delightful proofs that the Word is penetrating quietly but surely where we little expect to find traces of its power, and that the Christian spirit is working its way among those who have not yet accepted the Christian name. 'The kingdom of God cometh not with observation' in our day, any more than when the words were first uttered. Such thoughts as these were peculiarly suggested by a Sunday in the city of Rammohun Roy's labours, which was especially dedicated in my mind to the great reformer. I found, in a suburb of Calcutta, the young Brahmin convert, who had visited with me in Bristol the spot consecrated by having been the Rajah's last earthly residence, and the tomb erected to his memory. He had been intended for the ministry, but circumstances had been very adverse to him, and kept him somewhat isolated; he was, however, acquainted with some of the Brahmos, and I requested him to bring two or three of them, that we might hold a simple worship together, reading that grand fortieth chapter of Isaiah, which had been selected for reading at the Rajah's funeral service. He came accompanied by three Brahmos, each of whom I requested to take a part by reading a portion of Scripture. To one I assigned the fourteenth chapter of the Gospel of St. John, though with some fear lost it might not be read with much feeling. I then discovered that not one of the three had any idea of the circumstances under which that touching address was delivered. These I simply explained to them, and was listened to with evident interest. After a very touching prayer by my young Brahmin friend, the reading commenced. Anyone who has heard that grand portion of Isaiah's writings read in the pulpit with deep feeling and expression, will enter into my surprise, when one of these young Hindoos read it with a force and pathos which I have seldom heard at all exceeded. Another read a Psalm. He who was to read the Gospel, before commencing, solemnly prayed for a blessing 'on the holy chapter' before him, and then read it as one who deeply felt the solemn and affecting words he was uttering; this indeed he did, for he informed us afterwards that he had frequently perused with deep interest the words of Our Lord. Keshub Chunder Sen would have been with us on this very interesting occasion, but he was preparing for a service which he was about to hold that evening, in kind compliance with my earnest wish to hear him state his religious views. He usually conducts a service in Bengali on Sunday mornings, in his own large drawing-room; on this occasion he arranged to have also a special evening service in English, to which he invited the attendance of a few English friends, in addition to his ordinary congregation. On arriving after the service had commenced, I found that some one was engaged in prayer; and from the manner and the matter—full of deep penitential utterances—I should have thought myself in a Methodist chapel, and was quite perplexed who could be officiating, until a touching supplication for our 'mother country' and for perfect harmony between 'the conquered and the conquering races,' convinced me that he must be a Hindoo. He was indeed the same native gentleman who had read in the afternoon the fourteenth chapter of St. John. Mr. Sen read portions of the Hindoo Scriptures and of the New Testament, and an English gentleman engaged in prayer, while another conducted the singing of a hymn. Mr. Sen afterwards began his discourse, taking for his text, 'Except a man be born again, he cannot enter into the kingdom of God.' He most powerfully demonstrated the necessity of a change of heart, and in a deeply spiritual discourse developed his subject, in a manner truly astonishing to those who were not aware what progress he had made towards Christianity. On two other occasions I heard him give those remarkable extempore discourses, which rivet the attention of his hearers, and carry them with him in his spiritual flight.

English appears as familiar to Mr. Sen as his native language; indeed on these subjects it is probably more so, as his views have been formed by communion with minds who have expressed their views in our language. He is equally capable, however, of descending to the level of the capacities of the most ignorant. 'No one ever spoke to us in this way,' said the inhabitants of a mofussil town to him when he addressed them, in language which they could understand, respecting their duties one to another; he told them that they must be just and true in their dealings, avoid false weights and measures, and, in fine, do to others as they would have others do to them. They desired that those words should be spoken to them another day. Such teachings must come to the Hindoos with great power from one of their own nation; and, indeed, wherever Keshub Chunder Sen goes on his missionary tours, he is listened to by thousands. 'I never retrace my steps,' he has said. May he go onwards, until he becomes an apostle to call his people to accept Christ as their only Master!

On Saturday, Dec. 1, the Governor-General arrived. On the Monday following I was summoned to his presence. The interview was followed by a kind invitation from Lady Lawrence to take up my abode at Government House. This I thankfully accepted, with a grateful feeling for so much condescension; and on the following Monday was installed in my new quarters, where I was most obligingly treated as a guest during the remainder of my stay in Calcutta. I may be permitted here respectfully to offer my warm acknowledgments to his Excellency and his estimable lady, for thus showing their sympathy with the object of my visit, and affording me advantages which I could not otherwise have enjoyed. It was also regarded by my native friends as a token of sympathy with themselves; and they had as much facility for conferring with me, and visiting me in the rooms assigned me in Government House, as if I had been in a private residence.

Before taking leave of my friend Dr. Chuckerbutty, to whom I was so much indebted for his kind reception, I was anxious to see the Medical College, which was the scene of his daily official labours. This institution was founded by Dr. Henry Goodeve. Great anxiety was felt at the time lest the opposition it would excite in the minds of uninformed natives should defeat its objects; but science and enlightenment triumphed, and this institution has led the way to the diffusion of sound medical knowledge over the empire. The fact of Dr. Chuckerbutty being himself a native, and therefore acquainted with the habits and customs of the country, as none but a Hindoo by birth can be, is of great importance; it enables him in a variety of ways to adapt his teachings to the wants of his students, and to overcome their prejudices judiciously. The hospital wards presented considerable contrast to what I had seen elsewhere; they were provided with respectable nurses, chiefly East Indians, neatly and simply dressed; these were under the direction of a committee of ladies, with whom the surgeons communicated. The matron in charge appeared intelligent, and all seemed to be under good regulation. I afterwards learnt that this admirable state of the nursing department was probably due to the exertions of a society for training nurses, which was established some years ago in honour of the late Lady Canning. These results are very suggestive of the best mode of providing a supply of nurses elsewhere in India.

I had not yet visited the jails, and was especially desirous of doing so, having heard of the remarkable perfection of the skilled industrial work in that at Alipore. The printing, which has been introduced into that jail, has been developed in a very remarkable manner by Mr. Jones, now assistant-secretary to the Government; indeed, what I heard had been accomplished seemed hardly credible.

Through the kindness of the Lieutenant-Governor, Sir Cecil Beadon, his aide-de-camp obligingly called for me punctually at 6 A.M., on two mornings, to accompany me to this and some other institutions. The Director-General of Prisons, Dr. Mouat, was then absent in England; Dr. Francis, as superintendent of the jail, accompanied us, and gave us every information. There are from 800 to 1,000 prisoners in Alipore Jail. Some of them are employed in the rougher works, but the bulk of the prisoners are engaged in departments connected with printing, lithography, &c. Men, totally low and ignorant on their first admission, are taught the English letters in a month. I saw one, who had been there less than that time, select the different types quite accurately from a number, as they were called for. They are carried on, step by step, through the different stages, until they have arrived at as great perfection as if they were English printers. The very finest fancy printing is executed here, as well as Government despatches; and in the various workshops there is so much apparent freedom, that I should not have imagined myself in a prison, were it not for the presence of the guard who attended us round. All the prisoners were working with as much apparent goodwill as if they were free men; indeed, Mr. Jones assured us that he had ascertained that they performed more than a third more work per diem than ordinary workmen. This is the more remarkable, as there is no payment or reward allowed for industrial work; nor indeed have the prisoners any incentive, except the satisfaction arising from doing skilled work well. The healthy moral feeling and good tone thus engendered has the effect of lessening the need of officers, the incredibly small number of ten paid officials being found sufficient to maintain order, in addition to prisoners themselves, who are selected for good conduct to serve as warders. There is no provision for separate sleeping here, any more than in the other jails I had seen; but the injurious effects of association are diminished by the fact that the prisoners are fatigued by their work, and sleep soundly without giving any cause for complaint of disorder. This jail does more than support itself by the product of industrial work, and is in that respect perfect. It is to be doubted, however, whether the object of prison discipline does not require a more penal stage at the commencement of a sentence. I was indeed informed that the natives are so little deterred from doing wrong by fear of such a jail, where they have abundance of the necessaries of life, and no painful control, that they are in the habit of calling it 'My father-in-law's house;' this I heard respecting jails in various parts of the empire. Alipore Jail is, however, unique in its way, and well demonstrates many important problems in prison discipline. It would serve admirably as a second stage for long-sentenced prisoners, if the Irish or Crofton system were carried out in India.

We then visited the Female Prison, which is a completely distinct building, and the prisoners have far better premises than in any other that I had seen. The place was not originally intended for its present purpose, nor is it adapted to it. There is association without separate sleeping-cells. The jailer and his wife live on the premises, but there are male warders. A little instruction is given, though there did not appear to be any systematic attempt to improve the prisoners. Still, the place was such, that it would be very possible for ladies to come and visit these unhappy women, with every hope of conferring a real benefit on them. It appeared to me remarkable, that among the many benevolent works carried on in Calcutta by ladies, prison-visiting has not yet been included. Surely the want needs only to be known for it to be supplied. A woman approached me with hands folded in earnest supplication; the subject of her entreaty I could not of course comprehend, but was informed that she was soliciting my influence on her behalf, for her to be sent to the Andamans. These islands are a penal settlement for life-sentenced native male convicts. In the latter stage of their punishment, if they have obtained some degree of privilege by their good conduct, they are allowed to live in comparative liberty on one island. Having been separated from their families, it would generally be impossible for their wives to be brought to them, and yet domestic comfort was needed. A very large number of murderesses— I was told 150—were under life sentences. Many of these women did not appear to have acted form premeditated wickedness, but rather from sudden impulse caused by great provocation. Their condition was most deplorable, without hope of amelioration. The offer was made to them of going to this penal settlement with a view to marriage with these men; it was gladly accepted, and they were sent. To obtain a similar boon was the petition of this poor woman. Some of the prisoners had young children with them, which must indeed be a blessing to the parents. One small creature was lying in its mother's lap, stretching its well-formed little limbs in the sun with evident delight, and a ray striking on its dark eagle eye was so reflected back that it looked like a brilliant diamond. 'What a glorious spirit may be enshrined in the form that holds this young immortal!' I thought, as I kissed that tiny face. 'How unconscious is it of the degradation around it! What is to be the future of that little child? Whose duty is it to shape its destiny? The State has deprived it of its natural guardian—who is take her place?' An answer would involve many grave considerations.

After the jails, I visited a lunatic asylum, under the superintendence of Dr. Payne, which had some features so interesting and instructive, that another reference to such an institution will be pardoned.

There are two distinct establishments—one intended for Europeans and Eurasians, the other for natives. In the former, residence is usually a temporary one, as the English patients are generally sent home when proper arrangements are made. The object is therefore, in most cases, rather to promote the comfort of the patient during a short sojourn, than to attempt to carry out a system which would require a long period of discipline and care. A master and matron reside here, who have the care respectively of the male and female patients in separate departments. The premises are well arranged, with a nicely-kept garden. Every comfort and convenience is provided: there is a pleasant verandah, with a table on which are entertaining books and papers. All the sleeping-rooms are neat and cheerful. The matron threw all her energies and sympathy into the work, and treated the patients with the greatest kindness. They, however, had a most repulsive aspect. They were full of the most ridiculous self-sufficiency, and exhibited their peculiarities in a very disagreeable manner. The master endeavoured by his own example to induce the lunatics under his care to work in the garden as a pleasant occupation, but nothing effective appeared to be done; and the chief impression produced on me was, that great effort and kindness were being bestowed without more than a temporary result. The native asylum was very different. Here the same principle was developed as in that at Ahmedabad, with the addition of more skilled labour, which appeared a very important element. Extracting oil from the castor-nut was the manufacture adopted, as it involved a variety of processes, and was a kind of work with which many were previously familiar. Dr. Payne selected at all times the occupation which appeared best to fall in with the character and tastes of the patient, and to put him into as natural a condition as possible, the superintendent of the work carefully watching any symptom which indicated a need for change. The manner in which all this was being done was, to a passing observer like myself, so natural, that if the principles had not been explained to me, I should not have imagined that I was observing anything but an ordinary factory. Dr. Payne speaks most favourably of the result of his system, which indeed appears worthy of close study and imitation.

It is unnecessary to occupy the time of the reader with descriptions of the institutions which are well known to all who visit India. A passing reference only is needed to several of these, though all were very interesting.

The Museum of the Asiatic Society, with its rich stores of natural history, valuable manuscripts, relics illustrating Hindoo mythology, memorial busts of those who have recorded in their works their interest in India—all these recall especially to the mind its noble founder, Sir William Jones, whose virtues and learning embalm his memory in this country.

The Metcalfe Hall is a noble monument to the memory of the excellent Governor-General whose name it bears. Here are treasures of literature, which are highly appreciated and freely used, both by the English and by the native gentry; and a large saloon is filled with interesting natural productions adapted for use in manufactures, as well as valuable models of machines, and various works of art.

The Museum of Comparative Anatomy connected with the Medical College is an admirable one, and reflects the highest honour on its curator.

The School of Art is as yet young, but promises to be very valuable in developing native talent.

In the Sanscrit College is a wonderful collection of most valuable manuscripts. This institution carries the student through a highly-advanced course of study, as indicated by the examination-papers, with which the principal kindly presented me.

The Hindoo College, the school still called by the name of its excellent founder, David Hare, the large Martiniere School for Christian boys and girls, and other institutions of the kind, I could only see externally, as the vacation had commenced when I visited them.

The School for European Orphan Girls appears a well-managed institution, which has the merit of proving that, with a judicious system of education—mental, moral, and physical—English girls may be brought up in a healthy condition in India. I saw some respectable young married women, with their infants, visiting the school where they had been educated, and of which they retained a grateful remembrance.

The School of Useful Arts in Dhurmtollah, under the superintendence of the American missionary, the Rev. C. H. Dall, deserves especial mention. While combining with an ordinary Anglo-vernacular school a collegiate class, instruction is given in engrossing, lithography, and various other branches of manual skill, which may enable youths to gain a livelihood; and even fancy work, knitting, &c. are taught, which the boys in their turn teach to their sisters at home. I carried away maps beautifully drawn by the pupils, with specimens of well-executed lithography. There is also a girls' school on the same premises, which is regularly visited by an English lady who understands Bengali, who speaks highly of the docility and quickness of the little girls.

There are many other institutions in Calcutta which time did not permit me to visit. Most of them are intended to promote the welfare of the educated classes. It was most gratifying to an Englishwoman to find how much had been done, both by our Government and by private individuals, to promote the welfare of this great country; yet I could not but feel that the lower classes had not in any way shared these benefits. This is not entirely the fault of the English. The inferior portion of the population—in fact, the great mass of the inhabitants—are in a state of dense ignorance, which can hardly be conceived by those whose lot is cast in a civilised and Christian country. Most distressing as is the ignorance which still exists in our own country, and which must be regarded as a standing disgrace to it, until some active measures are taken by the educational department of the Government to grapple with it—yet in England none are in a state of absolute isolation from the educated part of the community. The institutions, organisations, voluntary efforts, Christian sympathy, which are in active existence and operation in our country, need only to be properly strengthened, aided, and wisely directed by the Government, to penetrate at once to the most remote and ignorant rural district, to the darkest corner of the most wretched court and alley in our great cities. It is otherwise in India. The educated natives, not having embraced Christianity, do not feel the impulse which animates us to seek and to save the lost; on the contrary, their religion, as far as it still influences them, would rather keep them aloof from inferior castes, than lead them to attempt to raise them by education to their own level. Even if they should theoretically accept the doctrine that 'God has made of one blood all nations of the earth,' and that all are children of one common Father, yet the despotic rule of custom compels them practically to ignore this great truth. There is no desire, then, on the part of the educated Hindoos to elevate the lowest grades; but, on the contrary, I have heard a native gentleman argue strongly against any attempt of the kind being made. These masses are, besides, separated by their language from imbibing any indirect civilising influence, still less any direct knowledge, from the English who dwell in their midst. Though official gentlemen master the vernacular of the district in which they are settled, and the English in general acquire such few words or phrases as may enable them to express their wants, yet there seldom exists a power of really communicating with persons speaking the very various languages existing in the country. Hence the masses remain quite isolated from all influences which might elevate them, and the rapid advance of education among the higher classes has not yet reached the lower. The educational arrangements for India do not appear to have as yet contemplated any effort to educate such children, nor indeed, under existing regulations, can any but very small pecuniary aid be given by Government.

I had been working at home now for twenty years, in practical efforts to raise the very lowest class, and had found these followed by far greater results than I could have anticipated; I had also learnt from experience that a very small seed sown in faith may grow to be a much larger tree than could have been possibly imagined, and that practical demonstration is more convincing than any reasoning. I therefore determined to commence a small school for such children as could not, by reason of their actual condition, be admitted, even if payment were made for them, into the ordinary existing schools. The Brahmin convert, who had studied my schools in Bristol, during his residence in that city, gladly accepted the office of schoolmaster. He considered that this would place him and his young wife in such a position, as not only to maintain himself comfortably, but to benefit his fellow-creatures. The house which had been consecrated in my heart by the

Brahmin prayer-meeting was then to be let, and I gladly secured it for a year. In that house, which proved to be most convenient, both for situation and accommodation, a few little boys were soon gathered, and were quickly brought under the influence of the master. As the school would not at present be opened on Sundays, I there met, on December 9, any natives who liked to join my young friend and myself in a simple service. On every subsequent Sabbath, during my stay in Calcutta, the afternoons were thus spent, and friendly conversations followed our Scripture readings. On one occasion Mr. Sen gave us an evening discourse on, ' The kingdom of God is within you.'

Tuesday, December 25, was a day ever to be remembered. The Court had retired, for the Christmas week, to the delightful country residence of Barrackpore. My arrangements did not permit me to accompany them. The day always recals to the exile the thought of many home joys, and of loving hearts far away. It is therefore a sad day, when strange attempts at merriment, and the substitution of heathen garlands for Christian holly, only remind one how many thousand miles are between us and our home. To draw off the mind from loneliness and painful thoughts, full occupation of a congenial kind had been planned by me for that day; it is especially sacred to me, because it is the anniversary of the union which was celebrated, more than sixty years before, of those honoured parents to whom the writer owes existence. The first event of the day was the baptism of our schoolmaster's two children, with that of his young wife, who, being the child of a Baptist, had not been christened. Familiar English names were blended with those of their country, and it was a touching service—performed by the father's own former preceptor, the Rev. C. Dall, in the library of the Mission School-house. Next was the festival of our school children. We could not give them the beef and plum-pudding which some 400 rescued boys and girls of our schools were then enjoying at Bristol, in their gaily-decorated schoolrooms; but the master provided such dainties as he knew would please them, and a few friends, native and English, assembled to see their enjoyment. Some poor natives also came, and they appeared thoroughly to appreciate the kind intentions which prompted the effort. The boys went through their exercises very creditably, proving that their wildness had been somewhat controlled; they showed a very fair progress in learning during the few weeks that they had been under instruction. A schoolmaster who was present was somewhat sceptical—as are many of greater experience than himself in England—as to the fact of these boys being unable to attend the ordinary schools; but a close enquiry, and observation of them, convinced him that he certainly should not wish to have them among his own scholars; and that even if he did, and free admission were obtained for them, they would not be likely to desire admission there if offered, still less would they seek it voluntarily themselves. Such children require here, as in England, a special school adapted to their wants; they also must be sought from the highways and byways, and induced by friendly influence to come under instruction. Our master was informed, however, that it would be his highest proof of success, to raise his scholars so much as to render them admissible to a higher school. With a view to improve their personal appearance, and to give them a little training to industry, a tailor was to be engaged to give lessons during part of the day.

This little school went on satisfactorily after my departure, and was pronounced a decided success by those who kindly visited it; it also gave satisfaction to the educational inspector. In the spring, however, the master was appointed to a Government post, and my responsibility in it ceased, further than the promised year's rent of the premises. The friends who had visited it were, however, so satisfied with its success, that they determined to continue it, with a 'grant in aid.'

After our children had left the premises, much pleased with their Christmas treat, we found that other visitors had arrived—the Brahmin ladies, with their husbands and a few friends. A short Bengali service in commemoration of the event of the day—the birth of the Saviour—was conducted by our Brahmin master, and then a copy of Rammohun Roy's 'Precepts of Jesus' in Bengali, kindly given for the occasion by the Rev. C. Dall, was presented to each. Friendly conversation followed, and the interchange of Christmas gifts, until it was time to separate; for our friend Dr. Chuckerbutty summoned Mr. Sen, the master, and myself to his hospitable board.

I hoped that the events of that day would leave on the minds of some present a lasting feeling of love to Him whose birth we so lovingly celebrated. I little knew how deep an impression had been made on the heart of one, at least, until the last post brought me the following most gratifying letter from one of those present—a gentleman who had been under Christian teaching, but had not become a professed Christian:—

'Ever since that memorable day, I mean that happy Christmas gathering in the outer verandah of the Ragged School, we have met every Sunday, five or six of us, with occasionally a visitor or two, for the purpose of worshipping "the Father, in spirit and in truth." To induce a devotional feeling, we generally read portions from the Works of Channing, Tayler, Clarke, &c., and after a few moments' social converse we have the service. Last Sunday we read from the New Testament that chapter which begins "Let not your heart be troubled," &c., and from the Old Testament that beautiful and refreshing Psalm, "The Lord is my shepherd, I shall not want," &c., a portion from your little book, and a sermon from Freeman Clarke's latest work, "The hour that cometh and now is." I can very well enter into the spirit of the prayer, a copy of which you have sent in your last. For if India is at all to be regenerated, it must be by the benign influence of Christ's teachings. We don't want speculation, we don't want wordy discussions about creeds and doctrines, but what is most urgently needed is a spirit of Christian philanthropy, brought to bear upon the everyday duties of life. I hope and despair not; for I verily believe that the day will come when every knee shall bend, and every tongue confess to the glory of that Name whose mission is peace on earth and good will towards men!'

During the whole period of my stay in Calcutta, it will be easily imagined that I lost no opportunity, either of becoming acquainted with native families, or of discussing the great subject of Female Education, advance in which entirely depends on obtaining a steady supply of trained female teachers. I had the pleasure of visiting many native ladies who impressed me very favourably. I could not, however, become reconciled to the fact of entering houses, the best rooms of which were not graced by the presence of the ladies who should preside over the household. I should gladly give some pleasing details of many of my visits to the zenanas, were I not withheld by feelings of respect to domestic privacy. It will be sufficient to state, that I was at all times most kindly received, the ladies evidently being gratified by the idea that sufficient interest was felt in them to have led to my journey. Many had made some progress in learning, and a great pleasure was evidently felt in fancy work; various kinds of this, especially worsted work, had been learnt from English ladies. It is to be regretted that their own taste and ingenuity were not more exercised in these matters, the patterns being always English. The desire to improve, even in fancy work, might be turned to good account.

With respect to the Female Normal Training School, a plan for which I took an early opportunity of laying before the advanced party, I found that by these it was earnestly desired, and a memorial to that effect was speedily prepared, and laid before the Lieutenant-Governor. But, on the other hand, a number of those influential gentlemen who are styled 'orthodox Hindoos' are decidedly opposed to anything which, they imagine, may eventually lead to some degree of change in the seclusion of the zenana, or the enlightenment of the female sex. 'I do not believe in Hindooism,' one of them was heard to say, 'nor does any educated man; but my ladies do, and it makes them virtuous and obedient to me. If they were instructed, they would see the folly of it, and I therefore do not wish them to be taught.' Reasoning is evidently useless with persons who avowedly hold such opinions, and it would be futile, as well as wrong, to attempt domestic interference. Such gentlemen do not appear to understand, however, that the proposed preparation of female teachers for these schools, only when managers wish them, can in no way interfere with their own social habits, and it is much to be regretted that they have as yet thrown obstacles in the way of those who earnestly desire improvement for the sake of their own female relations, as well as of the community. Native gentlemen of the advanced party assured me that they could at once find a number of respectable ladies who would gladly be trained as teachers. Others expressed a strong wish that arrangements could be made for their young wives to continue to attend school, by the provision of rooms in the Bethune School for private classes, since the education of native ladies is necessarily very imperfect, owing to the early marriages. It is to be hoped that these gentlemen will never cease their praiseworthy efforts, until they have obtained for the female part of the community all the advantages they require. The subject largely occupies the educated native mind, and has been always a special object of the Bethune Society. At a meeting of this institution, I was requested to give an address on Female Education, combining with this the treatment of criminal children. I had considerable hesitation in doing this, because in England I had been in the habit of reading papers only in the sections of the Social Science Association, and I had now no time for the preparation of any written address. Being, however, urged to give my views on a subject which was indeed my life-work, I ventured to deliver my experience to a meeting of the society.* At the conclusion, the following important statement was made by Baboo Kissory Chand Mittra, a native gentleman of great influence and experience:—

* *Vide* 'Addresses to the Hindoos,' pp. 1–11.

'Miss Carpenter has already brought her influence to bear on the Government for the purpose of establishing a Central Normal Female School. In order to strengthen her hands, a representation urging the necessity of such an institution has been submitted to the Lieutenant-Governor by several Hindoo gentlemen. Exception has been taken to this movement by some persons who profess to believe that trained female teachers to take charge of female schools are not wanted, inasmuch as school instruction is not now practicable. I am not ashamed to avow that I am a party to the memorial to the Government, and my friend on my left (Baboo Keshub Chunder Sen) is another. I have bestowed some thought on the subject, and have had ample opportunities of watching the operations of both school instruction and domestic instruction, and I have no hesitation in declaring my conviction, that the former is an immeasurably superior system to the latter. Those who underrate school instruction and overrate zenana instruction, are grievously mistaken. The zenana system may, in the beginning, be necessary in many cases—I do not depreciate it, I rejoice in its intention—but I can advocate it only as a tentative and a transitory measure, not as a finality and an ultimatum. It is dull and lifeless, whereas the other is instinct with life and animation. Fancy, sir, a governess teaching one or two girls within the four walls of a dark and perhaps ill-ventilated room! Why, it is very dull work, and both the teacher and the taught participate in the dulness. They cannot resist, so to speak, catching the torpidity of the thing. The efficiency of school instruction depends, on the other hand, on the living contact of spirit with spirit. It is to be ascribed to the sympathy of numbers, which has an electric effect, leading to the formation and development of right impressions and feelings, breaking up the old ground, and letting in new light. But, sir, whatever system may be best adapted to promote the enlightenment of our females, I earnestly beg my educated fellow-countrymen to remember that the social and mental status held by the women of a country is the true test of its civilisation. I would fervently impress on them the truth of what Tennyson has said—

> The woman's cause is man's—they rise or sink
> Together, dwarfed or godlike, bond or free.

Impressed with this view, I regard the mission which has brought out Miss Carpenter here as one of the noblest—one the fulfilment of which is fraught with results of the last importance to our country. In the interests of civilisation and humanity she should be honoured.'

The following expressions of opinion, inscribed in my book, is a brief but true record of what was frequently and strongly expressed to me by many:—

'Dear Madam,—Your visit to this great country, at a time when your valuable services are most needed here, seems to me to be providential, and I heartily thank God for it. The Hindoo female mind is just awaking from the deathlike sleep of ages, and has already shown in many quarters remarkable eagerness to receive the blessings of enlightenment. The means hitherto employed to promote native female education do not appear to me to meet all existing wants, and are not likely to achieve a desirable amount of success. The one thing needed, under present circumstanes, is a normal school for training up governesses for girls' schools, and also for the *zenana*. I feel highly gratified, therefore, that you have at once directed your attention and energies towards the removal of this want. May God bless your efforts, and may you become an humble instrument in His hands of promoting the true welfare—intellectual, social, and moral—of my unfortunate countrywomen!

'Keshub Chunder Sen.'

Calcutta, Dec. 21, 1866.

'To promote female education in Bengal we must have *good* books and *good* teachers. The idea of educating females by pundits must be abandoned. I cordially subscribe to Miss Carpenter's sentiment that trained females must educate the females, and I should say that any education of a superficial nature is of little use—it is the *soul* which must be educated and elevated.

'Peary Chand Mittra.'

Dec. 21, 1866.

Female education was not, however, the only subject which closely occupied my attention. In my intercourse with the native community, indeed, that was of course the one absorbing topic. It had long engaged the anxious attention of the more advanced among them everywhere: pamphlets had been written, discussions held, the puplic press had taken up the question, and, better still, many had steadily worked and made pecuniary sacrifices to promote the welfare of the weaker sex, who could not help themselves. All that was now required was to direct the movement into a channel which would secure its permanence and efficient working.

To subjects, however, which do not directly concern the interest of the educated portion of the native community, no attention appears to have been paid by them. English official gentlemen are usually so closely engaged in their own duties that they have no time or strength for anything which does not immediately concern them. One of these subjects was prison discipline, the condition of the jails, and the want of reformatories. How any attention could be excited to these and other social questions which have been referred to in the course of the narrative, was a perplexing matter of consideration. It was, then, with great satisfaction, that I learnt from the Rev. Mr. Long that he had been endeavouring to excite attention to these and other topics, and had even endeavoured to awaken attention to them among the natives by instituting discussion societies, both in Calcutta and in the Mofussil. Having become acquainted with the proceedings of our Social Science Association in England, he was anxious that such an agency should be established in Calcutta. This appeared a very desirable though almost a hopeless undertaking; for there are not in India, as in England, a number of gentlemen of both influence and leisure, who would make it no less a duty than a pleasure to promote the objects of such an institution, by taking the labouring oar in the management. Mr. Long was not, however, to be easily daunted by difficulties. Many highly intelligent and influential native gentlemen warmly seconded the idea, and promised to exert themselves in such an association, if some English gentlemen of position and influence would take the lead. The number of those interested rapidly increased, until the dozen English and native gentlemen who were to meet in the Asiatic Society's rooms to consider the matter, seemed likely to amount to fifty or more. His Excellency the Governor-General, with Lady Lawrence, and some other ladies, kindly attended; the Lieutenant-Governor presided, and the result of the meeting was, that a provisional committee was formed, to consider the practicability of forming a branch society, to be affiliated to the National Social Science Association of Great Britain.* This committee met at my rooms at Government House, and a sub-committee was formed, who were requested to draft a scheme for the constitution and organisation of the proposed society. The importance of this movement was becoming very apparent. It now appeared to me that Bengal required no support from a parent society, but was quite capable of standing alone. When, by request, I met the sub-committee at Metcalfe Hall, I was happy to find that this was also their view; and before leaving Calcutta, I had the great pleasure of being present when the provisional committee again met at my rooms, and a constitution was finally adopted. These proceedings were afterwards confirmed at a general meeting of the members at Metcalfe Hall, on January 22, 1867, at which the Lieutenant-Governor of Bengal presided.

The first session of the Society has been completed, and the volume of 'Transactions,' with the address of the President—the Hon. Mr. Justice Phear—has reached us now, in October. The constitution and working of the society may, then, be regarded as established. The papers are chiefly by native gentlemen, and give promise of great utility as well as interest. The cordial co-operation of Englishmen and Hindoos in the promotion of the social progress of India cannot but be attended with high results.

It will not be supposed that these grave subjects occupied the whole of my time at Government House. Cares of state so absorbed his Excellency that he

* *Vide* 'Addresses to the Hindoos,' pp. 19-24.

could rarely withdraw himself from them; but at the hours of meals there were constantly visitors, not only from the Court and official circles, but from every part of the world. Sometimes an American captain and officers received his hospitality; at others, an exiled French prince, with his suite. The Bishop of Bombay and his lady were at one time visitors—at another an English admiral. There was a constant succession of visitors, all receiving a cordial welcome from the Viceroy.

The drawing-room, which opened the festivities of the season, was an occasion of special interest. Native gentlemen, who have previously paid their respects to his Excellency at the levée, are privileged to attend, and many were expected. No native lady had, of course, been seen on such an occasion, but there was one who greatly desired to appear. Mr. Satyendra Nath Tagore was not yet sufficiently recovered to attend, as his position in the Civil Service would entitle him to do, but he desired that his lady should take the position to which she was also entitled. The lady of Mr. Justice Phear, who is always ready to show her sympathy with the native community, offered to present her in due form to Lady Lawrence; and the young lady went through the somewhat trying ordeal with great self-possession. With much good taste, she had retained the graceful features of the Hindoo dress, while she adopted only such portions of English costume as were essential to a public appearance. Her demeanour and appearance were the objects of much admiration, and the event was considered an important one in social progress. The assemblage was altogether unique of its kind. Some native princes were there in gorgeous attire; Keshub Chunder Sen, in his simple semi-clerical-looking dress. The learned professor Bannerjee, a Christian convert, introduced me to another native minister, who had married an English lady, and was there with her. There was a great variety of native costume, mingled with the court-dress of official gentlemen, and ladies in their gayest attire. The open verandah at the end of the great hall made the suite of rooms pleasantly cool, and there was no inconvenient crowding. Best of all, the truly kind and courteous demeanour of the Viceroy himself diffused an agreeable ease among the assembly, and made me almost fancy myself in one of the delightful soirées of the Social Science Association. This, Sir John Lawrence politely said, he considered a very great compliment on my part, but modestly disclaimed the large share of the pleasure of the entertainment, which everyone felt was due to his Excellency himself.

Many other matters of much interest arose from my sojourn at Government House, but space forbids further details respecting them. The visits I paid to the different suburbs of Calcutta presented so many distinct features that they cannot be passed by, and an account of these must be reserved for a separate chapter.

CHAPTER VI.

THE SUBURBS OF CALCUTTA.

BISHOP'S COLLEGE—HOWRAH—BHOWANIPORE—SERAMPORE—KONNEGUR—OOTERPARRAH—BURRANAGORE—RANAGHAT—KISHNAGHUR.

My first suburban visit was to Bishop's College, on Monday, Dec. 3. This splendid institution is on the other side of the Ganges, a few miles from the city; and I went there for a few days at the kind invitation of Mr. and Mrs. Woodrow, the former being the inspector of schools for the district.

A pleasant drive, through a rural wooded district, was an agreeable change after the confinement of the city, where custom forbade a lady to take a walk even to a short distance from her home. Crossing the grand and beautiful river had always a great charm for me, even though it had to be preceded and followed by a somewhat unpleasant transit over the muddy banks, which had to be effected by being carried in a unique way to and from the boat. It was delightful to find myself again, for the first time since my arrival in India, in what might be really called country, and in the midst of friends who have a warm and practical interest in the education of the native community. My hostess, indeed, takes a considerable share in zenana-visiting, and in other institutions connected with female improvement. My attention was particularly drawn by another lady whom I met there, and who is engaged in the same good work, to the miserable condition of the poor East Indians or Eurasians, as they have been called, who exist in large numbers in Calcutta. As these are half-castes and profess Christianity, they do not fall within the sphere of missionary labour; and since no special agencies are directed towards them, they remain in a helpless state, which they cannot hope to improve. I had not myself an opportunity of becoming personally acquainted with their condition; but the little I accidentally saw, both in Madras and in Calcutta, led me fully to believe in the correctness of the general impression, that they inherit many of the faults of the two races from which they spring, and that they have the sympathy of neither. Their position is one deserving of much commiseration, and it is to be hoped that some of the many Christian efforts which are made in these two cities will be directed towards them. It is not actual charity they so much require, as kind sympathy, and a judicious stimulus to exertion. The Rev. Mr. Bannerjee is a professor of the College, and with him I had much pleasure in making acquaintance. The students I did not see, as they were at Calcutta passing through the university examination. The education given in this institution is of a very high character, the need being strongly felt, by those who manage it, of giving candidates for the ministry such mental training as may make them, at any rate, equal the educational position attained by the native community. The library, staff, building, and general arrangements are calculated thus to train a large number of young men for the ministry. But, unfortunately, the institution does not appear to meet a generally existing want. There are not at present above twenty students, of whom most are East Indians, with one German. I could not but feel that the simpler and more domestic institution at Madras, was better calculated to prepare native Christian pastors for the people.

The great object of attraction in the neighbourhood of Bishop's College is the Horticultural Garden, which is an extensive and beautiful spot, filled with interesting tropical plants and trees. As it is situated along the river, it was the scene of terrible devastations at the time of the dreadful cyclone, which has left its traces far and wide in the province. One large and unique tree was entirely destroyed, as well as many smaller ones, and most were disfigured by the loss of some of their finest branches. Such was the case with two magnificent banyan-trees—the glory of the garden, —whose tall heads had succumbed to the fury of the hurricane. As I saw them, however, they were marvellous specimens of that remarkable tree, such as I had not before seen in India. When the banyan is within reach of animals, or in public places, as in the fine grove at Ahmedabad, the long fibres sent down by the branches become eaten or destroyed before they can take root in the ground; hence it is not common to meet with these trees of such extent as we read of, or see figured in books of travels. These, however, had been carefully protected, so as to shoot forth freely and to have their natural growth. That, indeed, had been aided by the careful gardener, who had frequently placed a hollow split bamboo for the root to drop through, that it may eventually become a fine straight stem, the parent of a large progeny of young trees. The ground being carefully kept clear and free from other vegetation, there was no cause to dread snakes or other reptiles; and we could wander at leisure among the varied trunks, which descended from some gigantic branchlike pillars supporting it, and then sprang out in a fresh direction, remaining as the grand parent of a new family group. One might write a long history of that old banyan-tree, illustrated with a number of picturesque engravings. I was told, however, that even this yields in extent and size to some that are met with in the district. Another object of great interest was a tree, believed to be identical with the fossil trunks found in the coal-measures. The grass was very wet with heavy dew in our early morning ramble, but a visit to such a rarity was indispensable. The cinchona or Peruvian-bark plants, which are very carefully cultivated here, are the subject of anxious speculation, as the production of so valuable a medicine as quinine in India will be very important. The little buds appeared very healthy, and gave promise of success.

I was still destined to be disappointed in flowers. The gardener informed me that this was the wrong time to expect them; they would not come out till February. Even that month did not satisfy my expectations of the floral riches of the country, and I gradually came to the conclusion that the want of care and interest in gardening makes it almost inferior in this respect to our ungenial climate.

Little did I imagine, while quietly enjoying this beautiful spot, to what a different scene it would ere long be witness, and what a catastrophe would shortly follow! On New Year's Day, a grand fête was held at the Horticultural Gardens, to which thousands crowded by steamers from Calcutta. The scene was animating, and his Excellency the Viceroy showed his sympathy with the general rejoicing by his presence there.

He returned by land—the bulk of the visitors were returning by water. A steamer was greatly overcrowded, and it struck against a sunken vessel, which had long been remaining in the river. With due presence of mind, all the passengers might have been saved, as the water was there very shallow; but those whose duty it was to direct did not appear in a condition to do so, and were quite powerless. A cry of fire was raised, and the passengers became quite frantic, many throwing themselves overboard in wild despair. For some time the scene was inconceivably frightful. Some gentlemen endeavoured to restore such order as might have saved life, but in vain. Even when the vessel began to sink, experienced persons knew that, even when it reached the bottom, those on deck might still keep above water. Many were rescued by boats, but numbers, in the confusion, sank to rise no more. To many families the year thus opened in deep sorrow. The scenes of distress may be imagined, as bodies were brought to shore of those who had gone forth that morning full of joy and hope. The loss of some forty or fifty lives at least was the more distressing, as it was generally believed to be the result of carelessness that the vessel struck, and to the want of proper control that the disorder ensued which caused the fatal termination of a day's pleasure.

Before leaving Bishop's College, my friend the Inspector took me a pleasant morning drive, through pretty country scenery, to visit a Hindoo boys' school. The entrance was not inviting, everything having a dilapidated air. We were surprised, at 11 A.M., to find the master not arrived, and the scholars amusing themselves. The house was not very airy, or well adapted for its purpose, in size or good order; and it was a matter of regret that boys so intelligent and docile as these appeared to be should not have greater advantages afforded them. A number of young boys were crowded into a separate bungalow, under the care of a master. The poor little fellows looked very dull, as they were poring over the perplexing mysteries of Bengali grammar, which appeared to be too abstruse for their juvenile capacities. I much wished that they could have been sent to one of our good infant-schools, and treated to an active game of romps! Children whose physical powers are so cramped, as they necessarily are in such schools as these, cannot grow up hardy youths or strong men.

HOWRAH.

We paid a visit to Howrah on our way back to the city, and there saw a school which presented a striking contrast to that which we had just visited. This was a large Government school, in fine buildings, with abundant room and excellent masters, all in perfect order. The school seemed much valued, as it was well frequented. Howrah is situated on the west bank of the River Hooghly, opposite Calcutta, and contains a vast heathen population, which may be fairly estimated at 70,000 souls, within three miles of the church. Here is situated the Calcutta terminus of the great East Indian Railway, which is now open for traffic to the distance of nearly 1,000 miles, and reaches almost to Delhi. Here are found nearly all the docks, in which the numerous ships in the port are received and repaired; and here, too, are several other large industrial establishments—such as ironfoundries, flour-mills, rope manufactories, distilleries, cotton screws, coal depôts, and salt warehouses, in addition to the extensive workshops for the erection of railway locomotive engines and carriages—which all give employment to an immense number of native artisans and workmen. Howrah has risen to importance through the traffic brought by the railway. The families of the officials employed in it are not neglected, and there is an excellent school for the children, which I visited with the Inspector. It was striking to observe that the girls in this school appeared of a superior grade to those whose parents would be of the same rank in England. They were being well taught, and had an air of refinement. The clergyman of this place (the Rev. F. Spencer) is active in his efforts for the social improvement of the inhabitants, and has instituted a 'Young Men's Debating Society,' where, from time to time, lectures and readings are given to the young Hindoos, and those of the English inhabitants who may like to be present. In the preceding August, the public papers gave an account of a lecture on Education in Bengal, given in St. Thomas's Schoolroom, by the Rev. Professor R. M. Bannerjee. 'At its termination,' the report says, 'a unanimous vote of thanks was presented to the learned professor by the Rev. Chairman; and the hearty applause which followed must have assured him, in spite of the difference of opinion expressed in the brief discussion which followed, how highly the audience appreciated his kindness in delivering the lecture.' Such gatherings on a common ground, without allowing difference of opinion to interfere with kindly feeling, must greatly tend to bind together in harmony the different races whom circumstances have thus brought together to form one community.

Having received a pressing invitation from the native secretary of the Howrah Young Men's Debating

Society, seconded by the chaplain, to give them my views on female education, I consented to cross the river for the purpose. I did so the more willingly, as an English gentleman from the Treasury had promised on the same evening (December 26) to give them some readings from Tennyson and other English poets. He kindly offered me his escort; and, as he was well acquainted with the locality, I was not afraid to cross the broad river by starlight. Yet it was a strange feeling to find myself on the surface of that mighty stream, little raised by the small ferry-boat above the level of the water, which reflected the many lights of the city of Calcutta, of world-wide renown! Vessels filled with many strange figures were everywhere around; the accents of foreign tongues were those that chiefly met the ear; but there was a home-feeling in the clear sense of an all-pervading, protecting Presence near, and I could yield myself to the marvellous beauty of the scene. The muddy banks ascended, we soon reached our destination, and were welcomed by the chaplain to a large well-filled hall. About half the audience were English, the ladies of course taking their proper place in such an assemblage. At first I thought that, among the native part of the audience, I saw several of the gentler portion of society. This was indeed an unexpected pleasure, and I began silently to moralise on the force of example which had conquered even Hindoo custom. I was, however, doomed to disappointment, as I soon perceived that those whom, from their style of dress, I had supposed to be women, were really persons of the other sex, closely wrapped in shawls, which enveloped their heads, in order to protect themselves from what is here considered cold weather! The readings were admirably given, with great animation and expression, but they failed to elicit much apparent interest in the native part of the audience. Even the 'May Queen' did not touch them. This surprised me, having supposed the Hindoos to be not only sensitive in feeling and fond of poetry, but sufficiently acquainted with our language to listen to it with as much facility as to their own. It soon occurred to me, however, that all the customs and emotions which are so exquisitely delineated in that touching piece, must be not only foreign to such an audience, but absolutely incomprehensible to them. May is not a 'charming month' where every one is suffering from intense heat, and anxiously anticipating the rains; no such joyous festival among innocent boys and girls as 'crowning the Queen of the May' could possibly be conceived by any one who has not been in England, or who has not become thoroughly familiar with its rural customs. The gradual change in the sweet little sufferer's feelings—the softening and purifying of her earthly affections—the gleam of glory from the other world hallowing this, and rendering its beauty more entrancing ere it disappears—all this cannot be comprehended by the Hindoo mind in its present social and religious condition; and if in such a poem any meaning is perceived, it must be of a vague mysterious nature, which they cannot grasp, and which only bewilders. Such thoughts brought into vivid contrast in my mind the condition of woman in England and in India, and her painful seclusion in this country from sharing the intellectual and social happiness of those bound to her by the closest family ties. I addressed my audience, therefore, in terms intended to awaken them to a sense of the needs of her intellectual life, and of the manner in which these should be supplied.*

BHOWANIPORE.

My visit to this extensive suburb was short, but deserves a record. Here is a 'Christian village,' as it is termed, existing as a record of missionary zeal in the midst of heathenism. The handsome large chapel and schoolroom are in constant use to benefit the surrounding population. I was invited here to meet a number of native Christians, with the families of the missionaries, in friendy socal intercourse; this was indeed most interesting, when we reflected on the amazing change which had been made in the lives of those who had thus abandoned heathenism. One of these was the minister whom I saw at the drawing-room, who appeared to be overtasking his strength in his zeal to help on his brethren. Only on one other occasion, and that in an evening party at Calcutta, at the house of the cathedral missionary (himself a Hindoo), had I an opportunity of associating with native converts. On this second occasion, one English gentleman alone, and myself, represented our country, and there were a few Brahmos; otherwise all were native converts, some of them gentlemen of education and position, with the ladies of their families. I heard very great regret expressed, then and at other times, that though native gentlemen are brought, by business connection and in educational institutions, into contact with Europeans, and thus acquire their manners and modes of thought, yet that the ladies of the family have not similar advantages; they have not those opportunities of friendly intercourse with our countrywomen which is peculiarly

* *Vide* 'Addresses,' pp. 30-35.

important to the younger members of it. The complaint is made, and doubtless with just cause, that efforts to proselytise direct the attention of English ladies to non-Christians, while those who have been converted do not share the same friendly sympathy, or receive the privilege of that social intercourse which would be to them of the greatest advantage. Hence these Christian Hindoo ladies, as well in general as the East Indians, have no opportunity afforded them of becoming suitable companions for cultivated and refined English ladies. So much work has to be done by our countrywomen in India, who desire to raise their Eastern sisters, that this important branch of it has probably hitherto escaped their notice. This work is not a difficult one, and only requires a sympathising spirit.

We must return from this digression to the evening at Bhowanipore. Many of the native non-Christian inhabitants of this suburb were much interested in the cause of female education, and regretted that the distance of the Bethune School prevented them from sending their daughters there. They assembled in the Mission Schoolroom to hear something on the subject, and a distinguished native gentleman presided, a judge in the High Court. It was my great endeavour, on this and on other occasions, to make it clearly understood that education does not mean simply learning to read and write, but the development of all the faculties graciously bestowed on us by the Creator, and the cultivation of the heart as well as the mind. I showed them that the customary inactive life of Hindoo women rendered it particularly desirable that they should have early as much physical development as possible, and that especially a garden should always be attached to a school. In reply to the ordinary plea of great poverty, and the need of Government help in everything, I assured them of my belief that they had ample means to do all they wish themselves, and that the desire only was wanting for the education of their daughters. The chairman stated his conviction that the ignorance and superstition of the female part of the family is a great drain on the pecuniary resources of the head of it. Hindoos are willing to educate their sons, because money so spent is regarded as an investment of capital; he had known an instance in which a man, whose income did not exceed 100 rupees per annum, spent 30 rupees in the education of his sons, for this reason. This was considered by those present far from being an unusual case. They all seemed at the time anxious to begin a school. Whether they have carried their wishes into effect I have not heard.

There is a kind of agency much required in this and other suburbs, which does not fall within the scope of the missionaries, and which cannot be accomplished by the natives unaided. There are not here, as in England, places of instruction and entertainment, where young men can go and spend an evening; or even public libraries, to afford them recreation at home. My native friend, who had commenced the little Sunday service above alluded to, resides at Bhowanipore, and felt most strongly the need of providing some such place of meeting as our Athenæums and Working Men's Clubs, adapted to the requirements of the Hindoos. Through the want of such institutions, or even a good popular library, I have been informed that great immorality prevails among young men engaged in offices after their day's work is over. Missionaries to whom the subject has been mentioned, all state that their already full engagements prevent them from undertaking what is not strictly a part of their work, being secular. The same feeling is probably universal. This is, indeed, a kind of work which properly falls within the province of the laity, though nothing can be foreign to religion which is calculated to advance social progress. The want being known, many gentlemen might supply it, even if closely engaged in business, by a little friendly sympathy or advice, or by gifts of books, or other means of intellectual improvement, which they could well supply. The mention in these pages of so simple a means of benefiting the rising generation of our Hindoo fellow-subjects, may lead some to proffer their help where needed; and the humble worker at Bhowanipore may thus be the means of commencing a movement very important to his countrymen.

SERAMPORE.

This is a very celebrated spot in the history of missionary enterprise. The name of Dr. Carey, one of the founders of the Baptist College in that place, will ever be remembered in that part of the world, not only for his piety and zeal, but for his scientific attainments. It was then with much pleasure that I accepted a kind invitation from the editor of the 'Friend of India,' and his lady, to pay them a visit. A railway ride of about an hour ought to have brought us to our journey's end; but an accident (not a very unusual occurrence in these parts) detained us so long on the road, that our arrival by this train was nearly given up. Serampore is not more than a village, beside the English residences and the college. There are some rich zemindars in the neighbourhood, but, these not being enterprising or friendly to progress, the buildings around are generally in a dilapidated condition: the country then does not lose the charms of wild nature by being traversed by well-made roads, or divided into fields by well-trimmed hedgerows. As our time was not limited, a ride through it in a somewhat primitive style was very pleasant. A little girls' school in an open bungalow is under my hostess's kind supervision; many of the girls looked intelligent, but it was sad to observe the significant red spot on the foreheads of the little creatures six or seven years old, and to know that the poor children were considered as married, and would shortly be removed from their homes, and placed in the zenana of their husbands' family! We saw another little girls' school under the patronage of a rich zemindar, but he did not honour us with his presence on the occasion. Probably, as he was far from being of the party of progress, he did not wish to encounter those who might be in favour of innovations which he did not desire. Serampore is indeed situated in the midst of a very unenlightened population. We used to suppose that the car of Juggernaut was a thing of the past. Here, however, I actually beheld it in all its native clumsy hideousness—a dreadful reality! On certain festivals the idol is conveyed in this car to visit his sister, in the midst of the greatest excitement of all the surrounding population; not many years ago, a man, wearied of life, actually threw himself under the ponderous wheels, and was crushed to death! Such an example is very contagious among these people, and it is found necessary to set the police on guard, at these festivals, in order to prevent similar catastrophes. It was a marvellous contrast to visit a little country church in the neighbourhood, very sacred from many old associations, and in a quiet rural spot.

A sunset walk on the banks of the Ganges was a

refreshment to the spirit. Only a tropical region can display such gorgeous tints, during the very short time before darkness closes in; these, reflected in the calm broad stream, are inexpressibly beautiful. The effect must be greatly heightened when the court is at Barrackpore, on the opposite side, and the music of the band reaches Serampore, softened by distance.

The next morning all the relics in the college were duly examined, and with great intrest; time, however, forbade me to linger in this honoured building as long as I should have desired. A venerable pundit paid me a visit, who was regarded as a wonder, having reached an age which in this country is seldom attained— seventy-four years. He inscribed some Sanscrit in my book, of which the following is a translation—

'Of all things in the world, education is the best, for no thief can steal it away. Though it has no fixed value, yet it is very valuable, because it cannot be spoiled by rust. Therefore nothing in the world is as good as education. A man who is not blessed with education is very like a beast. For the above-mentioned reasons education is very necessary for men, women, and children, irrespective of caste or creed.—Written by a Pundit of the College of Fort William, established by Lord Wellesley, and afterwards by Dr. Carey.'

The sentiment expressed by this aged pundit is more liberal than is usual to Hindoos of his generation.

KONNEGUR.

On my return I had been requested to visit the girls' school of the little town of Konnegur. It was evidently the object of much interest and care on the part of the native gentlemen of the neighbourhood, and did great credit to them, as well as to the young scholars, in the proficiency they had made. Then one of these gentlemen invited me to visit his family, which I did with pleasure. His was a large house, as usual built round a courtyard, and many of his friends were assembled there. The master of the house introduced me to the ladies of his household, who here occupied cheerful apartments, with access to a pleasant garden. It was an interesting family group, and the lady at the head of it is very intelligent and kind-hearted. She appeared to have infused those qualities into her daughters and granddaughters, in the latter of whom I recognised some of the most advanced scholars in the girls' school. The father showed me, with parental pride, in a Bengali ladies' journal, some poetry composed by one of his daughters, and he evidently took a warm interest in their improvement. I was much gratified by taking some refreshment provided for me in this pleasant room—those present themselves sharing it with me. 'You do not find zenanas so gloomy and disagreeable as is generally supposed?' asked my host. 'This indeed is not so,' I replied, 'but I fear there are not many like it.' The great secret of the advanced state of the ladies of this family is, that the head of it has completely thrown off idolatry and superstition; and instead of a Brahmin being retained, in the house or elsewhere, to direct the religious ceremonials of the household, and bind them down to the superstitions of bygone ages, this gentleman leads family worship himself. He showed me a Poojah hall, dedicated to the One True God, and every morning he conducts a simple religious service with his family. They were glad to learn that I could thus sympathise with them, as far as they went. Some of the Brahmo missionaries come here at times, and hold service, in his hall, for such as choose to attend; these, however, are not many.

The assembled friends had inscribed, during my absence in the zenana, an expression of their satisfaction with my visit to the school, and their approval of my suggestions. My host added the following:

'My wife is very anxious that cultivated English mistresses should come from England to teach the females of this country, and she approves of the plan of establishing a Female Normal School in Calcutta.'

(Signed) W. CHUNDER DEB.
December 20, 1866.

My return to Government House was not quite as easy and agreeable as might have been expected. I have heard, in some distant countries, of a railway accident being common on alternate days; I therefore thought that it was fair to expect none to-day, as we had had an accident on the preceding morning. I was, however, too sanguine. Being now quite alone, one of my native friends accompanied me to the station, to see me safely off. No train had arrived—it had broken down at a considerable distance. At these stations there is rarely any accommodation for ladies, and I was obliged to sit under a shed as a protection from the sun for about two hours, waiting for the arrival of another train. It was a strange feeling to be thus isolated; but I was beginning to feel quite at home with the natives, though I could not speak their language.

It was a matter of regret to me to learn that I had been expected that day at Rishrat, a village two miles from Serampore, and that considerable disappointment had been felt at my non-appearance by the managing commitee of the girls' school there. This was inevitable, as I had received no invitation, and was not aware of the existence of the place! It is, however, an interesting fact, that so many schools are springing up for the instruction of young girls, and that native gentlemen are taking so much interest in their management. 'This school,' the secretary writes, 'is of little more than three years' standing, during which period some of the girls were taught as far as Sanscrit, and double rule-of-three in arithmetic.' This is remarkable progress.

Another school I also much regretted not being able to visit—at Kurdah, about nine miles north of Calcutta. It consists of four separate schools—'one, the secretary writes, 'for boys who desire to learn both English and Sanscrit; a second for peasants of our country, whose characteristic features (as you will learn after a short stay in the land) are ignorance and superstition; a third for those who wish to learn Bengali exclusively; and, lastly, one for those who have attracted the attention of your compassionate heart, and upon whose welfare depends the welfare of their country.' The writer of this deserves especial sympathy, as his is the only case I met with in which there is a distinct recognition of the duty of attempting to raise the lower classes, by giving them education. May the schools at Kurdah prosper, under the management of their benevolent secretary! 'I have established them,' he writes, 'by my humble and stinted efforts, and—what is far more essential in such matters—the blessing of Him who mysteriously and permanently presides about and above us.

OOTERPARRAH.

On the morning of December 14, I set off to visit the institutions connected with the Hitokorry Shova, or Benevolent Society of Ooterparrah. Our party consisted of Mr. Atkinson, the Director of Public Education, Mr. Woodrow the Inspector, and the celebrated pundit, Isher Chunder Vidyasager. Ooterparrah is a native town a few miles above Barrackpore, on the Hooghly; and was but a small place when, in days long past, the Duke of Wellington (then Sir Arthur Wellesley) and the late Lord Combermere visited the spot. 'The heroes of Waterloo and Bhurtpore,' we are informed by a native journal, 'were delighted to see the infant village of Ooterparrah, and accepted milk and plantain, the simplest articles of a simple luncheon, offered them by their honest host, Baboo Ram Hurry Roy Chowdry. The moral effect of these visits was not lost upon the ancestors of the existing inhabitants of Ooterparrah, and the present prosperous state of the town may be attributed to the edifying and healthy example of men who were honoured by military men and civilians illustrious for their wisdom and probity.' The present very remarkable condition of this town is chiefly due to the enlightened munificence of two rich zemindars, Baboos Joy Kissen and Raj Kissen Mookerjee, who have for several years been directing their energies to the establishment of various institutions calculated to raise the native community. In December 1865, his Excellency the Governor-General paid a visit to this town, accompanied by Lady Lawrence, and several other ladies and gentlemen. This visit excited the greatest enthusiasm in the town and neighbourhood. Every possible mark of respect was shown him; and, though the announcement of the visit was made only the day before, two most appropriate addresses were presented to him. 'The Viceroy's replies to them, as well as his other remarks on the state of the town, were remarkable,' says the native journal, 'for their sententious brevity, and for the uncommon condescension which was testified in almost his every word.' 'The effect of this visit,' says the 'Bengali,' 'will long survive. Already Baboo Joy Kissen Mookerjee stands pledged to Sir John to found an agricultural school, on the plan advocated in his well-known letter to Government. The Baboo is prepared to lay out 30,000 rupees for that object; and the money cannot be more usefully or reproductively, as regards the country, spent. A vivifying spirit of emulation will be infused into the surrounding districts, by a condescension which has unequivocally proved, that if any town or village be ambitious of attracting the applause of the representative of the Majesty of Great Britain in India, who is greater than even the Emperor of Delhi was in his palmiest day of glory, it must first deserve, by the same means by which Ooterparrah has been reclaimed from a mud village into a smiling garden, the splendid honour.'

These anticipations were not disappointed. In a pamphlet published afterwards on the subject, we find the following statement, which shows how gratefully kind sympathy is received by the Hindoos, and how great a stimulus is imparted by it:—'The moral effect of Sir John's visit upon the town itself has been so great, that a remarkable quickness in its growth is already perceptible. All classes have felt the vivifying influence of the inquiry and interest of the man first in the realm, and are striving to exhibit and put forth higher energies against the next viceregal visit, whenever that may be. An honest pride in the appearance of the town, both physical and moral, has been infused into every householder; and if patriotism means such a condition of the public mind in any place, it may be confidently asserted that it is a virtue, the value whereof is now practically appreciated in Ooterparrah, and is undergoing a speedy development in it.'

The gentlemen who are carrying on the good work in Ooterparrah are Brahmos, and it is observable that an open relinquishment of idolatry appears, in all cases, to be the first step towards enlightened benevolence; in fact, I may venture to assert that, except in the relief of the hungry and starving, I have never found this virtue manifest itself practically among the Hindoos, unless where idolatry was abandoned. The recent dreadful Orissa famine proves that native liberality may then be relied on.

The Hitokorry Shova (or Sabha), a benevolent institution whose operations we were invited to inspect, was founded in April 1864. Its intention is thus described in the first Report: 'The great objects of the Hitokorry Shova are to educate the poor, to help the needy, to clothe the naked, to give medicines to the indigent sick, to support poor widows and orphans, to promote the cause of temperance as a branch of the Bengal Temperance Society, and to ameliorate the social, moral, and intellectual condition of the members themselves, and of their fellow-inhabitants of Ooterparrah and its vicinity.'

The efforts of the society have been chiefly directed to female education, which especially required their attention; and in the promotion of this, great zeal has been displayed by a body of young men interested in the training of their sisters and daughters. 'They have laid,' the last Report states, 'the foundation of the system of female education, upon which, it is hoped, Government would raise the superstructure. It is time for the State to give its utmost attention to the education of girls—to offer them as much encouragement as is bestowed upon their more fortunate brethren.'

Attention to the poor and sick has continued to be a prominent object of the society. The literary branch has made efforts for the improvement of the moral and intellectual condition of the members themselves, and of the population generally, and lectures have been delivered to the society by English gentlemen as well as by natives.

The following reasons for publication, given in the preface to the Report published in the present year, strikingly show the difficulties under which the supporters of this society labour:—' Experience has taught the Hitokorry Sabha to bring to light at once even its most trivial proceeding, lest Bengal darkness, which has eternally swallowed up many a useful institution, should destroy the Sabha also. The fear of exposure at the bar of public opinion may be one of the considerations that actuate the originators of societies that have seen the light to improve gradually their vital powers; but such is not the case with those who, having nursed in secret the objects of their care, are little troubled about their fate, and apprehend reproaches at their dissolution neither from their own hearts, nor from the voice of public opinion.'

We first proceeded to the girls' school, where we found the secretary of the society—Baboo Peary Mohun Bannerjee—with its most distinguished supporters. The young ladies looked bright and intelligent, and we went from class to class, which was being examined by the pundit. All the girls answered well. A considerable stimulus is given by a general examination of all the schools affiliated to the Hitokorry Shova, in the month of March every year. Scholarships of one rupee and two rupees per month are awarded: this continues for one year, on condition that the holder prosecutes her studies during that time. The examinations are in writing, and the answers indicate good mental powers and considerable proficiency.

Young ladies who are obliged to leave the school on account of marriage, are permitted to continue their studies in the zenana, and to hold scholarships. A native convert female teacher, who is employed in the school, visits them at their homes, and conducts the necessary examinations. Specimens of good needlework were shown to us; and here, as in many other schools, I was strongly impressed with the great capabilities of Hindoo girls, and with regret that these have no adequate means of development. The younger classes here, as elsewhere, suffered from the want of proper teachers.

My expectations were highly raised by my friend the Inspector respecting my next visit, which was to the library; the reality, however, greatly exceeded my anticipations. A large and commodious building, of which two spacious rooms were filled with a complete and well-chosen library at the entire cost of one individual—a native gentleman—was indeed a subject of admiration. There were also suites of pleasant airy rooms, looking out on a garden and the river, which were intended for social entertainments or club-rooms. These were not, however, yet fully occupied; their existence will doubtless in future be a stimulus to the young men of the town to engage in intellectual recreations, for which they are so well adapted. An account of this remarkable institution, kindly drawn up for me by the librarian, Baboo Koilas Chunder Mookerjee, will be interesting to the reader:—

THE SUBURBS OF CALCUTTA. 245

'Some twenty years ago, Baboo Joy Kissen Mookerjee, having got an English school and dispensary endowed in the town of Ooterparrah, perceived the growing want of a library, with a reading-room attached to it, for the benefit of his countrymen. In order to supply this desideratum, the Baboo applied to Government, through the Commissioner of Revenue, Burdwan Division, to establish one on similar terms with those of the English school and the dispensary; but not succeeding in his attempts, he undertook the work without any extraneous aid from the State. With this view, he caused a suitable building to be constructed upon the river-bank, at a cost of 85,000 rupees; and when the same was completed, he commenced the inauguration of the library, by collecting books and pamphlets from different places. At the time when this public library began, the books of the old Hurkaru Library were advertised for sale, and the Baboo availed himself of the opportunity to buy some of the oldest works from the same for his own library. These, added with those bought from the Calcutta China Bazaar booksellers, amounted to 5,000 volumes only. The Baboo, not being satisfied with such a meagre collection, resolved to extend the institution by purchase of additional books from hawkers, whom he invited over from Calcutta, to supply him with rare and valuable books and magazines, &c. at fair prices. Thus, when the books were purchased in the manner narrated above, to the number of 12,000 volumes, he set about working the library in the year 1859, by appointing a librarian, an assistant librarian, one duffturee, one forash or sweeper, one durwar, and two mallees or gardeners. These formed the constitution of the library establishment, for the management of its duties in the beginning of the institution, and the same is continuing unaltered up to the present day. To ensure proper supervision over the library, and to secure its permanency, the Baboo has appointed a body of native gentlemen as curators of his library, to whom he has made over a landed estate, yielding 1,800 rupees a year; but as more works in English and Sanscrit are yet to be added, he has made a separate provision for the purchase of the same. It is endowed in perpetuity, the proprietorship being vested in the eldest male issue: accordingly his eldest son, Baboo Horrow Mohun Mookerjee, is at present the proprietor.

'It will not be out of place to mention it here, that the lower story of the building contains the library, and the upper rooms are reserved to accommodate respectable visitors, as well as to hold public meetings and deliver lectures—in fact, to serve the purpose of a Town Hall. A garden of choice fruits and flowers is attached to the institution, for the resort and recreation of the community, which is largely availed of by them.

'The library subscribes to the leading journals of the day, and also new publications from England to the value of 1,000 rupees, which the proprietor of the library pays from a separate fund annually.

'Besides the 12,000 volumes of English books above referred to, the library has a separate department of Bengali and Sanscrit works, containing 2,500 volumes, which being considered as insufficient, Baboo Joy Kissen Mookerjee has resolved upon adding as many of the latter as he can collect, and with that view has got himself enrolled as a member of the society formed under the patronage of the Prince of Wales.

'In order to extend and diffuse a taste for reading among the educated people of Ooterparrah and its neighbourhood, the Baboo has offered a gold medal, as a prize to any one who would pass an examination in the reading of the best books of the library.

'In conclusion, permit me to state that the library is largely availed of by the educated natives of the place, and by Englishmen residing on the railway line and in the Ballee papermill; and its circulation of books is calculated, on an average, to be 350 volumes in a month.'

The Government boys' schools were excellent, and we were much pleased with the thorough knowledge of the English language displayed by the first classes of the High School. They analysed Gray's 'Elegy in a Country Churchyard' admirably, and were fully acquainted with the meaning of the passages respecting the 'mute inglorious Milton,' and the greatness of the human soul, independently of external condition. The zemindars did not neglect the opportunity of urging the official gentlemen present to grant their request to found a college for them, they themselves taking half the cost. I could not forbear expressing my surprise that gentlemen of affluence and liberality should wish to be dependent on Government for the higher education of their own sons, since the Government had already done more for them in this respect than for British subjects; and millions of their countrymen were still remaining in gross ignorance, without the blessing of education, and perfectly unable to procure it, even if they desired it. These remarks did not meet with a response from these gentlemen, who did not appear to like the practical application of the poetical sentiments they had admired.

We then repaired to the residence of Raj Kissen Mookerjee, who had kindly prepared refreshments for us. I was afterwards invited to the zenana, where a number of ladies had assembled in large cheerful rooms. They received me in the kindest way, with the remark, 'We are very glad you spent your own money to come to see us;' and were evidently gratified by my assurance that many English ladies took a warm interest in them, as well as myself, but had not had an opportunity of showing it. I promised them, however, that on my return home I would endeavour to excite the sympathy of my countrywomen for them.

After warm thanks to our hosts, we proceeded to Bally, a primitive-looking native village at no great distance. After wending our way through some narrow lanes, we came to a girls' school, carried on in a small bungalow. This had been founded chiefly through the efforts of a very intelligent young gentleman, whom we had remarked as one of the most advanced students in the Ooterparrah High School. This is another instance, among the many we witnessed, in which young men, who have themselves felt the value of education, are anxious to impart it to the other sex.

BURRANAGORE.

On Sunday morning, September 10, 1866, occurred an examination and prize-giving at a small girls' school in the suburban town of Burranagore. This place does not present any peculiar attraction to the stranger, but is now rising into some importance through the establishment there, by an English house, of a large gunny-bag factory, which is giving employment to 4,000 men, women, and children. The school itself contained 75 girls, of ages varying from six to ten, who are taught, in addition to grammatical instruction in their own language, geography, arithmetic, and needlework. It is superintended by two pundits and a mistress, 17 rupees per mensem being contributed by Government towards the whole expense. Though this school does not present any peculiar feature, yet to trace the steps which led to its present condition will be instructive. The following passage, from the pen of an 'Englishman,' is therefore extracted from the 'Indian Mirror' (a native paper) of that month:—

'The Burranagore Girls' School traces its origin to the family of the founder, who commenced it by teaching his wife and one or two relations in his own house. It was then increased by the addition of some girls who were desirous of obtaining instruction; and so great was its success, that it was removed from the sacred precincts of the zenana—or, to speak more correctly, zenana education was given to grown-up persons, and a school for girls was opened under the superintendence of a pundit. The movement received much encouragement from the inhabitants, and the school increased rapidly. But a sudden stop was put to its progress, by the fact of the founder having embraced Brahmoism. A revulsion of feeling took place; all the pupils of the zenana, and many from the school, were withdrawn, and all were warned from further contact with the heretic who had forsaken his ancient religion. The heart of the young reformer was not to be discouraged by persecution, and he manfully stood his ground, kept open his school, and has lived down the tyranny of his persecutors. The result of his perseverance was last Sunday's gratifying ceremony, which was attended by a large number of his neighbours, and a few English gentlemen. . . . The chair was taken by Professor Lobb, of the Presidency College; and the Report, which I hope we may see printed, was read by the founder of the school, who is also the secretary to the managing committee. The prizes (which consisted of books, slates, clothing, &c.) were distributed to the youthful, intelligent, and, I must add, in many cases comely recipients, who received them with evident satisfaction and glee. The chairman, and one or two of the European gentlemen, addressed a few words to the meeting; but it was left to Baboo Bacharam Chatterjee, the celebrated Brahmo Somaj preacher, to make *the* speech of the day. I am really sorry, owing to its having been spoken in Bengali, and my ignorance of the language, that I cannot give its substance to your readers. It was very fluent, and repeatedly elicited the applause of the audience, and, I am told, chiefly related to the importance of female education in many of its most prominent aspects.'

On Wednesday, December 12, I set off to visit the school, under the escort of the secretary, Baboo Soshe Pudo Bannerjee, a Brahmo, and one of those who had accompanied his wife to the tea-party at Dr. Chuckerbutty's. He informed me that, when he openly renounced idolatry, he was excommunicated, and exiled from his ancestral home, receiving only a portion of his patrimony; this, however, gave him a degree of freedom in which he rejoiced. His is the only case I met with, throughout India, in which excommunication was not regarded with the greatest dread by the Hindoos. This first step having been courageously taken, he secured a small separate house for himself and wife, and then devoted all the leisure he could command to movements connected with social progress. The diffusion of the knowledge of One True God was his first concern, in connection with the Brahmo Somaj. He devoted himself also to the temperance movement, for which he had to suffer much persecution, being once imprisoned on a charge of murder by a publican whom he had offended. The murdered man having been produced, alive and well, the next morning by his friends, he was released, but not without much expense and annoyance. This peculiar mode of revenge is not, I am informed, uncommon in India.

The girls' school, as well as that for boys, is in small and inconvenient premises, being the only ones that could be procured with the very limited means at command. It does indeed seem extraordinary, that while so much money is bestowed on boys' schools—while no expense is spared which is necessary to obtain them suitable buildings — such real efforts as these are cramped for want of means. The natives are thus led to infer that the Government does not value the education of girls as much as that of boys.

After visiting the schools, I was anxious to see the factory. It was near the hour of closing, so that there was not time to inspect all the works; but the natives

—men, women and boys—were all working in a regular and orderly manner, as in a factory at home. There is no school at present attached to it, but the managers have secured a piece of land, where it is intended to build one. This will be very important. Education will be secured to those who are at present entirely without it, if the regulations of our Factory Act are introduced.

The influx of money into this town is very great, numbers thus obtaining good regular wages who were previously in receipt of small precarious earnings only. But this increase of the resources of the inhabitants has not hitherto been productive solely of good effects. These people are quite content with what we should deem a low, miserable way of living, in poor huts; they are without any education, nor have they the wants of civilised life; they spend their money, therefore, in vicious indulgences. An evening school, to give some instruction to these young men, appeared likely to be very useful, and this was commenced in the little room of the girls' school. My next visit was to this, and it was very gratifying to observe how much the scholars valued the unbought services of their teachers. The following address, here presented to me, from some of the inhabitants of the town, indicates their spirit:—

'We, the undersigned inhabitants of this place, have the sincerest pleasure in adding our share to the cordial welcome which has been universally accorded to you by the liberals of every denomination of all places you have visited in our great country. We had intended to dispense with the ceremony of this address, as a thing which in itself could neither augment your pleasure, nor tend to our honour. Considering, however, that even the local ventilation of the address may be the cause of the contemplation of a career such as yours by many of our brethren and sisters, who would not else hear of it, and therefore an indirect aid to your mission, we determined otherwise. We wish we could rather give a welcome of deeds. We regret our inability for female improvement here, and even male has hardly yet begun. And this is more urgent reason of our welcome of you. No town, suburban or provincial, this side of India, offers a more inviting—we do not mean a more promising—field for the exercise of your mission than Burranagore. Here indeed, of all places of equal importance, can you exercise your double genius for influencing both the male and female heart. This is not the medium for an *exposé* of our weak points, else we should have gladly expressed to you in detail the wants of our town, and of course received your valuable suggestions.

'The reasons for shyness, however, which exist in a public document, do not exist in private intercourse. We therefore give you a general hearty welcome to spy the nakedness of our place, and we entertain the hope that your visit may be of a more than formal character.

'And may God prosper you and your mission!'

   '(Signed) NOHAKRISH MASKERJEE and others.

'December, 1866.'

Though it was becoming late, my young friend would not allow me to depart without a visit to his abode, as his lady was expecting me there. And well indeed was I rewarded for any trouble I may have taken to come here. For the first, and for the last time, during my whole visit, had I the happiness of being in a simple native dwelling, which had the domestic charms of an English home. The young wife came forward gracefully to welcome us to her pretty sitting-room, where well-chosen prints covered the otherwise bare walls, and a simple repast had been prepared for us. Her little boy, a fine child, was quite happy to see his father, and be noticed by him; and the only drawback to the pleasure of the visit, was my inability to converse with my hostess, through her ignorance of English. Now that the Hindoo ladies are beginning to understand that we have a real interest in them, they will, I trust, overcome this obstacle to friendly intercourse, by acquiring our language, and becoming thus acquainted with our habits and thoughts, as expressed in our literature. In the meantime it is pleasant to know that she, and doubtless many others, are able to divine feelings without the aid of words. 'She talked to me so kindly by pressing my hand,' was said by one, but perhaps felt by many.

Burranagore does indeed present, as stated in the address, a very wide field for the labours of those who desire to advance social progress. The fact of even one inhabitant of a place being zealously bent on promoting improvement, prepares the way, and renders efforts made by others productive of good results. This suburb is fortunate in having such a factory established in it, with managers who are willing to co-operate. Before my final departure, therefore, I requested my young friend to give me an opportunity of making the inhabitants of his town acquainted with some of the movements in England, which have in view the elevation of the working-classes. An evening was agreed on, and when I arrived at the place of meeting, I found the only room which could be procured densely filled with intelligent natives, and several English. The doctor of the town kindly presided. The scene presented a strangely different aspect from a meeting of English operatives assembled to hear an address on subjects connected with their social condition. Our operatives comprehend what is meant by the dignity of labour, and do not think that their social position is lowered by engaging in it. Here, on the contrary, I found that I had unwittingly offended some of my turbaned audience, by addressing them as those who were engaged in factory-work, that being performed, they considered, solely by persons who were ignorant and illiterate; the fact of their being able to understand me proved the contrary with regard to themselves. I apologised for my error, requesting them to explain to their less favoured fellow-citizens what I had said. The time will come, I earnestly hope, when Hindoo factory-workers may be an educated class of society, as well as English operatives; and when a knowledge of our language may enable them, as well as the higher classes of the native community, to receive the benefit of a knowledge of our civilisation and institutions.*

The meeting did not conclude without passing a resolution, proposed by my friend the secretary, Baboo Soshe Pudo Bannerjee, that a committee should be formed, of English and native gentlemen, to consider the formation of a society for the improvement of the working-classes. This was not a mere formal resolution, barren of results. The disinterested zeal of this young man, who had already given so much practical proof of his earnestness and perseverance, enlisted the warm co-operation of some enlightened and benevolent gentlemen; and in the 'Indian Daily News' of July 24, 1867, we find a report of the first half-yearly meeting of the 'Burranagore Social Improvement Society,'—Dr. Waldee, president, in the chair. A committee was organised, a public library commenced, and arrangements made to obtain a room for the proceedings. A valuable address was made by the chairman, and he showed how much might be done by even one true-

* *Vide* 'Addresses to the Hindoos' pp. 40-45.

hearted individual, by remarking: 'A girls' school has been in progress for some time, and with as much success as in the circumstances can be expected. For the institution of this, and also for the night-school for men and boys, and mainly also for carrying them on, we are indebted to the highly praiseworthy labours of the secretary, Baboo Soshe Pudo Bannerjee. But in my view it is unfair to leave such institutions so entirely under his care, and the society ought to make it their business to assist him.'

May this grain of mustard-seed, so carefully planted and watered, grow up to be a large tree at Burranagore, overshadowing and blessing the whole population!

RANAGHAT.

Early in December, three students of the Presidency College addressed to me an earnest request that I would visit a small girls' school they had commenced in this place, hoping by this means that some interest may be excited in it, and additional help obtained for it. Feeling always a special interest in unobtrusive efforts of this kind, and sympathising greatly with young men who are thus struggling nobly to emancipate from the thraldom of ignorance the weaker sex, I was desirous of giving them, if possible, any small help which my visit might afford them. I was therefore glad to find that Ranaghat was a station on the way to Kishnaghur, a place I proposed to visit. A friend, acquainted with a zemindar of that neighbourhood, wrote to request a kind reception for me; and as Baboo Keshub Chunder Sen intended to visit Kishnaghur before commencing his missionary tour in the North-west Provinces, he kindly gave me his escort, together with an English friend.

We set off early in the morning of December 27, and, on our arrival at Ranaghat, were received in great state by the zemindar, attended by a large elephant with suitable trappings, and a number of retainers, one of whom carried a large gilt umbrella. We formed quite a procession, of which the noble animal formed a distinguished part, not being employed as a beast of burden, but taking a position as one of the household. We proceeded to the little school. There, as at Ooterparrah, the movement had been commenced by the establishment of a benevolent society, for the proceedings of which a room was provided. Female education was here, as there, the most important object of their efforts. They were not able to raise funds to pay a teacher, and some of the members devoted their spare time to the instruction of little girls. They had improved wonderfully, to the satisfaction of the parents; and on the present occasion their performances were exhibited, and prizes were distributed—the zemindar presiding, and apparently taking a warm interest in the proceedings. The young gentlemen who had invited me were members of his family or their friends, and their exertions were most praiseworthy. The zemindar then requested us to proceed to his residence. We passed by many somewhat dilapidated buildings, and arrived at his abode—a large mansion round a quadrangle, capable of accommodating at least a hundred persons. A number of guests were assembled kindly to welcome us; the younger members of the family were gorgeously dressed in the rich brocade so peculiar to India. The students expressed the warmest anxiety for the support of the school; they cannot obtain any help from Government in procuring a teacher, unless they raise half the salary, and this they had found impossible under the impoverished circumstances of the district. It need hardly be stated that I expressed my hopes, as strongly as politeness would permit me, that my wealthy host would use his powerful influence to accomplish so desirable an object. The young students themselves had no means at their command, having no allowance of money from their parents, as in England, for their private expenditure. A liberal repast was provided for our party by the hospitality of our host; it lost its charm, however, to me, here as elsewhere, by not being shared by those with whom we had just before been enjoying agreeable intercourse. The beautiful drawing-room, too, looked sadly desolate without the presence of the ladies of the family. I had not, indeed, the pleasure of seeing them at all. Their apartments were in a remote part of the building, and we were informed that the chief lady was subject to hysterics, which would render her unable to receive me. This malady, I was informed by a medical gentleman, in large practice among native ladies, is not uncommon among them. Nor is this a matter for surprise, condemned as these poor ladies are to a seclusion in which they have no healthy occupation for the mind, no physical stimulus for the body. The doctor, being well aware of their mode of life, and of the probable cause of the hysterical affection of one of his patients, prescribed for her a jumping-board! His advice was adopted, and on his next visit, he saw his patient laughing instead of crying!

KISHNAGHUR.

After thanking our polite host for his hospitality, and wishing my young student friends success in their undertaking, we proceeded by rail to the nearest station on the way to Kishnaghur; my English friend returned, since my first fellow-traveller, Mr. Ghose, had come to escort me to Kishnaghur, where his family reside. We had to cross a river and take a carriage, the driver of which continued to importune us most vociferously for some time, demanding an exorbitant payment, because, though there were two native gentlemen, there was an English lady, and it was always the custom to make an extra charge for the English! This hint may be useful, if any of my fellow-countrymen or women travel this way. The country was not devoid of beauty, exhibiting many trees that I had not seen before; among others, that producing the india-rubber. Occasionally, even here, we saw some of the effects of the cyclone. But what was most painful was the number of deserted buildings, and these evidently belonging not to the lowest class, where whole families had been swept away by pestilence. The town itself, from the side on which we entered it, was anything but attractive; streets with low native houses on each side, bad drainage, and, in harmony with these, a heathen temple with wide open doors, displaying a most hideous idol to the gaze of all passers-by. The minds which could accept this as an emblem of deity, could not be expected to rise high in social progress. Mr. Ghose had spoken to us with pleasure of Kishnaghur as his home, but evidently felt ashamed of it, now that his English education had raised his standard. At the other side of the town, however, were pleasant English residences and institutions; and I was soon most comfortably installed in one, the residence of the Church missionary, the Rev. Mr. Blumhardt, and his family. It was very pleasant to find myself here quite as much at home as altered circumstances would permit, with morning and evening worship, and the sweetest possible sacred music from the young ladies every evening; such domestic privileges are very precious in this heathen land, and help to keep oil in the lamp. Morning revealed fresh sources of pleasure. Around the compound were erected a chaste and simple village church, a school-house for the children, taught by native converts, and superintended by the ladies of the family; also a college for native students, superintended by the worthy pastor himself. Cottages there were besides, neat little Indian dwellings for a few native converts holding some office; one I entered, to give my good wishes to a catechist and his family, as well as the girls' school; the students were absent, enjoying their Christmas holidays. On the other side of the house was a pleasant garden, carefully laid out and attended to, with flowers in bloom, or soon to burst from their buds. The lady of the house was, as in England, the unobtrusive director of all the movements of the household, the source of all its comfort and order; she must have diffused an influence around, on those who otherwise would not have known the nature of an English home.

When the good missionary came here some five-and-twenty years ago, this place was comparatively a wilderness; the converts being in the lowest depths of ignorance, being, as such are called, 'rice-Christians,'— *i.e.* they accepted the religion of those who showed them mercy, without much comprehension of its nature. The change effected by persevering work is most encouraging. Mr. Blumhardt devotes himself also to city improvements, and during the famine, which to some extent reached this place, exerted himself to provide some public work for the starving families, who were thus saved from being pauperised. I saw them ranged in his compound to receive from him their small daily stipend.

The proceedings of the next few days were so well delineated by a native pen in the columns of the 'Indian Daily News' of January 2, 1867, that I shall beg permission to transcribe the passage, as it will give considerable insight into the Hindoo mode of viewing things:—

'*December* 30, 1866.—The arrival of Miss Carpenter has created a great sensation in the Kishnaghur community. She reached the station on the evening of the 27th, and is a guest of the Rev. Mr. Blumhardt. The object of her visit to India is too well known to need a particular notice. In her way hither, she paid a visit to Ranaghat, whither she was attracted by the existence of a female school. The rich baboos of the place received her with all the honour due to her, and her philanthropic endeavours for the regeneration of her sisters in India. They, however, seem to have disappointed her in a most material point. She did not expect to be dazzled with the *kinkhaff* dresses and *ashaghotas* of her hosts, while at the same time there was no care for the support of the school, the better condition of which would have given her real satisfaction. What must have been her surprise to find that those among her hosts, who vied with each other in the display of their wealth before her, did not pay a pice towards its support? The school has come into existence, and is being maintained by the zeal of the young students, and some young educated men of the place, but receives little attention that deserves the name from the baboos. The benevolent lady exhorted them in her most persuasive way, and I hope they will take to heart what she said. It is really to be regretted that while the zemindars elsewhere are daily changing character under the influence of the enlightened age, those of Ranaghat should lag so far behind it in every social improvement.

'On the 28th, Miss Carpenter, accompanied by Miss Blumhardt, the Maharajah Suttish Chundra Roy Bahadoor, and Baboo Monomohun Ghose, paid a visit to the Belliadanga female school. She was evidently pleased with all she saw there. The arrangements made for her reception were excellent, and the courtesy with which both the Rajah and his cousin Baboo Judoonath Roy treated her did them credit.

'This school was established four years ago, and has hitherto been enabled to maintain itself in fair progress, mainly by the unflagging zeal and fostering care of Baboo Judoonath. Owing to the vicissitudes it has undergone, by the prevalence of the epidemic fever, its numerical strength does not appear to be so satisfactory as could be wished. On the day of Miss Carpenter's visit, the number on the rolls was thirty-four. The girls are all of respectable families, some of them being the connections of the Maharajah, who took a particular delight in pointing them out to the lady. The first-class girls read Charoopat, No. 1 Byacoran, and were examined in geography and arithmetic. Mrs. Blumhardt, the Maharajah, and Baboo Monmohun, examined them in several branches of their study, and the readiness with which they read, explained, and answered the questions put to them, reflected great credit on them.

'Miss Carpenter was next taken into the zenana of Baboo Judoonath Roy. Before noting down what passed there, I would give you some idea of the sort of family into which our visitor was introduced.

'Baboo Judoonath is a cousin of the Maharajah, and is of a most respectable family. He has a widowed elder sister, a most intelligent lady, and, as Miss Carpenter styled her, "a superior woman." The Baboo took an early opportunity to teach her reading and writing, as well as to communicate to her the most valuable information on various subjects. Besides this, her natural good sense has rendered her a model of domestic economy. Amiable to a degree, she has not been wanting in a stout heart, in purging her mind of some of the most pernicious prejudices that fetter our women in general. Yet she is not fond of violent and indiscriminate innovation, and would not for the world give up one old idea or habit in which may be found the faintest trace of good. Her influence over her brother's family has been marked, inasmuch as there is scarcely a female in the family who does not know her book, and cannot talk sensibly. Among the many good things resultant of this happy state of affairs, may be pointed out one in particular, that the children of the family, unlike those of the other rich families, in which the women are ignorant, are taken better care of in all matters by their own mothers, instead of being consigned to the baneful influence of the ignorant, and not unfrequently vicious, servants and maidservants. The above points a moral which we should do well to study—that in each family, if we take care to pick up one or two intelligent women, and train them up carefully, a considerable amount of good might be effected in female education, and with it a thorough reformation in our domestic economy. Such families are rare, indeed, in which there cannot be found out at least one worthy female, who, when properly trained, could not fail to exert her influence over the rest. At Kishnaghur may be named several other families in which the same satisfactory results have been arrived at by the same means. Miss Carpenter's Commonplace Book will show the signatures of several Kishnaghur ladies, given her at her particular request, none of whom ever went to school. Female schools must be for the girls, but no method could be better adapted to the education of the grown-up women.

'To return to my subject. Into such a family, then, Miss Carpenter was introduced; they gave her a hearty greeting. Miss Carpenter must have seen how unostentatious were her female welcomers. Entering so rich a family, she perhaps expected to see women covered with gold and silver; but to her delight, she saw no such thing. A clean *perhan*, a neat *sharry* gracefully worn, a pair of white stockings and soft shoes, with a pair of earrings to give effect to the face, were all that the women had on them.

'After the interchange of civilities between the parties, Miss Carpenter went on explaining the object of her visit to India. She said there were several other ladies at home who were as much interested in, and anxious about, the amelioration of the condition of their sisters in India as her own self,

THE SUBURBS OF CALCUTTA. 263

and that it would give them an infinite delight to receive a cheering account of them on her return home. The Baboo's sister then read an address, which she had composed beforehand, in which she cordially thanked the noble lady in the name of her sex in India, for whose welfare she had left home and friends, undergoing all the inconvenience and hardships of so long a journey, and at such time of life. The Maharajah and the Baboo acted as interpreters on the occasion. Miss Carpenter was next taken to another female school in the Laheeree Parah, with which also she was well pleased. On her return, she attended a lecture on " Faith " at the Kishnagur Brahmo Somaj Hall, delivered by Baboo Keshub Chunder Sen. This closed the business of the day.

' The next day the native ladies of most of the respectable families gathered at the Maharajah's to receive her. When Miss Blumhardt had done playing one or two dulcet tunes at the pianoforte, Miss Carpenter rose to express her satisfaction at meeting so many intelligent and clever women. Among other things, she said that should it please God to prolong her life, she would in all probability take another opportunity of visiting India, and enjoy their company and conversation, when she hoped their number would be vastly increased. Baboo Judoonath Roy's sister then rose, and in some very appropriate terms returned thanks for Miss Carpenter's kind wishes. This lady spoke so well and fluently on the occasion, as to elicit Miss Carpenter's praise. The Maharajah's nephew acted as interpreter at the meeting.

' At 7.30 P.M. Baboo Monomohun Ghose invited the *élite* of the Kishnaghur Society to a *soirée* at his house, to meet Miss Carpenter. About thirty-five of the most influential and educated men of the place were present, and Miss Carpenter talked to them in her usual lucid and fascinating manner. The conversation, however, proved to be of a desultory character. Two or three subjects were proposed by the lady, but none were discussed to a satisfactory issue. Social science was, of course, the chief topic of the evening, in talking of which she repeated what had passed in the meeting held in the rooms of the Asiatic Society the other day. She was surprised to find that the subject was nothing new to the company, they having taken the initiative some months before, to form a Social Science Association at Kishnaghur, and having already produced two papers, one in English, and another in Bengali, on two of Mr. Long's five hundred questions. She expressed her satisfaction pretty much in the following terms:—" Mr. Ghose," she said, addressing Baboo Monomohun, "these gentlemen already know and appreciate the importance of social science, and are quite willing to undertake to produce valuable papers. I see the Kishnaghur community is in advance of the Calcutta one. I never saw so large an assemblage of respectable and clever native women, as I had the pleasure of meeting in the afternoon at the Maharajah's,'and here again is a most agreeable and sensible company around me. You are on the Calcutta committee, and you will tell them on your return all that you hear just now." The Rajah thanked·her for the compliment she paid to Kishnaghur, and Baboo Monomohun said he had always been of the same opinion, though he might be partial.

'Baboo Monomohun having requested her to speak a few words for the edification of the company, expressive of the interest that the people of England feel in the welfare of India, she said it was one of the most cherished objects of the English at home. They were at all times very kind to the natives who visited England, received them in their families, and tried everything in their power to make their stay as comfortable and agreeable as possible. They were the best friends of the natives, and would do anything and everything that lay in them to advance their interest. But, she continued, the English at home were in profound ignorance as respected the wants ot India. If the natives could only furnish them with information about themselves, the English at home would at no time be found lacking in zeal and earnestness to turn such information to good account. She said she had been pained to hear that some of the English in India, had brought a stain on the character of the nation by their unkind treatment of the natives. All she would say of such Englishmen was, that they were " low-bred and vulgar-minded," and were no more representative of the nation, than the same class of the natives in England would represent them! Some one of the company happening to say how the natives were called "niggers" by some of the whites, she added, "Don't name it—it is vulgar, and the language of the vulgar-minded. Why, Mr. Ghose," she continued, "you can tell your friends how you were treated in England. Your testimony will be of far more weight than all I could say in favour of my countrymen." Baboo Monomohun expressed his acknowledgments of the kindness of the English at home in very handsome terms. Here is the testimony of one of the best of England, in corroboration of what we have heard from time to time from others of the same class, both in England and India. Her " low-bred and vulgar-minded " means nothing less than Baboo Rajendro Lall Mitter's " sweepings of Europe." Yet what measures were not resorted to some years back, to heap disgrace on the head of the Baboo for his expression! Let the " nigger "-hating Europeans take note of this.

'It is not in my power to speak sufficiently of Miss Carpenter. The earnestness and the suavity of her manners have already won her the golden opinion of the Indian public, and her talents have called forth their admiration. She has nearly realised the expectation entertained of her, in her mission of peace and progress. Her manners and conversation are well worth the study of our mofussil rulers, or of all our rulers in general. They would do well to attend one of those social gatherings in which, in a foreign land, she is surrounded by all who have the best power of appreciating worth, and listened to with a degree of fondness which nothing less than genuine goodness can excite. If they shared in the tenth of the amount of kind feeling and sympathy of the noble lady, and of her class in England, for the good of India, what might not have been achieved by this time?

'I have digressed rather a little too far. Night advancing (it was nearly 11 P.M. when the company dispersed), it was proposed and agreed that a public meeting, including both the

European and native gentlemen of the place, should be convened on Monday next, to hear Miss Carpenter on the subject of social science. I will take an early opportunity to let you know what transpires at the meeting.'

The address alluded to was delivered on the last day of the year; a brief account of it is contained in 'Addresses to the Hindoos,' pp. 26-39.

An early morning visit was paid to the jail, where I found the same very bad features as in other jails—association in dormitories, women of the worst character locked up together under male warders, and no provision for instructing or reforming either male or female prisoners. There were at that time about 350 in the jail, and the place was calculated for 400. On one occasion, however, 600 were crowded into it, and 100 died! It is astonishing that such mortality does not lead to an investigation of the cause, and a prevention of its recurrence by a reconstruction of the premises. This would not be expensive, for there is abundance of ground, and the labour of the prisoners could be used. The poor fellows seemed wonderfully docile, for we saw them working, apparently quite freely, in fields beyond the boundaries, just as do our own reformatory boys. Under such a system of prison discipline as was developed in Ireland under Sir Walter Crofton, and is now being introduced into England, how much might be done for Hindoo culprits, in preparing them to be useful members of society!

What I heard from the gentleman who accompanied me, as well as from the very intelligent native physician of the place, perfectly appalled me, as to the want of provision for the disposal of the filth of the city. It was too shocking to be here recorded, and elicited from me the remark that, instead of wondering why I had seen the desolated village, and why so many died, I marvelled only how any human beings lived in an atmosphere so poisoned. Surely every means should be tried to rouse public attention to so important a subject. The fact that a branch Social Science Association already exists here, leads to the hope that the enlightened and scientific men of Kishnaghur will never let the subject drop, until they have provided at least pure air for the inhabitants.

The hospital and various public offices appeared here, as elsewhere, to be well cared for. The educational institutions of this city I had heard spoken of highly; but, unfortunately, I had no opportunity of judging of them, as this was holiday time. The college buildings are, however, admirable in the accommodation they contain, as well as in their external appearance. They are an ornament to the town, and must be a convincing proof to the inhabitants of the interest of the British Government in their improvement. May the time come when it shall feel prepared equally to make efforts to aid in the elevation of the other sex! The progress which has already been made in female education in Kishnaghur indicates a strong aspiration after better things. The managers of the schools gladly accepted the offer of visits to them from the accomplished daughters of my host, and several families expressed a desire to receive instruction at home from them. The want of female teachers here, as elsewhere, is strongly felt by the natives, and one excellent mother of a family expressed her wish to be the first subscriber to such an institution as would provide them. All things are ready for an onward movement: if it is guided by wisdom, patience, and the dictates of experience, it will surely succeed.

An afternoon ride in a very extensive park in the neighbourhood which is secured to the public, was a pleasant change after some of the scenes of the morning. There are splendid groves of teak-trees, with their majestic trunks and large leaves. Occasionally I saw a bare white trunk and branches of a tree which appeared dead: it was the cotton-tree—still alive, only slumbering to refresh its energies, and enable it to throw out in some two months splendid scarlet blossoms, which precede the leaves. Monkeys abound in these parts; I saw very large ones gambolling over the fields. They have, in fact, at times committed such ravages on the crops intended for the food of the inhabitants, that, notwithstanding the strong objection to destroy animal life in general, and monkeys in particular, it has been found necessary to put a price on the heads of the devastators, and encourage wholesale slaughter.

The country in this district appeared to present numerous objects of attraction, which I regretted being unable to visit.

And now the moments of the departing year were numbered; the last day of its existence was drawing to a close! It had been a very eventful one to me: it had bestowed on me the crowning privilege of my life. After our very interesting evening meeting, above referred to, I rejoiced to close it in prayer and thanksgiving to the Giver of all good, with my kind missionary friend and his family.

CHAPTER VII.

FAREWELL TO CALCUTTA—RETURN TO MADRAS—CALICUT.

CALCUTTA, *Jan.* 1, 1867.—The dawn of the new year rose brightly upon me. Every morning is generally a glorious one in India—it is expected as an ordinary occurrence, and does not usually elicit the mutual congratulations which are common in our duller climate. This morning—the first of the opening year—was full of joy and gratitude in all our hearts, but it was somewhat shaded with the thought that it was to be our last together. The good pastor inscribed in my book some treasured words, together with a verse in Anharic, the dialect of Abyssinia. He had been a missionary in that country, but now had given his heart to India; he and his whole family had devoted their lives to this land of his adoption.

It was a pleasant surprise, after taking farewell of these friends, to find that the doctor had paid early visits to his patients, with the kind intention of accompanying me to the station, and that Mr. Sen was prepared to do so too. This was, then, a very happy morning; for each had much to say about future progress, and we parted with the mutual promise to mark permanently this New Year's day in the note-book of our memories.

Farewell to Calcutta itself was to be the next

parting, and for this much preparation was to be made.

My first care was to complete the work for which I had traversed the empire—to lay before the highest authority in it that result of my observations, which had been asked for by the Government of Bombay, but which, I perceived, concerned not one presidency, but the whole of India. I requested permission, therefore, to present to his Excellency the Viceroy the observations which my experience had enabled me to make, aided by the facilities which had been so kindly afforded to me, on female education, reformatories, jails, female convicts, and prison discipline generally. These were graciously accepted, with the promise that they should be laid before the different departments. These observations and suggestions will appear in a subsequent part of this volume.

The provisional committee of the Social Science Association held its final meeting at my rooms, and I had the pleasure of believing the Society now an absolute fact, and of paying the first subscription to its funds.

One more school had to be visited, for it was supported and managed by native gentlemen, who desired my presence there. It did great credit to their zeal. I had also a pleasant interview with the ladies of their families, all anxious to show me their progress in learning.

Another proof was given me of the efforts which are being made by one section of the native community. A deputation from an existing society presented to me a beautiful volume, consisting of the numbers of a journal printed in Bengali, for ladies, and containing many contributions by them. Diagrams illustrating subjects connected with astronomy, natural history in its various branches, and botany, indicate the instructive nature of the contents. The following address, presented with it, shows the views of the Society and its methods of action :—

'Madam,—We, the undersigned members of the "Bamabodhini Shova," a society established in 1863, for the improvement of the women of Bengal, heartily welcome your arrival in India. We cannot sufficiently express our gratitude and admiration to you for having exposed yourself to countless dangers and sacrifices only for the good of India, and especially for the good of Indian females. We feel we are bound to you in deep obligation, and therefore venture to hope that our humble expressions of thankfulness may not be unacceptable to you.

'The suffering women of this land do, indeed, deserve your sisterly sympathy and care, and we expect much benefit to them through the exertions of a lady of your rank, experience, and exemplary character. We do sincerely believe that you have been sent by Providence on a sacred mission, and doubt not but your labours will be successful. You can look for little encouragement indeed from the quarter you have come to enlighten; perhaps, on the contrary, you should expect some opposition. But we are aware your wishes are too hard, and your affections too deep, to be affected by the influence of any external obstacles. We observe with great delight and astonishment the warmth and enthusiasm of youth in a life loaded with years, and the labours and energies you have shown during your short stay in this country, inspire our hearts with sanguine hopes for the regeneration of the females of India. May the all-merciful Father sustain your health and strength, and enable us to receive all the good that we expect from you! We humbly beg to present you with a set of our monthly journal, called the "Bamabodhini Putriku," published in Bengali by the Bamabodhini Society for the Improvement of the Women of Bengal. We hope you will be delighted to learn there some signs of progress, both intellectual and moral, which are now manifested by the women of our country. The measures we have adopted to contribute to their progress, are noted below.

'We will receive with thanks any suggestion, advice or assistance, that you may be disposed to offer for the better execution of our objects and plans.

'We beg to state, for your information, that the project of instituting a female normal school, for which, at your suggestion, several respectable members of the native community of this town have, we understand, memorialised Government, was laid before the public by us some time ago, and it was only for want of co-operation and encouragement that we were obliged to drop it. We shall be extremely glad, therefore, to see the success of this project, so that a sufficient number of female teachers may be made ready for our girls' schools.

'The following measures have been adopted by the "Bamabodhini Shova" for the improvement of native females:—
1. By publication of papers and periodicals to improve the intellect of native females.
2. Establishment of a system of prize essays for the encouragement of educated native females.
3. Establishment of schools for the education of adult females belonging to gentle families, of an approved system of zenana training, as well as that of conferring prizes for encouragement.
4. Offering every assistance that may be in our power for the promotion of girls' schools.

'We have the honour to remain, Madam,
'Your most obedient servants,
'KHETTER MOHUN DUTT, and others.'

'Calcutta: December 26, 1866.'

Finally, on the last evening, a number of those who had shown the most practical interest in female education met at my rooms; and there, after long discussion on the important subject, appended their names to the following statement:—

'Our acquaintance with Miss Carpenter, and the views which she has expressed on the subject of female education, and on other subjects, have *intensified* our ideas as to the excellency of female education, for it has not been our lot to meet with a lady so large-minded, able, earnest, and practically devout. She carries with herself our best and most sincere wishes for her health, happiness, and success to her noble mission. We now form a society to carry out her plans of female education.'

It was now necessary to take farewell of my noble hosts, with sincere gratitude for their great kindness to me, and thanks for that of each one of their staff. My reception in Government House had certainly been not only very agreeable and gratifying to me, but had shown to those with whom I was more especially concerned the sympathy in my work of the head of the Government. Again I beg to tender respectfully to them my sincere acknowledgments.

Many of my native friends accompanied me to the ship for a last farewell. With much regret I saw recede the harbour of Calcutta, where I had found among many a warm sympathy, and had learnt from experience that the higher feellings of our nature are not dependent on clime or colour.

The following parting address I left among my friends:—

'Being about to leave Calcutta, after a residence of six weeks in your city, I beg to express to you, and to all the Hindoo gentlemen who have given me a kind and friendly reception, the gratification I have experienced in having been so fully assured of their confidence in me, and in the motives which prompted me to visit your country. The results of my visit to you will not be temporary, for, on my return to my native land, I shall always retain India in my inmost thoughts, and shall ever esteem it no less a pleasure than a duty to do anything that lies in my power to promote her true welfare. You will, I trust, remember this, as you cannot gratify me more than by freely informing me of anything I can do for you.

'The subject of Female Education was the leading motive which prompted my visit to this country. I discovered in the first Girls' School I entered in India, the grand obstacle to its advancement, in the want of Female Teachers, and I saw the absolute necessity for measures being promptly taken to ensure a permanent supply of them. From that time, till now, I have been labouring, both publicly and privately, to effect that object. I am happy to say that the views of enlightened Hindoo gentlemen are in full accordance with my own. I am aware of all the difficulties which exist in the way of the accomplishment of this great object, but I know by past experience that strong faith, untiring perseverance, and a zeal undaunted by apparent failures, can and will surmount them!

'The time is now, I believe, fully come when we must make a united effort to obtain the adoption of such measures as will inaugurate this great work. While I honour and highly appreciate every effort which is being made by individuals or religious bodies to aid in Female Education, and while I am aware that the Government has always been ready to second these by grants-in-aid, yet we all know that the education of the male portion of the community could never have attained its present condition if Government had not taken the *initiative*, in founding schools and in training teachers. It did so, as soon as it was evident, from private efforts which had been made, and from the reception which those had received from enlightened Hindoos, that the time was come when these were required. The country was not then prepared to ask the same thing for the other sex, whose wants are yet more pressing. The enlightened portion of your countrymen do desire it now, and should never *rest* until equal justice is done to both sexes, to which our Heavenly Father has given powers to be cultivated to His glory, and for the welfare of each one immortal being, as well as of society in general. The work will require the greatest wisdom, judgment, and freedom from low and narrow prejudices, but it must be done; and woman must be raised to her true sphere, before India can rise to the position for which I trust she is destined.

'I beg then, as my parting request, that you will form a small society of true-hearted persons who desire to effect this great object, and that you will do me the favour to keep me informed of your proceedings, and to let me know how I can help you in England. Should God see fit to spare my health and strength, I shall hope again to come among you, to witness, I doubt not, the fruits of your exertions.'

The morning of Sunday, January 13, found our vessel off Madras. A government boat conveyed me to the pier, and a pleasant drive brought me to the beautiful country residence of his Excellency the Governor, to which I had been invited by telegram while at Calcutta. After a kind reception from Lord and Lady Napier, I was installed in a room such as only an Anglo-Indian house can furnish: a shady verandah on three sides enabled me at all times to enjoy the air, and the sight of a luxuriant tropical garden; gorgeous flowers were in profusion on my table, and chief of all was the charm of seeing a beautiful blossom of the Victoria Regia, gathered for me from a pond in the garden. The members of the household having attended the cathedral in the morning, an evening drive took us to the little church of St. Thomé, which is almost on the seashore. A small refuge for young orphans, chiefly East Indians, is near the church, delightfuly situated, so as to give these poor little weakly creatures the benefit of good physical, as well as moral influences. This receives the kind notice of her ladyship, and we paid it a visit. An evening ride home by moonlight, along roads shaded by palm-trees and other tropical foliage, is one of the great pleasures of Eastern life. A morning ramble in the garden was also delightful, before the sun was too powerful to allow an umbrella to be a sufficient protection. The various kinds of trees were a never-ending source of gratification. Sometimes we came to one we had often heard of but never seen, even in a hothouse, such as a fine old cinnamon-tree; and again, were amused at finding that some plant, carefully cherished by us, was only a weed here; the gardener complained that he could hardly clear the ground of the sensitive plant, which I saw crawling over some neglected spot. Vines, of course, required to be shaded rather than protected from cold; and near these, which reminded me of Europe, were beautiful plantains, with their graceful long leaves and heavy bunches of fruit. Cabbages here receive a degree of attention which is not bestowed on them in England, being cultivated in pots, that they may be removed from the scorching heat of the sun, and kept sufficiently moist. The Anglo-Indians greatly prize anything which reminds them of home. A gentleman once remarked to me, when looking at a neat Chinese vegetable garden, that he never thought he should delight to see cabbages growing—they reminded him of Old England! My favourite walk, however, was to the large pond devoted to the Victoria Regia; it was extremely interesting to watch its growth, and see its splendid large leaves floating on the water. In Madras most of the servants can talk a little English. It was very pleasant to hold needed conversation in one's own language.. On remarking to one of the under-gardeners on the beauty of a flower, he immediately told me its Latin name! To hear our learned language from a native in the semi-nude condition common in these parts, had a very strange effect. My first anxiety was to learn what progress had been made in preparing a memorial to Government, praying for a Female Normal School, as had been proposed. Some of the leading native gentlemen had called a public meeting on the subject; but considerable discussion had arisen, through the apprehension felt by some, that this was a covert attempt to force the English language into their girls' schools, and the meeting was dissolved without coming to any resolution. I therefore asked my friend, the Director of Public Instruction, again to call a meeting of native gentlemen to his house to discuss the matter. This he kindly did, assembling all those who apprehended difficulties and objections, as well as those who entered warmly into the matter. A memorial had already been prepared, and they were all quite satisfied when they understood that the training of teachers did not in any way involve these teachers being employed in their schools, unless desired by the managers, and that, when so employed, they would teach nothing but what the managers wished. The fear entertained by these and other natives, not of the progressive party, appears to be, lest the introduction of the English language into their girls' schools should lead the way to a change in their religion and customs, which they do not desire. 'We do not wish our ladies to be made humble Christians,' a native gentleman once said to me. This is, I believe, the underlying feeling which causes hesitation as to accepting help from the English. It is to be regretted that they should have any cause to dread interference which they do not desire. The adoption of the Government principle of non-interference with religion or social customs, is, therefore, essential to the success of any effort to introduce an improved system of female education, which is now so much desired by the enlightened portion of the native community. The memorial was soon completed by them, and having been signed by most of the influential Hindoos, was presented to his Excellency the Governor. It was as follows:—

'*To the Right Honorable Francis Lord Napier, K.T., Governor in Council, Fort St. George.*

'The humble memorial of the undersigned Hindoo inhabitants of Madras, respectfully showeth:

'That your memorialists crave permission to address your Lordship in Council on the subject of Female Education, a subject so important, and so closely connected with the future welfare of their country, that they cannot but feel that it will meet with the warmest support of your Lordship's government. That your memorialists are convinced that the absence of intellectual culture at present characterising the Hindoo female, is one of the main causes of the tardy progress of Hindoo society; and that, though many are anxious to do all in their power to remove this evil, yet, with the limited resources at their command, they feel that they would fail to achieve success without the help of Government.

'That in the vernacular schools now existing in Madras for the education of Hindoo girls, it has been found impossible, save in exceptional cases, to procure other than male teachers; that this drawback has placed the schools under serious disadvantages, and rendered them less attractive in the eyes of native parents than they otherwise would be; and that, therefore, good female teachers are amongst the foremost wants of the native community.

'Your memorialists therefore pray that a Normal School may

be established for the training of respectable female teachers, to supply the want complained of.

'And your memorialists, as in duty bound, shall ever pray.

'C. RUNGANADA SHASTRY, and others.

'Madras, January 17, 1867.'

My native friends, being anxious to hear particulars of what had been done in Calcutta on this and other subjects, requested me to meet them at the beautiful country residence of one of the leading citizens, Mr. Veccatasawrung Naidoo, which I did with pleasure. Friday, January 18, was the day fixed, and I gladly accepted an invitation to visit first the families of my friends, Rajagopal Charlu the president, and Subroyalu Chetty the secretary, of the Veda Somaj. It was most gratifying to observe how much these gentlemen were doing to elevate and educate the ladies of their families; the only drawback was the want of a common language, which prevented any communication of thought. All that I saw at Madras of these and other native ladies, convinced me that they only want suitable education to render them intellectual and cultivated in manners. On arriving at the house of meeting, I was agreeably surprised by being presented with the following address. I hope I shall not be thought guilty of egotism in copying this and other documents, my object being to show the reader how susceptible this nation is of grateful feeling for kindly sympathy, and how ready they are to give their confidence when they are sure that there are no concealed motives:—

'*To Miss Mary Carpenter.*

'Madam,—We, the undersigned inhabitants of Madras, beg permission to present you with an address, in token of the respect and esteem we feel for you.

'Long before your arrival in India, the reputation of your goodness and benevolence had reached us. Now, after having had the pleasure of making your personal acquaintance, we see how fully that reputation is supported by your feelings and acts. We will not offend your modesty by enumerating all those acts of pure philanthropy which have distinguished you, whose whole life has been devoted to the cause of humanity. But we cannot let you leave these shores without offering to you our sincere and heartfelt thanks for the benevolent solicitude you have displayed for the welfare of the inhabitants of this land, by coming over here, at the risk of health and with the sacrifice of comfort, to promote female education. We assure you, Madam, your visit has stimulated us to fresh exertions in this noble cause, and hope Providence will crown our efforts in this direction with success.

'Again, we humbly beg that you will accept our thanks for your benevolent intentions toward us. We feel that to dwell more upon your undoubted claims to our gratitude is unnecessary, when we remember we are addressing a lady whose heart, love, and griefs have always been given to her fellow-beings, while to say less would not merely be a positive dereliction of duty, but would deprive us of what we regard as a high gratification.

'Fervently praying that Almighty God will pour his choicest blessings on you, and prolong your life—so valuable to the cause of humanity and progress—to the fullest period allotted to mortals,

'We beg to subscribe ourselves,

'Your sincere friends and well-wishers,

'C. RENGANADASHASHY, and others.

'Madras, January 18, 1867.'

The next day a party was assembled at Guindy, consisting of a number of the leading native gentlemen, as well as English, with several ladies, to have an opportunity of free conversation respecting the great question of female education. This kind consideration of his

Excellency was highly appreciated, as such friendly intercourse between the two races had not been common hitherto—the native gentlemen not having been in the habit of attending receptions at Madras, as at Calcutta.

On Wednesday, January 22, I paid a visit to the Veda Somaj, and once more had the pleasure of joining with my Hindoo friends in an English prayer. I little then anticipated that only a few months would pass before he who led our devotions—one of the most estimable and earnest of those present—P. Subroyalu Chetty, should be called away from this world, after a painful illness, leaving his sweet young wife to lifelong widowhood, his religious society to mourn the loss of their excellent secretary, and his friends (myself among the number) to lament the departure of one from whom we hoped much in the work of progress! We must trust in the wisdom and love of the Heavenly Father where the reasons which guide Him are inscrutable. May those that remain feel only an increased stimulus to carry on the work to which he so earnestly devoted himself!

Whenever it was possible, during my stay in India, I devoted one portion of the Sunday to worshipping with the natives, either in a mission chapel, or (as in Calcutta), with the more advanced in their own worship in English. It was then with peculiar pleasure that on the morning of January 20, I set forth to find a little native church, of which I had already heard much. Its history is remarkable. More than fifty years ago, a native servant of an English gentleman, who attended his master to England, became converted to Christianity by the study of the Scriptures; he fell in with the works of Rammohun Roy and of Dr. Channing, and the perusal of them led him to embrace the doctrines of Unitarian

Christianity. He adopted and took the name of William Roberts. He was strong in his convictions, and, on his return to Madras, endeavoured to convert the poorer natives. Being anxious to establish a place of worship, he took other voyages to England, in order to raise funds by his own personal efforts; having saved his earnings, he bought a piece of ground and built a chapel, where he formed a congregation and preached. He obtained books and tracts from England, and himself published tracts, which he distributed. On his death, his second son, who bears his name, deeply reverencing his father, and sympathising in his work, determined to qualify himself for preaching, by studying his father's writings, and his various English books, which now formed a good library. The congregation were too poor to raise any salary for him; he therefore engaged in secular occupation, devoting himself on Sunday to his little church. I had visited his abode during the preceding week; it was an ordinary Indian bungalow, but neat and respectable, as were his wife and children. His superior in business gave him a high character, and expressed to me the hope that means would be found to give him a salary, and thus enable him to devote himself entirely to the ministry. My Hindoo friends of the Veda Somaj spoke favourably of him, and aided him in the printing of a little magazine. Some Mahometan gentlemen also, with whom I became acquainted, were on friendly terms with him. He had been ordained as a minister, had registered his chapel for the performance of marriages, and kept as neat and careful a family register of births, deaths, marriages, and baptisms, with full particulars of name, age, &c., as can be found in an English church. He has not, of course, many converts; but some are occasionally added, besides those springing from the natural increase of the families of his flock. He has assumed the dress of an English minister, not the style generally adopted by Christian converts. These particulars are mentioned, because it is instructive to observe how a little church has sprung up and established itself without connection with the English missions around.

An English lady accompanied me, and it was somewhat difficult to find the way, through an obscure part of the city. The approach to it was swarming with uncivilised-looking heathen children. It was an agreeable surprise to see a very neat chapel, with a portico and a flight of steps. It was shaded by palm-trees, and a church-bell summoned the worshippers. The service was serious and earnest, the congregation very attentive. It was a happy sight to see husbands and wives sitting together with their children. There were also several of the scholars from Mr. Roberts's little schools, who presented, by their dress and deportment, a striking contrast to the untaught creatures whom I had noticed outside. A servant belonging to the Governor's household was there, being a member of Mr. Roberts's congregation. Though the Madras Government livery does not greatly differ from the ordinary native dress, yet I remarked that he had changed it before taking his place as an independent member of a congregation. He bore a good character in the discharge of his duties, and, though Christian servants do not always do credit to their profession, it was pleasant in his case to be reminded of the text, 'Even in the household are some obedient to the faith.' At the conclusion of the service, a woman came forward, with an infant in her arms, and knelt down to be churched; she was the wife of the Governor's servant, and they had their other children with them. A very aged woman, older than any one I had seen in India, was near her. She had never married, but had lived with a brother, who was now dead. She was kindly received into this truly Christian family, and resided with them.

The interior of the chapel was very neat, the congregation at times raising a small sum for its repair; they had also purchased a handsome altar-cloth, and some of them had presented the bell. There is a small cemetery which had been purchased and presented to the chapel by the founder.

This place seemed an oasis in the midst of a moral desert. May it prosper under the Divine blessing!

Not far from Mr. Roberts's residence is a large mosque, with many buildings around; it is, indeed, the centre of a district inhabited by many Mahometans. I went to visit this, but the Mahometan servant who accompanied me having intimated that this was a particularly sacred period, I did not of course make any inspection of it. Not far off is a famous Hindoo temple, in the district of Triplicane. There are extensive premises round the temple, which is a large and picturesque one. An air of dilapidation prevails, as usual in such enclosures. One could not wish it otherwise, in a place devoted to superstition and degrading ceremonies. A great lumbering ceremonial car is kept under one shed, and under another, an unfortunate elephant, whose lean appearance indicated a scanty supply of food; he seemed to me sadly degraded by an idolatrous mark of the presiding goddess painted on his forehead! Looking into the temple, I observed several priests, and a number of fine Brahmin boys; it was dreadful to think of their being brought up under such influences. Attracted by curiosity, they came out to take a closer view of a stranger; I told them I had travelled from a great distance—from Bristol, in England. They immediately said, 'That is in Gloucestershire, on the River Avon.' Knowledge derived from English education sounded strangely in this heathen place.

There is a large tank near, with a building in the middle for ceremonials. Nature adorns everything alike, with her beauties of light and shadow profusely shed on all. This temple, with the tank reflecting the architecture around, makes lovely photographs, which I brought away with me, endeavouring to forget the scenes that take place within these buildings. May the time come when the knowledge of the Lord shall cover even these dark places of the earth!

The sanitary condition of Madras occupied much of the attention of the Governor, Lord Napier. As he wisely considered that good air and water are essentials, he desired, as a first step, to procure these for the inhabitants, by improving the present bad, unhealthy state of many parts of the city. Desiring to see things as they really were, he proposed to pay a visit to some of the worst parts of the city, if possible incognito, but, at any rate, without preparation being made for his Excellency's inspection. I gladly accepted an invitation to accompany him, and we started at 5.30 A.M. on the morning of January 23; at that hour there was a degree of coolness in the air, which made a shawl agreeable. On arriving, we found a most suspicious state of extra-cleanliness; there were, however, indications of the want of any arrangements for ordinary decency. We went into several parts of that district of the Native Town known as Triplicane. Some streets were very picturesque, terminated by a palm-tree; but when I penetrated into small courts, and found miserable abodes without any current of air through them, and scarcely any hole for a window, one house opening into another,—I did indeed wonder that dreadful pestilences did not more frequently devastate the city— unsparing avengers of the neglect of nature's laws.

An interesting institution which we afterwards visited, was the Monegar Choultry, or Pauper Asylum for Natives. It appeared under admirable management, and kept in an excellent sanitary condition. The least satisfactory features were the hospital, and the house for stray children. The want of trained nurses, here as everywhere, is painfully evident; and the impossibility of finding any native women who understand the duties of matron, resulted in the poor orphans being left in a state very different from what they are in our institutions at home. They did not appear to have any instruction, difficulties arising from the fear of proselytising. This is to be regretted, for there are many educated native masters everywhere, who would doubtless be able to give these children not only intellectual but moral instruction, with some general principles of religion. The report of this institution for the year 1865 states, that the average daily number of paupers, including foundling and stray children, was 306. The total expense of the whole establishment, including clothing and diet for the year, was 2,196*l.* An idiot asylum is connected with the Choultry, the expense of which for the year is 509*l.* This annual expense is chiefly met by voluntary contributions, of which about one-sixth in amount is from natives. This was the only institution of the kind I saw in India.

At this time, considerable preparations were being

made for the reception of the Maharajah of Travancore, who was coming to pay a ceremonial visit to the Governor of Madras. The Government House was being arranged for his reception. This is a handsome and very commodious residence, situated in a beautiful park, through which the public are permitted to drive. There is a large detached building, which can be used for public ceremonies, or as a ballroom. This is a great advantage, preventing the necessity of disarranging the household on occasions of public festivities. At Guindy Park no such convenience existed, but it was marvellous how rapidly transformations were made in the saloons, to prepare them for a government ball. One would suppose that India was too hot a country for dancing, but it appeared to be a recreation highly appreciated by the resident English gentry; and, certainly, large airy ballrooms opening on verandahs appeared pleasanter than crowded hot rooms at home. These amusements are not shared by the natives in Madras, nor would it, indeed, seem congruous for them to come as spectators only, until they are accompanied by their wives and daughters. The receptions were highly agreeable and informal, being held in the grounds under the shade of beautiful trees. One evening, when the company was assembling for a party, a native gentleman brought three young ladies, members of his family, to call upon me. They were beautifully dressed, decorated with jewels, and very intelligent: one of them had written some sentences in Tamil in my book. They were desirous of the honour of an interview with the Governor's lady also, which was kindly granted, and several of the ladies of the company also came in to visit these novel guests. No gentleman was of course admitted, except his Excellency, though several showed considerable anxiety for a similar honour. It was an amusing scene to see these ladies of different nationalities surveying each other with admiring curiosity, but unable to interchange sentiments. The young Hindoo damsels were compared to birds of paradise, which they certainly rivalled in the brilliancy of their ornaments; they retired much gratified with their reception. I returned the call with an English friend, and was introduced also to the lady of the house. This gentleman is so anxious for the education of his daughters, that he takes them to his town-house several times a week, to receive lessons from an East Indian teacher. We visited also another family, where similar efforts are being made to promote female education practically.

A Mahometan gentleman of rank likewise requested a visit, and we went to his house with considerable ceremony, where we were introduced to a large number of ladies of the family, of at least three generations; an East Indian lady gave instruction in this family, and served us as interpreter. The ladies appeared disappointed at not seeing us adorned with rich jewellery, and intimated that we were reserving the display of them for some more distinguished occasion, not imagining that we had not as valuable a collection of jewellery as themselves. Rich scents were poured on us from handsome chased silver bottles, used for such occasions. Then, and very often, I was reminded of the 'alabaster box' and fragrant offerings, when 'the house was filled with the odour of the ointment.'

Among the charms of Guindy Park, I must not forget to mention the pretty little school-house for the servants of the household; this is under the special supervision of the noble lady at the head of the establishment. The orderly intelligent look of both boys and girls proved the benefit of such influences, and they showed with pride the books and silver medals they had received from her. Surely such kind interest in the children of those of humble station, exhibited by persons holding the highest rank in the Presidency, must shed around the most beneficial influence!

My pleasant time at Guindy was drawing to a close, and I could not accept the kind invitation of my noble hostess to prolong it; as I had not paid my promised visit to the institutions of Bombay, and the time fixed for my return home could not conveniently be altered. I was also obliged to decline a very tempting offer to accompany a party to the much-desired Neilgherries, proceeding straight thence to Beypore. I had no strength or time for anything but the objects of my journey.

Fully to explain the nature of the proposed Female Normal School to those who had been working in the great cause of female education, I gave on Monday, Jan. 21, an address on the subject at the Evangelistic Hall, chiefly to English, though with some natives present; and on Thursday, Jan. 24, I gave a public address to the native community in Patcheappah's Hall, presided over by Mr. Ranganada Shastry, Judge of the Small Cause Court.* After this I reluctantly bade my native friends farewell, fully satisfied with the anxiety they then manifested to carry out, as far as laid in their power, the great object—a Female Normal School.

After taking leave of the many agreeable English acquaintances whom I had met at Madras, especially of my noble hosts, to whom I felt so much indebted, I again set forth on my solitary journey, very early on Saturday morning, January 26.

* *Vide* 'Addresses,' pp. 47-52.

It is sometimes good to be alone for a time, after weeks and months crowded with new and deeply interesting incidents, with important work opening out before one, and with treasured memories of intercourse with those now numbered among my valued friends. A quiet journey through beautiful scenery, such as met the view on each side of the carriage, was a true refreshment to the spirit; and having before passed through it during the night, it had all the charm of novelty. The day, therefore, did not appear long; but on reaching Coimbatore, at ten o'clock at night, the very unpleasant announcement was made that, as the next day was Sunday, the train would not proceed until one o'clock on the morrow. This delay would probably cause my losing the vessel by which I was to proceed to Bombay; there was, however, no help for it, and I was now very thankful for the kind consideration of Lord Napier, in sending his Christian servant to see me safe to my journey's end, so that I was not without protection. The accommodation was indeed miserable; nothing could be obtained but a half-furnished waiting-room with a cane sofa, with food very bad in quality, and difficult to be procured at all. Travellers must learn contentment under all circumstances. A brilliant morning was gratefully welcomed after the troubles of the night; here, far from the conventionalities of city life, which in India prevent ladies from taking even a short walk, I was able to ramble along the road towards the glorious mountains, in the midst of a country where 'all but the spirit of man is divine.' A year after that day I chanced to be detained on a Sunday morning at Holyhead. What a contrast! A somewhat bleak rocky coast, and bare landscape, but neat well-built houses, orderly streets, many chapels and churches, and none in the streets but people decently dressed, proceeding to their places of worship. May the Hindoo people rise from idolatry, and make their country what nature intended it to be! I was glad to find from the Christian servant, who could speak some English, that he was much attached to his little chapel at Madras, and understood the grounds of his faith; that he highly esteemed his pastor, and wished much that he could devote himself entirely to the ministry; and that he and two others, one of them his brother-in-law, united to support one of the little schools; he was not, then, one of those merely nominal Christians, who bring so much discredit on the cause they profess.

After proceeding some stages from Coimbatore, we came again into the region frequented by the Moplahs; half-naked, but armed with a knife, they were some of the most savage-looking beings I saw in India. The stations were all in some degree of extra excitement, owing to the approaching visit of the Maharajah of Travancore. I was agreeably surprised by being accosted by a native gentleman from Calicut, who expressed the hope that I should wait for the next vessel, and see the lions of his town, whither he would shortly return.

As the day declined, we were passing near the coast, and crossed some of the backwaters, as they are termed; a more lovely view I never beheld! The deep rich red of the sky was reflected in the water, and along the near horizon was here and there a palm-tree, calmly rising towards the heavens, and doubly revealing its loveliness in the water. Little jutting peninsulas, covered with darker masses of foliage also reflected, enhanced the brilliant beauty of the sky, and invited the eye to penetrate into their secret recesses. We were swiftly borne away from these beauties, and others succeeded, until we reached the end of our journey—Beypoor, where a gentleman brought me a kind invitation from the Collector of Calicut, to take up my abode at his house, which I thankfully accepted. I did not feel quite sufficient courage to proceed some miles in an open boat, after ten o'clock at night, to the steamer, which had not yet proceeded from Calicut. I was therefore soon in the ferry-boat, to which my escort, David John, waded through the water to bid me farewell, and I sent by him my thanks to my late kind hosts.

It was a long drive to my new abode, but very beautiful; we passed along a road bordered with palm-trees, forming a canopy through which the bright rays of the diamond-looking stars could hardly penetrate. The residence of Mr. Ballard, the collector, is on a hill, three miles beyond the town. From thence the morning rays revealed a splendid view over extensive woods of cocoanuts and richly cultivated land, to the grand range of the Western Ghauts. Tropical trees were in rich luxuriance around the house—the stately mango with its masses of foliage, the plantain, the slight elegant bamboo, and hanging creepers, with trees of greater variety of tint than I had yet seen. Various pretty animals were rambling tamely about, the pets of the lovely little twin daughters of my host. It was, indeed, delightful to sit under the shade of the verandah, in such scenery, and preserve the vivid picture of it by the pencil.

Calicut was the first port visited by Vasco de Gama in 1498. He then found here a very powerful race of warriors, named Nairs. These at present constitute a large portion of the population, but have turned their energy into better channels. My first introduction here was to a gentleman of this race, who called on the

Collector to bid him farewell before his departure to a town at a little distance, to fill the office of magistrate, to which he had been appointed. Many peculiar customs prevail among them—among others, inheritance by the female side only. This custom was adopted when the rights of marriage were little understood or respected, and when this was considered the only means of transmitting property by a certain lineal descent. At present, great difficulties arise from this practice, and many would be glad to relinquish the custom. The British Government, however, on this as in other matters relating to the social habits and customs of the people, very wisely declines to interfere, and the Nairs themselves are not sufficiently united in their wish to make the change. Though Calicut has the elements of British civilisation introduced into it by the presence of the various official gentlemen connected with the Government—a collector's office, various institutions, an excellent High School, a factory, &c.—yet these do not appear to have produced as much effect on the general habits of the educated portion of the community, as in the Presidential capitals; but, on the other hand, there is not that air of dirt and dilapidation, which was so painfully depressing and repulsive in many parts of the empire which I had already seen. The country realised one's ideal of a rich tropical region, in the luxuriance of the foliage, and the evident fertility of the soil. This is probably due to the fact that here there is rain, to a greater or less extent, during about six months of the year.

The native gentleman whom I had met on my journey, kindly offered to accompany me on some visits in the neighbourhood. It was striking to observe that the roads, and even the lanes, between different properties, were well-made and neatly bordered; every six inches of land, he remarked, was so valuable, that they wished to make the most of it, and to lose nothing by want of care. My escort had been a great traveller. He had spent some years in Calcutta, which he contrasted very unfavourably with this part of the country. He had been educated at the Presidency College of Madras, and, like all others who had studied there, when the present director was principal of it, spoke of him in the highest terms. After riding through many pleasant lanes, we reached his abode, which was shaded with trees, and with a garden and tank near. It was neat and well arranged, in purely native style. In his own study I was surprised and pleased to see lying on a table a volume of the works of my brother, the physiologist; my friend had evidently devoted some time to the study of it, and said he proposed making a popular abstract of it, to give his countrymen some idea of the laws of health. The lady of the house, with her daughters, soon entered, and gave me a kind reception; they appeared to be well educated. We next visited the house of a Nair gentleman. Though no intimation had been given of my probable visit, the house was beautifully neat and clean, and an air of finish pervaded the whole premises. He was considered an elderly man, being about 60, and told us with pride of ancient deeds of prowess which he had performed, in favour of the British, showing us many presents he had received from persons of distinction, in token of approbation. A little boy of six years of age, the child of his old age, appeared to appropriate all this glory to himself, and to claim the privilege of a favourite. The ladies entered after some time, carefully dressed, and highly decorated; they also had been educated at home. The superior families of this neighbourhood seem to attend to the education of the ladies, and not to keep them in that painful seclusion and constraint which I observed in Calcutta. I did not, however, hear of any girls' school here. Both these families appeared to reside alone, not in association with relations. In the case of this Nair gentleman, family difficulties were arising, from the strange custom of inheritance above alluded to. His sister claimed the family property for her own daughters, and was displeased, because he had built this house for his wife, and wished his little son to have some benefit from it.

Owing to the retention of antiquated and sometimes barbaric customs, complications exist in these parts, which we, at a distance, can hardly realise. I had noticed that a servant who had been sent to fetch something for me from the carriage, instead of handing it to me, put it down at a little distance, and quickly retreated; the customs of his tribe made him cautiously avoid incurring the danger of touching me. Persons of different castes are here so careful not to come within a certain distance of each other, that when one sees another approaching in the road, the superior cries aloud, 'Aha—aha!' *i.e.* 'Avaunt—avaunt!' The inferior must then retreat into the paddy or rice-field, until the other has passed by. On one occasion, a woman saw a man of inferior grade approaching, and warned him, after her fashion, to go aside. He was by no means disposed to do so, and saying, 'This highway belongs to the English, not to you,' walked on, without troubling himself at her indignation, and she was obliged to go aside if she wished to sustain her dignity. So these prejudices will gradually disappear, with more intercourse with a civilised nation.

Little progress has, however, been made in one

respect, which appears to me essential to proper self-respect—viz., suitable covering to the person. The native costume is here, simply, a piece of cloth tied round the loins. Those natives who are connected with government offices, of course wear neat white clothing, such as I had seen elsewhere, when they are on duty, or visiting the English; on other occasions, however, they indulge themselves in native freedom from the restraints of clothing.

My friend now conducted me to the High School, which is a commodious building for 400 scholars, and well provided with teachers; what was my amazement at being introduced to this large body of young gentlemen with only this scanty costume! They were well educated, and polite in their manners, though their appearance was so uncivilised. I could not but think that a little kind influence, on the part of their instructors, might lead them all to take that first step, so necessary to civilised social intercourse, before proceeding to book-learning. Some words, kindly inscribed by some of them in my book, showed that their education had not in other respects been neglected.

On Wednesday morning, Jan. 30, I visited the Calicut Jail. This building is stated (in the Government Report for 1865-66), to be unsuitable for its purpose, and to have been already condemned. It is to be hoped that one will shortly be built on an entirely new principle, and adapted to carry out the grand ends of punishment, which it certainly cannot do in its present state; it is calculated to contain 260 prisoners. During the previous year there was considerable overcrowding, and the mortality was very great, amounting to 165; of these, 48 died of cholera in less than a month. This jail has always, the Report states, been considered unhealthy, and twelve others are mentioned with it as increasing the rate of mortality in the Presidency, which is 12·944 per cent., or nearly 130 in every 1,000 prisoners. Surely such a state of things calls for speedy reform!

On arriving at the jail, I was surprised to see a large number of men crouching on the ground, half-naked and manacled, outside the walls; these were the prisoners, who were waiting to be taken, by labour-warders and the police, to work on the roads or elsewhere. As this jail is condemned as unfit, it is unnecessary to describe it; but here, as elsewhere, women were locked up together, of whom one was a murderess, and one a criminal lunatic; they had no instruction, and were under male warders. One spectacle of unrivalled horror struck me, and I have never since been able to banish it from my mind. Passing a grated cell, I observed five men, in a state of extreme excitement, wildly crying out, and piteously holding up their hands in supplication. These wretched creatures were under a death sentence! While capital punishment remains on our Statute Book, a remnant of a barbaric code, are unhappy beings, ignorant and helpless as these are, to be treated with so little consideration of their condition by our nation? In several other jails there had been men under sentence of death; they seemed dull and apathetic, and I did not look at them, as I could do them no good; here the spectacle was so full of horror, that it forced my unwilling attention.

It was indeed a pleasant change to turn from this to a large coffee-factory. There all the processes are performed, from the first state in which they are brought by the bullock-carts from the Mysore Hills, to the final packing for exportation. The history of the growth and preparation for use of this valuable berry, with an account of the individuals who are employed, might fill an interesting volume. It was very gratifying to see about 400 strong-looking women and children employed in what was by no means hard work—winnowing, sizing in cylinders, and sorting—under the kind superintendence of the manager. He spoke in very friendly terms of them, and evidently took a warm interest in the people under his charge. On enquiring from him whether any attempt had yet been made to instruct the girls employed in the factory, he said that they had no desire to learn, and that this had not yet been attempted; he appeared to feel, with me, that this would be an excellent opportunity of endeavouring to improve them.

On the return home we passed a building intended for an industrial exhibition. The undertaking excited warm interest, being mainly carried out by the Collector and his friends. It seemed a wonderful move in this part of the country. It caused a great sensation, and the photographer prepared to perpetuate the memory of it. Since my return, the post has brought me a packet of very interesting views, two of the exterior, six representing the different departments—('Woods and Machinery,' 'Jewellery, &c.' 'Grains and Pottery,' 'Textile Fabrics,' 'Embroidery,' 'Miscellaneous'); also a group, consisting of the Collector of Malabar, assistants, deputies, and tahseldars. The exhibition took place in the spring, and the Collector writes:—' On the whole, the thing was a success. I am sure many of the visitors, who numbered upwards of 30,000 (you must remember I speak of Calicut, not Paris—of the population whose scanty clothing you so objected to, and whose ideas are about on a par, and not of an intelligent European community)—many of the visitors, I say, went away with ideas that they had not when they came. Some ten years ago an exhibition was attempted, and it was currently reported among the rural population, that the scheme was to cover a sort of Tippoo-like design, of deporting the whole assemblage *en masse*. We are a little beyond that now, but I believe a sort of phantom of taxation pervaded the very pretty show. In an out-of-the-way place, the other day, I was told that some of the rajahs rather inclined to father the exhibition with the licence-tax (the great staple of controversy and reprobation of late), and it was not without some difficulty that they were induced to yield to the chronological argument. But it was a great thing to get so many visitors, all of whom went away surprised and pleased; and, indeed, the universal remark was, that had people known there was to be so gallant a show, both contributors and visitors would have been far more numerous.'

The subject of the Female Normal Training School was not of course forgotten, and the Collector kindly asked a number of Calicut native gentlemen to meet at his house to discuss it. I explained the whole plan to them, and they appeared to enter as fully into the idea as could be expected.

My visit here was short, but very delightful, and without it I should have lost an agreeable experience of tropical life. I bade it adieu with regret.

END OF THE FIRST VOLUME.

LONDON: PRINTED BY
SPOTTISWOODE AND CO., NEW-STREET SQUARE
AND PARLIAMENT STREET

www.ingramcontent.com/pod-product-compliance
Lightning Source LLC
Chambersburg PA
CBHW050844090925
32259CB00016B/1411